Living a Delusion

A MEMOIR FROM
SOVIET RUSSIA

OLGA MOROZOVA

For my grandmother, Katerina

Oshun

Published by Oshun Books
an imprint of Struik Publishers
(a division of New Holland Publishing (South Africa) (Pty) Ltd)
PO Box 1144, Cape Town, 8000
New Holland Publishing is a member of Johnnic Communications Ltd

First published 2004

www.oshunbooks.co.za

1 3 5 7 9 10 8 6 4 2

PUBLISHING MANAGER: Michelle Matthews
EDITOR: Helen de Villiers
COVER AND TEXT DESIGN: Natascha Adendorff
TYPESETTING: Bev Dodd
PRODUCTION CONTROLLER: Valerie Kömmer

Set in 10.5 pt on 13 pt Bembo

Reproduction by Hirt & Carter (Cape) (Pty) Ltd
Printed and bound by Paarl Print, Oosterland Street, Paarl, South Africa

ISBN 1 77007 033 8

DISCLAIMER
Certain names have been changed to protect the privacy of individuals and
institutions. Any similarity to persons living or dead is purely coincidental.

www.imagesofafrica.co.za
IMAGES OF AFRICA
PHOTO LIBRARY

Contents

Susie Moffatt Moscow 2005

Prologue

O<small>NCE</small> I <small>HAD LEFT MY NATIVE</small> R<small>USSIA</small>, <small>PEOPLE</small> I <small>MET EXPRESSED</small> interest in my origins, and in the fact that I had once been a member of the Communist Party. Many of these people cited sketchy information and isolated details they had picked up about the Soviet Union, such as the repression of opinion, the harshness of ordinary life, the reputations of some leaders, and, more recently, the introduction of *perestroika* and *glasnost*.

While I certainly had opinions on many issues and tried to answer questions honestly, I didn't want to denigrate the country of my birth unnecessarily; nor did I want to paint it as paradise on Earth, which it definitely wasn't. When I started answering questions and relating some of my life experiences, friends suggested that I write a book. I initially demurred, thinking it too much of a challenge. However, on reflection, I decided to take up that challenge in the interests of telling a fuller story and painting a much bigger picture; in this way I could avoid overemphasis of some aspects, and complete neglect of others.

Many have been inspired to tell their stories of life in the Soviet Union in the particularly 'unusual' circumstances of the twentieth century. Gorbachev and Yeltsin have both written memoirs that have shed light on some of the more political aspects of that part of the world, but which reveal less about the effects such policies and doctrines had on the lives of ordinary Russians.

I recently came across a copy of *First Person*, a frank self-portrait by President Vladimir Putin. I find his considerable achievements all the more admirable when I realise how similar our childhoods and upbringings were. He tells of his young life in a communal flat, with no hot water, a smelly toilet and constant bickering. So many of us were fated to endure those unfortunate conditions, but Vladimir Putin is living proof that success can be achieved from humble beginnings.

I have not emulated his rise to fame and I don't envy him his huge responsibilities. However, I have succeeded in my own way and managed to find a happy life – far removed, as it turns out, from the circumstances of our youth.

I have not left Russia, the country that gave me a life for 38 years, without some sorrow. It has meant leaving my immediate family – my mother (my father died shortly before publication of this book) and my brothers. I am grateful to them for the love, warmth and support they have always shown me. Their generosity of spirit will always remain with me and be a source of inspiration. In writing this book, I have drawn heavily on their memories, and I thank them for having had the patience to provide me with so much detail.

I thank those kind people who urged me to write this book and hope they will find it interesting. Hubert and Dianna Goetsch, thanks for your valuable assistance. Your input has meant a lot to me.

My gratitude is also extended to the following people who made publication of this book possible: Frances Bond, Eileen Molver, Marlene Fryer, Georgina Hatch, Michelle Matthews and Helen de Villiers. Your kind encouragement and assistance always kept me focused on the task.

Special thanks to Roger Cartwright who has worked tirelessly with me and had the patience to convert my broken English into eloquent prose; and to cushion my frustration over not being able to write it all myself. Without his hard work, determination and continual encouragement, this book would never have been written. Roger, I love you.

OLGA MOROZOVA

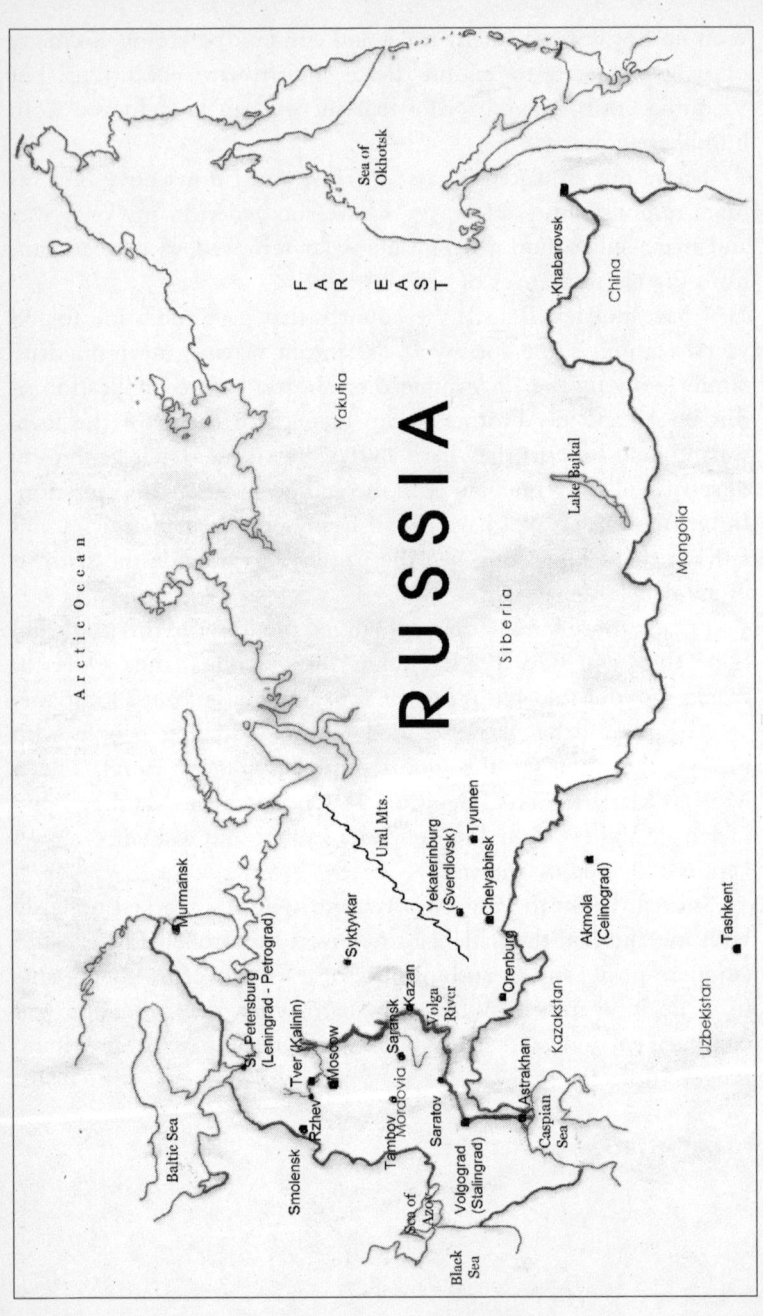

I

Roots

WHEN I WAS FIVE YEARS OLD, I ASKED MY FATHER WHAT Communism was. 'Communism,' he said, 'will be the happy life that we are building now.'

My name is Olga Danilovna Morozova (née Devjatkina). These names may sound exotic to a Westerner, but to a Russian they are quite ordinary. Olga is a popular girl's name of Greek origin; Danilovna, my patronymic, means daughter of Daniel; and Morozova is from the Russian word *moroz*, meaning 'frost'. So, it translates into English as 'Olga, daughter of Daniel, Frost'.

I grew up in what was then the city of Kalinin, which is situated 160 kilometres northwest of Moscow on the road and waterways to St Petersburg. Originally a trading post named Tver, it was first settled by people from the Novgorod region in the late eleventh century.

Catherine the Great had a castle, church and belltower built there in 1760. She and subsequent Tsars used it as a stopover point between their palaces in Moscow and St Petersburg.

The church was destroyed by the Communists, who set in its place a statue of Kalinin (Stalin's deputy) after whom they renamed the city in 1930. In 1991, as change swept the country, the city's name reverted to Tver.

As a good, patriotic citizen, I longed for the privilege and prestige of belonging to the Communist Party of the Soviet Union. Finally, I succeeded in qualifying for membership. However, seven years later, my growing disillusionment caused me to resign. Not long after this, rejecting my upbringing and education, I adopted capitalism as a way of life. From my childhood in the heart of the

Soviet era, I had journeyed from an early, unquestioning acceptance of the doctrine of Communism to take my place in the free world.

Following the tragic murder of my father-in-law in 1993, I fled my country, leaving behind family, friends and hard-won assets.

This is my story, and that of my family, as we lived through political upheavals, experienced the rise and fall of the Soviet State and witnessed the dawn of the new Russia.

Ours was a typical Russian family. My father's family came from Mordovia in central Russia, and my mother's from the northwest. I have never visited Mordovia, but I am told it is not much different in character from the northwest part of the country, which I know well. Both sides of the family were serfs, working the land for the landowners. The abolition of serfdom in 1861 took a long time to come into practical effect, so years passed before my antecedents were able to call a piece of land their own.

Bortnikovo, a village 40 kilometres from the city of Tver, was the birthplace of my mother and her ancestors. The word has its roots in old Slavic language. It means 'collecting honey from wild hives' and points to an earlier, simpler lifestyle.

Mixed forests of silver birch and pines surround Bortnikovo. Some areas are swampy, caused by many springs that ultimately feed the Volga River. Slavic peoples settled the higher ground in the area before the ninth century. Nobody knows why they settled in that wild place with nine months a year of bitter cold and icy rain. Perhaps it was simply in pursuit of independence or freedom from oppression.

Establishing any form of agriculture was a challenge and feeding livestock was only possible in the few grassy fields found in the forests. Existence revolved around hunting, fishing and collecting whatever honey, berries, mushrooms and herbs nature provided. A typical Russian country village, such as Bortnikovo, might have up to 100 wooden houses constructed in close proximity and facing each other on either side of the only village road. Larger villages would normally have a church, so that people in the smaller settlements, usually within a few kilometres, could reach it on foot.

Every family owned a small piece of arable land of around 4 000 square metres, where they cultivated rye, wheat, potatoes, cabbages, onions, carrots, beetroots and, in more modern times, cucumbers and tomatoes. Russian summers are short, lasting only three months in those regions, so farmers were obliged to work hard during that time to plough, plant, tend and reap vegetables and fruits, as well as make hay for winter animal feed.

Some enterprising villagers would build mills and charge farmers a share of their crop to have it milled. Mill owners invariably became the wealthiest village inhabitants. Others built extraction plants to produce oil from indigenous flax seeds. The residue was used to feed young domestic animals. A cheese factory was built in yet another village, to use milk that was in excess of family requirements. Later, flax was cultivated to produce linen, for which the area became famous throughout Russia.

However, Bortnikovo was without mills of any kind, or a church, but it could boast a manufacturer of sheepskin clothing, which was necessary for everyone in winter. In an adjacent village was a church that served the devoutly Christian communities from birth to death. Usually a school would be set up at the church and sometimes an old-age home or infirmary. Time was measured for the locals by the church bell, calling people to services.

The calendar was made up of religious celebrations, which were of such importance to the communities that they could not imagine life without their regulatory influence. Every aspect of their lives was dictated by the church: when to sow crops, when to harvest, when to put the bull to the cows, when to marry.

Prior to 1917, the forests were controlled by the *Zemstvo*, elective district councils responsible to the government for all inhabitants of prescribed territories. One of their duties was wood distribution wherever it was required – for example, to hospitals, schools and offices. All villagers had, by law, to provide the *Zemstvo* with the best quality logs before taking any of their own. Men cut and stripped, while women loaded the logs onto horse-drawn sleds and drove them to the *Zemstvo* storage sites, which were sometimes many kilometres away. Every able-bodied person would turn out to take wood for their family's needs once the *Zemstvo* had its quota.

My maternal great-grandmother, Avdotja Saveljeva, told my

mother of times when she had worked in waist-deep snow, blizzards and freezing conditions of minus 30 degrees centigrade. The job was particularly hard and, in many cases, reduced life expectancies. My great-grandfather, Osip Saveljev, died at 46, leaving his wife of 44 with five children. She also suffered because of the punishing work, which affected her legs, making walking difficult.

Life was tough for my forebears and got even worse with the advent of the First World War (WWI). My paternal grandfather, Mikhail Devjatkin, was conscripted, leaving two small boys and his pregnant wife Elena Devjatkina. He never returned from the war, simply vanishing, with no report of his death ever received. My father Daniel, his third son, lived without ever knowing his father.

My mother's uncle, Nikoli Saveljev, who was 18 and the one expected to work to feed his sick mother, younger brother Ivan and three sisters, was also called up. Nikoli was lucky to survive the war. Many men fought and died at the front, leaving the women to feed their families, and do the work of their absent husbands and sons in addition to their own chores.

While WWI was raging, there was growing dissatisfaction in Russia with the rule of Tsar Nicholas II, a groundswell that had been building for some years. The people were tired of food and fuel shortages, and the repressive nature of the Tsarist government. Military incompetence in WWI further damaged the government's reputation. In 1917, war abroad turned into revolution at home; the Tsar was deposed and a provisional government established. Later the same year, the Bolsheviks, led by Vladimir Lenin, seized power, establishing a Communist Soviet (council) 'State', the Union of Soviet Socialist Republics (USSR).

A year later, a bloody civil war broke out with the Bolsheviks (Red Army) fighting the Tsar's (White) Army, which included foreign troops, particularly from monarchies abroad. Both sides called for more conscripts and boys of only 16 years of age were obliged to join up. Propaganda from both sides was strong and it must have been very confusing for 16-year-old country boys, who had little or no idea of which side to join.

Sometimes the result was to split families. Nikoli, who had been at the front, returned to join the Bolsheviks fighting for the Red Army. His younger brother, Ivan Saveljev (my grandfather), and a group of friends, in Kronstadt at that time, the very heart of the Revolution, were deeply confused as to which side they should be fighting for, particularly when they were called up to serve the Tsar. They ended up deciding not to fight for either side, which meant that they risked falling foul of both armies. The chance of being discovered as deserters, or even non-combatants, and punished accordingly, was doubled. When Ivan arrived back in his home village one night, his mother, Avdotja, hid him in the cellar, where he remained until 1919 – a period of some two years.

Nikoli, an invalid after losing a hand, was by then a committed Communist. Demobilised, he returned home and was so incensed when he discovered his younger brother hiding, that his immediate inclination was to shoot him on the spot. Only the intervention of their mother saved Ivan.

When he found out that there were other deserters, also hidden in their families' cellars, Nikoli organised a search, dragged the boys from their hiding places and had them tried before a hurriedly formed military tribunal.

The boys were turning 18 at the time and the decision of the tribunal was that they should be made to join the Red Army, which was desperately in need of conscripts. Back they went to Kronstadt, where Ivan was based until 1922. The civil war ended then and he returned to his village of Bortnikovo.

That same year, he married my grandmother, Katerina Rodionova, who had fled the death and anarchy in Petrograd (formerly St Petersburg) during the Revolution, and returned to her home village.

A year earlier (in 1921) there had been a drought that crippled the area, killing all crops and causing dramatic food shortages. Many villagers died of starvation. In that difficult time of political turmoil and widespread famine, Ivan and Katerina's first child, my mother, was born.

In 1923 the civil war was over and the Bolsheviks set about consolidating their grasp on the country. One of the steps they had decided upon, in principle, was to collectivise agriculture. Lenin proclaimed the land nationalised, but farmers continued to farm it for themselves until collectivisation happened in earnest – at different times in different areas. Reforms were first implemented in the cities of Petrograd and Moscow, from where they would eventually spread to the countryside.

People's lives in post-Revolution Russia changed fast and dramatically. The Bolsheviks renamed themselves 'Communists'. One by one, their congresses arrived at new ways of developing the country. The Fifteenth Communist Party Congress was held in December 1927 and the first of many Five-Year Plans for national development was adopted. It included, among other things, plans for developing heavy industry and finalising farm collectivisation.

The province of Tver, because of its proximity to Moscow, was affected before the reforms reached central Russia. For that reason, my mother's family became members of a collective farm (*kolkhoz* in Russian) before my father's. All land was nationalised and farmers were pressured 'voluntarily' to join the collectives.

The Communist government's aim was to make everyone in the countryside 'equal' – in effect, equally poor. Poverty and hardship were publicly upheld as virtues necessary for the long-term building of a perfect, fair Communist utopia. The worker's hammer and the *kolkhoznitsa*'s (female collective farm worker's) sickle were adopted as symbols of the State.

New rules dictated that, in the first instance, all land, farm animals and implements were to be handed to the collective. For generations the peasants had known only one kind of farming, and that was for themselves. Now, no exceptions were tolerated. All that the peasants were left with were their tiny wooden houses and a small surrounding area to cultivate in their 'free time'.

The Communist government saw fit to divide agricultural people into three categories, for ideological purposes, and to name them accordingly. 'Kulaks' was the name given to those who had been the wealthiest farmers, usually owning large tracts of land, many animals, modern equipment and who, in season, hired the labour of other families. This group of relatively wealthy peasants earned the particular wrath of Stalin, who called for their 'liquidation' as a class.

Serednjaks were the middle group who owned less, but whose people were hard working, self sufficient, and able at times to employ others. *Bednjaks* were the poorest people in the villages. They were the small landowners with perhaps only the ground around their houses, one horse, a cow, a few sheep and chickens. There were many reasons for their poverty, but they, too, were reluctant to give what little they had to the collectives.

In 1928, resistance to collectivisation resulted in a bloody civil uprising, little of which was reported outside of Russia. The Kulaks and many *Serednjaks* resisted with all of their strength, obviously unwilling to hand over assets accumulated over generations of hard work. Only under severe pressure did most finally submit.

In order to overcome the resistance, government developed a special system executed by the OGPU (forerunner of the KGB) of expropriation and dislocation to wild and uninhabited areas in northern Russia, the Urals, Siberia and Kazakhstan. Many died in transit and those who survived created the first 'gulags'.

The gulags were a system of Soviet labour camps situated in remote areas of the country. Extreme conditions such as very long working hours, harsh climatic and other working conditions, meagre rations and summary executions resulted in limited life expectancies. Anyone who failed to co-operate in the Communist plan, or who had in some (often undefined) way offended those in charge, was liable to end up in a gulag. It has been estimated that up to 30 million people died in this system between 1918 and 1956.

The pressure and resistance to collectivisation continued. In 1930, in response to the unpopular and chaotic system, Stalin published an article in *Pravda*, the newspaper mouthpiece of the Communist Party, stating that he was unaware of the blood that had been spilled. He claimed to know nothing of the banishments to Siberia or any executions, pleaded his innocence and strongly criticised the Communist leaders responsible for the methods they had adopted. He was of the opinion that farmers should have joined collectives 'voluntarily', but it was too late: most of Russia had already been collectivised without option, and those who resisted had been dealt with.

Once a collective farm had been established, a meeting of *kolkhozniks* would be called to elect a *kolkhoz* board and chairman. Because the majority was invariably *Bednjaks*, and because the Communists controlled the elections (if necessary through the barrels of guns), those elected to office were inevitably Communists, whether they had any knowledge of farming or not.

Every *kolkhoznik* was obliged to work some 250 days of the year for the collective and was paid annually, when the crops had been harvested. The board would keep track of the days and quality of work of individual *kolkhozniks*. When the time arrived for their annual payment, those who had not done their quota would be penalised. Shoddy work or neglect of some duty, such as irregular feeding of livestock, would also result in a penalty – something *kolkhozniks* could ill afford.

Although grains such as wheat, rye and corn were produced on collectives, as well as meat and dairy products, *kolkhozniks* were expected to farm their own small allotments of land to produce most of their own food – and were therefore considered to require little money.

Collectivisation was completed by 1936. Prior to that, *kolkhozniks* were unable to get internal passports in their land of birth, so they could not change residence inside their own country. They were virtually slave labourers and prisoners on the collectives. For a people accustomed to freedom of movement in a vast country, it must have been a bitter pill to swallow.

My father, Daniel, was from a *Serednjak* family. Initially they resisted collectivisation, but, with no father at the helm (Mikhail had disappeared in WWI), capitulated in 1931. My father was 18.

My mother, Antonina, was from the *Bednjaks,* who did not resist in their area. Only two *Serednjak* families lived in that region: one was occupied with agriculture and the other made sheepskin clothing. These families were to lose everything they had – their land, houses, factory and sheep. None of the *Bednjaks* felt much sympathy for the *Serednjaks* as they had always regarded themselves a little above the other villagers because of their relative wealth. However, the villagers would come to regret their departure when they were unable to get the necessary clothing for the icy winters.

The *Bednjaks'* domestic animals had been their treasures. Some, rather than concede them to the collectives, slaughtered their animals. Others, even after being obliged to hand them over, continued to be concerned for their welfare. They would try to find the time to get to the collective sheds to feed or groom them, as if they were still part of the family. Later, when everyone was working with animals they had never owned, concern for the poor beasts' welfare dissipated. The Communist State had been determined to destroy all feelings of pride in private ownership, and collectivisation was an ideal vehicle for achieving that aim.

In 1930, the province of Kalinin suffered another serious drought. Crops died and the population was unable to find enough food for winter. Memories of the starvation that occurred in 1921 were still fresh and people desperately tried to obtain food by going to other regions, even as far off as Tashkent.

Bread was rationed and people would walk many kilometres to scavenge what they could for their families from bakeries or army barracks. This, together with the few vegetables people managed to scrape together from their failed crops, and wild berries and mushrooms collected in the forest, made up their diet. Discipline was the key to survival. Those who stuck to the rationing mostly lived to see the next summer.

Across Russia, Stalin's brutal repression gained momentum. By 1938 his tyranny was in full swing. People could not understand why relatives or neighbours were suddenly arrested and accused of being 'Enemies of the State'.

Nikoli, my mother's uncle, was fanatically supportive of the Communist government and by then chairman of a *kolkhoz*. One night a black government car, known as a 'voronok' (a black crow, a bird that lives on carrion and is a symbol of trouble for Russians), arrived in front of his house. It carried a number of OGPU agents who arrested him in full view of his family. He was not seen or heard of for decades, and never returned. Nobody knew who had denounced him.

To ask reasons of the authorities was very dangerous and could easily invite similar charges against those who asked. Nobody felt free to discuss these developments. Even in families, political discussion was avoided. Any family having a member arrested would immediately find itself distanced from all others. To be seen to be friendly, or to associate with them, was looking for serious problems. Fear is still alive and well among people of that generation.

After being out of the country for a few years, I learned that Putin had been elected president. During a routine, cheerful call to my parents, I asked my mother her opinion of Putin, and if she thought he had taken office with a positive attitude. There was a sudden deathly silence. I realised immediately that this was the wrong kind of question. I had broken the unwritten law from Stalin's time: to refrain from any political comment whatsoever, for fear of denunciation.

Even my generation, born after Stalin's death, has inherited fear and mistrust from our mothers' milk. Try talking about Russian politics with any middle-aged Russian, anywhere. You will feel the shutters come down. It is a hangover from those dreadful days.

Hot on the heels of Stalin's purges came the Second World War (WWII), which robbed my parents of their youth, but was not enough to stop two young people falling in love and marrying. Their first child, a son, was born in July 1945, soon after the capitulation of the German army in Russia. Five years later they had another son and, in 1955, two years after the death of Stalin, I was born.

This was the backdrop to the lives of my grandparents and my parents and, indirectly, of my life too. It moulded our characters and our outlook.

2

My grandmother, Katerina

OF MY FOUR GRANDPARENTS, I KNEW ONLY ONE – MY MOTHER'S mother, Katerina. Her husband, Ivan Saveljev, was lost in the winter of 1942, fighting the war at Smolensk. My paternal grandfather, Mikhail Devjatkin, was lost in the first year of WWI. His wife, Elena Devjatkina, died before I was born.

I consider myself lucky to have had even one grandparent survive the disasters of WWI, the 1917 Revolution, the civil war that followed, Stalin's repression, WWII and the famine that was just one of the consequences of that unfortunate conflict.

Katerina was born in 1899 in Bortnikovo, a village on the eastern side of the Volga River. She was the last of 19 children, with only the first two and last two having survived, all four girls. Her mother, Lisaveta Rodionova, was 51 when she was born. A strong woman blessed with entrepreneurial skills, Lisaveta was married to Mikhail Rodionov, whose passion, other than for her, was for the apple orchard he had developed. The only one of its kind in the region, which was generally considered too far north for this type of farming, it provided the family with an income a little better than the average villager's.

Every autumn Lisaveta would take the crop of apples to town to sell at the market and, with the money she raised, buy tea, sweets and sugar to enable her to run a tearoom from their house that provided a small source of extra income through the winters. While hard working in his orchard, the old man possessed few other skills and was content to leave the business side of their enterprises to his wife. He was a happy man, and enjoyed the company of his friends at the local pub on weekends.

Katerina, the youngest in the family, was a naturally active child. Before the Soviet era, children were able to start school at the discretion of their parents, providing the teachers agreed. So, at age seven, Katerina went to school at a neighbouring village church. She was intelligent, learned fast and absorbed everything 'like a sponge'.

At the age of only 11, however, her childhood and schooling were over, when she was sent to St Petersburg to look after the seven children of her eldest sister, Liza. Her sister had married a baker and they were both busy for long hours, baking products to sell. By the time Katerina was 17, the children had grown, affording her more time to work in the bakery. Although she had completed just four years of formal schooling, she always wanted to learn as much as possible, and found opportunities to read library books and wrote regularly to her relatives.

Her favourite job was serving behind the bread counter. She enjoyed interacting with the customers and they with her. She was always neatly dressed, and she was pretty, with dark curly hair and dark brown eyes. I remember her telling me that when she was on duty they always sold more bread. Some people even waited until she was behind the counter before coming in to make their purchases.

Her sister and brother-in-law were very happy to have her help and, for her seventeenth birthday, gave her a Singer sewing machine with pure silver fittings. They were keen for her to create an independent future by becoming a dressmaker. Life in St Petersburg was good for her in that it taught her the civil niceties expected of a well brought up young woman. She had expectations of a good future in the city.

Even after the Revolution had started, they continued with what they considered a normal life. However, things beyond their control started happening. Because they were independent bakers and running their own little business, they were considered capitalists. One day, their house, bakery and shop were confiscated by the Bolsheviks, who were enthusiastic about demonstrating their newly established authority. They were allocated a single room in which to live. All their possessions were taken too, supposedly to be distributed among the poor.

Their neighbour was less fortunate. After being dragged by his beard from his food store, he was shot in the street in front of his family.

Life in St Petersburg was becoming dangerous, with fighting breaking out everywhere. When the Bolsheviks, with the object of freeing the Tsar's political prisoners, stormed the jail of Peter Paul Fortress, many bystanders watched the battle. By chance, Katerina and her best friend happened to be in the vicinity. Although they were some distance away, on the opposite bank of the Neva River, a stray bullet hit her friend. She died in Katerina's arms.

Without sufficient living space and no job, Katerina had to leave the city; her life was altered forever. But somehow the Bolsheviks had overlooked her pride and joy, and her only asset, the Singer sewing machine. She returned to her home village of Bortnikovo, taking the sewing machine with her.

Because there was no employment available and her parents were elderly, she was obliged to help out on the small, general-purpose family farm. She learned how to do all the necessary tasks, including the heavy work normally done by men.

Being of marriageable age, she looked for a suitable partner – but men were scarce. Many young men had lost their lives in WWI and in the Revolution, which was continuing in the form of a civil war.

In 1922, at the age of 23, she was encouraged by her parents to marry a local man, Ivan Saveljev. He was able-bodied and unharmed by conflicts, although his means were limited. Nobody appeared to consider love a factor; practicality was the driving force. She had to move in with her new in-laws, a family consisting of her husband's three unmarried sisters and her mother-in-law, Avdotja. Katerina's sister, Sasha, was left to help out on the farm.

Ivan's three sisters had passed the customary marital age, but had found nobody to marry. At every opportunity, the jealous girls would mock, sneer at and humiliate Katerina. She lacked any support from her husband, who himself was brow-beaten. The only one to take her part at times was her mother-in-law, who appeared to love her, but was often reluctant to take sides against her own unkind offspring. When Katerina fell pregnant with my mother (Antonina), the eldest of the three sisters (who had suffered an injury falling from a horse, and had few prospects in life) was particularly spiteful.

Gradually, my grandparents were able to put aside sufficient funds to build their own house, which they embarked on after the birth of their second child. Russian farmhouses were fairly basic log cabins, consisting of one large room with a big brick oven for warmth, cooking, and on top of which people could sleep on cold winter nights. Blankets or wooden partitions were sometimes used to provide privacy. As a rule, the community would assist in the construction, which was often completed in no more than a week.

In the interim, Katerina's two younger sisters-in-law had somehow managed to find husbands of their own. Because Ivan was responsible for his old mother and injured sister, these women came to live with them. Throughout her life, Katerina was destined never to have a house exclusive to her own family.

The 1927 Five-Year Plan would in time result in the confiscation of all land, farm animals and implements, so that only their tiny houses remained in the hands of the people. My grandparents were obliged to work the collective farm and try to find time to work their own little piece of land, granted to them by the system and intended to enable them to feed themselves. Short Russian summers afforded little time to do what was necessary to grow crops. For that reason, ploughing had to be started at a time when the ice had only just melted, making it extremely hard work, especially for women.

Three days after giving birth to her third child, in early May 1930, Katerina was forced back to their land to hand plough behind a horse. Ivan could not leave the collective and someone had to tend their private plot to ensure that the family would not starve the following winter. Katerina's plough became bogged down in the sodden, icy earth; she tried to lift it, but it was too heavy and she overstrained herself, causing serious internal injury. From that moment on, she was unable to lift any weight of more than a couple of kilograms.

The village doctor said that she would now be capable of only light duties, which counted her out for work on the collective – and raised the serious question of who would now tend their own little plot. Ivan, bound to the collective, had insufficient time off to be of any real use at home.

It took three years and one more child before they were finally forced to give in. They had little choice other than to abandon the country and head for the city of Kalinin, leaving behind everything they had built up over the years – their house, the land and their horse, all of which were, at this point, taken over by the collective, which was standard procedure for those leaving, no matter what the reason.

With four children, a mother-in-law who chose to live with them, little money and no assets other than the Singer sewing machine, they set off on a hired wagon for Kalinin. They had initially to find lodging with distant relatives, had no jobs and were not qualified to do anything in particular, other than farming.

Life was tough and an unrelenting battle. There was even a time when Katerina was forced to ask her mother-in-law if she would not agree to go back to her two living daughters (her handicapped daughter having meanwhile died), so that she might be better fed, but the old lady begged to stay with Katerina.

Fortunately, with Government emphasis being placed on the development of heavy industry, jobs were becoming available and Katerina was eventually able to find employment as a cleaner in a clinic.

Ivan found work on a building site, far out of town, and was able to come home only once a month. He developed a liking for vodka, not uncommon among his peers. Typical of Russian men of the time, when he worked, he worked hard; but once he started drinking, it was a party until the cash ran out. Many times he would arrive home having blown most of his monthly salary on vodka. Things haven't really changed much; even now, alcoholism is a huge problem in Russia.

They were so short of money that Katerina had to take on extra cleaning work to try to make ends meet. The situation obviously led to friction between the couple, and their previously reasonable relationship began to suffer. As Katerina's children grew, they attempted to assist her, within the limits of their ability. They understood and felt sympathy for her struggle.

She had given birth to a total of six children, the first being my mother. Her second child, a daughter, had died at seven years of age from diphtheria. The loss of this child, of whom Katerina had been passionately fond, was to affect her deeply. Then came a boy, two other girls and, finally, another girl, who also died in infancy. Katerina seemed to take that death with less pain, since she knew that another mouth to feed would be placing even more strain on already inadequate resources.

She was totally against having more children after that. Bringing up the four she already had was quite enough of a challenge and there would be no material help from her relatives. Her mother, Lisaveta, had died shortly after her marriage and Mikhail, her father, had passed away in 1935 at 90 years of age. The second eldest sister, Sasha, the only family member left in Bortnikovo, had 'inherited' the family assets, including the old apple orchard, in which the *kolkhoz* had shown little interest.

In 1938, the Soviet government, without consulting the local inhabitants, decided to build a huge dam on the Volga River that was to flood Bortnikovo, including the family farm, and many other villages. The now homeless residents were relocated to other areas, but the loss of the old family orchard was a particular blow to Sasha, who might otherwise have been in a better position to assist Katerina. Sasha moved to the village of Rozhdestvenno where she occupied a small house until her death.

Life provided another test for all of Russia when the Germans invaded in 1941. On the third day of the war, Katerina's husband Ivan was called to report for military duty. Seven months later she was told that he was 'missing in action'.

During Stalin's rule, any missing soldier was deemed a traitor and regarded as a coward for having 'surrendered'. They remained so accused unless hard evidence to the contrary were established. Official punitive action was taken against the families of men missing in the war. People in their community regarded such families as pariahs. Even school children victimised the offspring of missing men.

Families of soldiers known to have given their lives in the war were much better off. They received war widows' pensions, child support and their children were given preference in admission to university and in obtaining better jobs.

For Katerina's family there would be no government support, no pension, no chance of ever improving their standard of living, because the government controlled everything, including the allocation of apartments. Higher education for the children of a missing soldier was also a problem. At this time, the NKVD (later the KGB) controlled every aspect of people's lives. If they wanted higher education, a job, an internal passport – without which it was illegal to travel inside the country – or to undertake just about any other activity, people were obliged to complete forms that had been drawn up by the NKVD.

One question was common to all forms: 'Is there anyone in your family who was missing or in captivity during WWII, or who is in prison?' An answer was compulsory, even up to 50 years after our victorious end to the war. Very few of those involved in the war had survived for that length of time, but the authorities kept asking the question of participants' grand- and even great-grandchildren, which was very disturbing to me and I'm sure to many others. Whenever the occasion arose for Katerina or any of her children to complete one or other of those dreaded forms, they were obliged to write that Ivan had gone 'missing in action'.

As a child, I recall asking where my grandfather was and being given evasive answers. We, the grandchildren, were simply told that he had died while serving in WWII, like millions of other men, but that nobody knew where. Our parents obviously wanted to keep the matter confidential so that we would not be tarnished by the event and would not have to suffer the indignities they had borne.

By the time I could understand the issues, so many years had passed that the scorn heaped upon my parents and others of their generation had, to a large extent, abated. Older people were trying to forget the terrible suffering that the war had inflicted and, over time, were becoming more forgiving.

A memorial to 'The Unknown Soldier' had even been constructed outside Moscow's Kremlin wall, and was unveiled on 8 May 1967. Later, similar memorials were erected in other cities and towns all over Russia. That made ridiculing the families of those missing in action a little less appropriate. Since nobody at that time was able to account for what had happened to my grandfather, he might well have been 'The Unknown Soldier'. Who knew?

In the years leading up to WWII, Katerina worked in the city of Kalinin as a security guard at the chemical plant. When the Germans invaded Russia, their main objective was to capture Moscow. Kalinin was only 160 kilometres northwest of the capital. The Volga River, a formidable barrier for any advancing army to cross, runs through Kalinin. Although the Germans did not actually cross the Volga at Kalinin (the Russian forces having destroyed all the bridges in advance), they took the city itself and the main road to Moscow that lay to the southwest.

Katerina remained at her post until the day Kalinin fell. When the advancing German artillery rained shells on the city, her only thought was to save her children's lives. Her eldest, my mother Antonina, had just finished school and been mobilised for work in an armaments factory in the Urals. Katerina took her two youngest girls, Lydia (9), Nina (11), her son Alex (15), as well as her old mother-in-law to Rozhdestvenno, after narrowly escaping from the city.

The Russian army liberated Kalinin after two months of Nazi occupation. The citizens began to return slowly to what was left of their ancient city. It had been almost totally destroyed. Katerina also returned with her children, leaving her mother-in-law in Rozhdestvenno with a family that had shown her great kindness.

Luckily, the building that contained the room occupied by Katerina before the war had remained standing, but everything of any value had been stolen. Jobs were impossible to find. The only employment available was cleaning up the ruins of the city.

The food stores had all been looted, so returning citizens went hungry. As Russian authority was slowly put back in place, rationing of a little food began. By then, Katerina could not look into the eyes of her starving daughters. Alex, her son, now 16, had volunteered as a tank mechanic and left for the front.

By the time spring arrived, with new crops still a couple of months away, Katerina was emaciated and unable to get up from her bed. Neighbours contacted the authorities who finally sent word to Antonina in the Urals to come home and decide what to do about her two sisters, who they thought were about to become orphans.

The authorities gave permission, on compassionate grounds, for Antonina to leave her work and travel to Kalinin. When she arrived, she found her mother very close to death. There was only one thing she could do. She traded her clothes and shoes for food, enabling her mother and sisters to get some nourishment and, very slowly, to gain a little strength. Fortunately, Antonina was soon able to get a job and, with the little she earned, feed the family and help them back to better health. For another year, Katerina was so weak that she was unable to work, but also unable to get any assistance from the State.

In 1944, Antonina married Daniel Devjatkin, a young man she had met at her place of work. Together, they tried to get the most nutritious food available for her mother. In 1946, when the war was finally over and Katerina was strong enough, she returned to work at the rebuilt chemical plant. Her younger daughters continued their schooling, which had resumed in the autumn of 1942 after the liberation of Kalinin. In due course they finished school, obtained jobs and were able to buy their own food. They both married and left Katerina's room. Alex returned from the army and also became self-sufficient. By about 1952, Katerina was able to breathe a little easier.

In 1953, trouble began again for Katerina; she was diagnosed as having cancer. Radiation treatment was in its infancy and she became a 'guinea pig'. Fifty sufferers underwent treatment, three of whom survived. She was one of the survivors. After 17 treatments with radiation, she had lost all of her teeth and suffered other physical side effects. But she was cured and carried on living for another 40 years – testament to her fortitude and tremendous will to survive. By the time she was 55, however, the cancer had taken its toll – Katerina was no longer able to work.

The archives in the city had been completely destroyed during the fascists' bombing, so records of Katerina's working life were lost. Without her working records, the State would not give her a pension, particularly as in the chaotic situation no witnesses could be found to substantiate her claims to having worked at the chemical plant. The result was that, in spite of her diligence and hard work before the war, she was entitled to no retirement benefit.

At that time in Russia, accommodation was impossible to find. Families were often obliged to live in one room, sometimes as small as 10 square metres. Alex was the last of her children to marry and when he did, because of the lack of housing, was obliged to bring his wife to live with Katerina. Her daughter-in-law did not have the kindest temperament and did her best to get Katerina out of what had been her own room.

Watching their unhappy mother's and brother's lives being ruined was unbearable for Katerina's daughters. They invited their mother to stay with them. Finally, Katerina succumbed to the pressure and left the only room she had been able to call her own home since leaving the country village of Bortnikovo 23 years earlier. For the rest of her life, she lived with her daughters in turn, helping to raise their children.

Katerina helped to bring up my two brothers and me. She also raised her middle daughter Nina's son, and the two daughters and one great-grandson of her youngest daughter, Lydia. All of us loved her very dearly and missed her terribly if we didn't see her for any length of time.

As I was growing up, Katerina taught me to do whatever she could and was unstinting in her love for me. She always encouraged me to gain as much knowledge and education as possible, because she herself had never had such opportunities. My first attempts at reading, writing and arithmetic were under her tutelage.

Since my parents were required to work full time, she felt obliged to do all of the domestic chores in our small flat. When I was still little, she taught me the essentials of housekeeping. She always treated me as if we were friends, with no age gap.

I had so many questions during those years. I remember asking her which of her three daughters and one son was her favourite. She told me to open my hand and look at my fingers.

'They are all different,' she said. 'But if you hurt one it won't matter which, because they all feel pain the same way. My children may be different people, but if anything happens to any one of them my heart feels the same pain.'

Then I remember asking her if she didn't get bored doing the same work every day. I wondered why she would continue doing it if she really didn't like it. She said there were some jobs that people enjoyed and some they didn't, but that they were a duty and had to be done regardless.

'Don't think that everything everybody has to do in life will be a pleasure. Who wants to clean a toilet? But everyone wants a clean toilet and that's why someone has to do it.'

She continued, 'You already have some duties and you can expect more obligations as you grow up. It's better simply to accept them, without giving them too much thought.'

At the age of five, I didn't like this particular advice at all. I thought life was there to be enjoyed. All I wanted to do was play with other children out in the yard, dress my doll, paint or draw and read fairy stories.

She taught me to be economical. Some things were sacred to her. Children should always respect and care for others, and their parents in particular. Another sacred thing, for her, was bread. During the war, bread had saved lives. She taught her grandchildren to respect bread as something holy. We were not allowed to throw bread away, even if it were mouldy – she insisted that we feed it to the birds or animals. If it were dry, she would cut it into pieces and make rusks. We were not allowed to put a loaf upside down on the table because she thought that indicated disrespect.

She also regarded money as sacred; she had so little of it during her lifetime, and not one kopek of government pension until very late in her life. Although the money my parents gave her to buy food for our family was never checked, she would always account for every kopek and ensure the leftover cash went back to them. Never would she consider spending anything on herself. So she taught us to respect our parents' hard work and the money they brought home. It was never to be spent on trivialities.

I recall, at the age of 12, running an errand to the bakery just before dark. On returning home, I gave the change to my mother and, to my surprise, a three rouble note was missing. Mother thought that I had lost it and sympathetically accepted the situation, but Granny Katerina found it hard to accept and kept asking me where I thought I'd dropped it.

The next morning, at first light, she woke me and said I should go with her. I hurriedly dressed and followed her down to the street, unhappy because my sleep had been interrupted. A miracle happened: we found the money lying on the pavement exactly where I thought I might have dropped it.

I was still grumpy from waking early and, on the way back home, I asked if waking me at that hour was worth three roubles; I thought our family would have survived without it. She was very angry and said it was a shame to listen to me. For three roubles, she said, our family could have enough food to survive for one day, and my parents had worked hard to earn it. I should learn to pay more respect to money as it was not easy to come by.

As had been the custom before the Revolution, Katerina had been baptised in the Russian Orthodox Church. She was fully conversant with all the traditions and ceremonies, but never tried to teach us about God. Maybe our parents were not in favour of it. Perhaps she understood that making us religious was running a risk, since the Communist authorities opposed it and promoted atheism.

When I asked her if there was a God, she said simply that when she was growing up there had been, but that now there were some doubts because our cosmonauts had returned from space and told us that there was nobody there. She sighed thoughtfully and said, 'Everyone has God in their souls because, without Him, they cannot be human.' Her life was rather like God's toughest examination, and she passed it with great dignity.

When I was old enough to analyse her situation, I realised how difficult it must have been for her – without her own room and without any source of income for much of her life. And, during her later years, being totally dependent on her daughters' families meant that she was always obliged to maintain good relationships with everyone. She was never independent in any way, but always at the beck and call of others.

Despite this life of deprivation, she never complained. In fact, to the contrary – she always appeared happy, knowing that she was loved and needed by everyone in her daughters' families. Even during the hardest of times, when my family was obliged to accommodate six people, including Katerina, in a 14 square metre room, sharing kitchen and ablution facilities with our neighbours, we never considered her to be in the way. I am proud that we kept her within the family, right to the end of her life.

In 1983, the Communist government passed a new law. WWII widows who had no pensions and had not remarried were to be given a widows' pension and could apply for a small flat. Katerina, as the widow of a missing soldier, was not eligible. That motivated my mother to approach the State Archives in a final attempt to establish what had really happened to her father.

All previous enquiries had yielded only one answer, 'Missing'. Finally, an answer to her latest enquiry arrived from the Moscow Archives. Her father, reportedly at the battle for Smolensk, had lain on the snow for many hours and contracted pneumonia. He had been too sick to fight and, in a barely conscious condition, confined to a military hospital. The hospital had been completely destroyed in a fascist bombing raid and no hospital records had survived. That was the reason why the authorities had listed him simply as 'missing', regardless of the disgrace and problems it implied for his family.

Obviously the chaos that prevailed after the war ended had not been conducive to caring about the reputations of lone soldiers. What had really happened to him must have come to light only years later, by way of a survivor's report. His status was changed to 'killed in action'. Katerina was, at that late stage of her life, elevated to the position of a WWII widow.

We were not pariahs after all, but we had known that all along. Justice had finally been done. Our dearest grandmother, who had been so deserving of better treatment by a government she had defended with all her strength, at last had what she so richly deserved, although she had unjustly been made to wait 40 years. It took my mother a further two years of running around administration offices before she finally had all the necessary documentation for her mother's pension and flat.

When Katerina heard about her entitlement, she told us that, in her youth, she had seen a gypsy fortune-teller who had told her that she would have a long life, that in her last years she would live with her youngest daughter and that she would die a rich woman.

She said, 'The gypsy was right. Everything she told me has come true. I have even become a rich woman.' When we heard her say those words, we cried. Katerina was then 86 years old. A small, one-roomed flat was like a castle to her, but the sad thing was that she was now unable to enjoy the 'luxury' of the privacy previously denied her. She was simply too old to cope on her own. On her grand monthly pension of 38 roubles, she would never have survived. (The official breadline figure was 90 roubles.)

If there was any joy in it at all, it was that at least, before she died, she might be able to regard herself as a normal and self-sufficient member of society. It afforded Katerina great pride to hand her pension money to her daughter as a contribution to the family budget. I'm sure that her food tasted better once she knew that, at last, it was her money paying for it. Her buoyancy throughout life, her great compassion for others, along with her simple lack of animosity and bitterness towards society, touched us deeply.

She passed away in 1994 at the age of 95, surrounded by her children, grandchildren and great-grandchildren, all of whom loved her dearly. I can confirm that the gypsy was right: she died rich – in the love of her family.

3

Daniel, my father

ALTHOUGH THEY CAME FROM DIFFERENT BACKGROUNDS AND regions, my parents shared certain common experiences. Neither had been able to enjoy a normal, carefree childhood and their youthful experiences had been gained in very tough times, through the turmoil and dramatic events sparked by the 1917 Revolution. They were ambitious in the sense that, above all else, they wanted a good education to provide them with opportunities. They both desired a better quality of life than their parents had managed to achieve.

Daniel was born in a village in the Chamzin area of Mordovia in December 1913, the third son in a family that was to lose its father; Mikhail Devjatkin, in WWI. In fact, Daniel never met his father; he died before he was born. His mother, Elena Devjatkina, never remarried, waiting in vain for the return of the husband she loved.

As was the case with his two elder brothers, he attended school in the village and spent the rest of his time helping out on the family land, taking care of their animals, and cutting and stockpiling the wood needed to survive the bitter winters.

When he was 18, his family was collectivised and became *kolkhozniks*. His hard work on the *kolkhoz* paid off and he was promoted to a managerial position. In 1932, he was selected to go on a course to qualify as a *kolkhoz* accountant. A year later, the *kolkhoz* board recommended Daniel attend a two-year study course at the Soviet Party School, which he completed in 1935.

Those schools had been set up all over the country by the government, with the aim of training Communist devotees. His education there was intended to prepare him for a future leadership role in the Communist financial hierarchy and to implement their policies. Qualifications from such a school provided opportunities in many areas of the national economy not open to others. Teaching Party principles to carefully selected candidates, and honing their Communist zeal, was one of the many arrows in the political quiver of the Communist Party, intended to hold control over the minds of the people.

Daniel's attendance there had precluded his being drafted into the army, but as soon as he had qualified, he was sent for basic military training. While at the school, he had met and fallen in love with a beautiful young girl. He was completely overwhelmed by her and felt compelled to marry her before being called up for military duty. He did and she fell pregnant immediately.

From 1935, he performed his duties as a soldier in the Soviet Army, undergoing training in the Khabarovsk region in the Russian Far East. There, he received the happy news that a son had been born.

Unfortunately, during the final month of his military duty, while on a training exercise, tragedy befell him and his fellow soldiers. They were living in a two-metre deep camouflaged dugout to help escape the bitterly cold weather. The sides, floor and roof were made of heavy taiga forest logs and the men had covered the roof with soil for added protection from the cold and possible shelling.

Under the added weight of a heavy snowfall, the roof caved in without warning, burying the occupants. Daniel was one of only a few survivors, but was left unconscious for many months. During that time, he was transferred from one hospital to another, ending up in Khabarovsk. When he finally regained consciousness, he had no idea of what had happened to him or his colleagues, or of where he was, or how he got there.

A year passed before he had gained sufficient strength to care for himself; then he was invalided out of the army by the doctors, who relegated him to the ranks of the handicapped. In place of the bright career he would have hoped for on his release from the military, at 25 years of age he was discharged with the gift of a new uniform (since he had no other clothing), an army blanket, intended to keep him warm enough for the journey home, and a little money for his travels.

When he finally reached home and met his wife and son, Daniel was shocked to find that she had decided she had no need of an invalided husband. She had found another man with whom she intended living.

Devastated, he left and went home to his mother in Ruzaevka, in the Chamzin area. He would care for her as best he could for the rest of her life. In order to feed himself and his mother (his brothers having married and left their village), he tried to get employment as close as possible to his home.

Because of his medical status as 'invalid', however, he was unable to get any sort of job. Life had turned sour on the young man. He had lost his wife and son, suffered bad headaches from the accident and could not find employment.

Depression set in, but Daniel was not the kind to give up. There was no choice – he had to leave the village to find a job where he was unknown. He had learned sad lessons through being honest enough to show the papers listing him as an invalid. Not even his wife had needed an invalid.

Aspiring to a career as a detective/investigator, Daniel was led to the city of Kazan, where he decided to make a new life for himself. There, without proffering his army medical discharge document, he took a clerical job in a KGB office and attended night classes at the School of Justice, where he hoped to qualify. Whatever he could afford was sent home to support his mother.

At this time there was an orgy of misguided State power in the Soviet Union. Stalin's grip had tightened around the throats of the Russian people. Individuals were being denounced as traitors for no reason other than, perhaps, having offended neighbours, who reported them to the KGB as 'Enemies of the State'. With hindsight, we recognise this as violent repression, but at that time the people, including Daniel, did not understand what was happening around them. Misinformation by organs of State led the trusting proletariat to regard Stalin as a hero and 'father' of the nation.

As a young man, Daniel was convinced that he had found his vocation in the investigative services, but being a detective meant it was essential to work under the KGB. I remember once asking him what he did there.

He smiled ruefully and said, 'The KGB office was just like any other, with a huge amount of paperwork. Don't think that everyone in that office must have been a murderer. We really believed, most of the time, that the young Soviet State had many enemies hidden among the people. The tragedy was the discovery of people's innocence after it was too late.'

That period has not gone from my parents' psyche. It has left indelible marks on their attitude and behaviour. Throughout their lives they have never spoken aloud about anything even remotely connected to politics. Criticising Communist Party officials is still taboo. They don't even complain about their lives or the circumstances surrounding them – 'the walls have ears'. It is still difficult for them to discuss what took place in Stalin's time, let alone what their opinion of it is now, or was then. Life has taught them that silence is safest for them, their family and those with whom they are connected.

It is extraordinary that my father, back in 1938, could have risked hiding from the KGB the documents that related to his invalid status. It may have been the rashness of youth, or simply that people at that time had not yet learned that nothing could be hidden from the tentacles of that monstrous, octopus-like organ of the State.

The KGB checked everything, especially the backgrounds of the individuals working for it. After a few months it came to light that Daniel had not been completely open when applying for the job. He felt sure that exposure would lead to his dismissal, or worse. But he had worked hard, without complaint, and so managed to conceal his disability from his colleagues. In fact, his superiors thought him diligent and patriotic. Luckily for him, they left him alone. Daniel was able to continue with his studies and hold down his daytime job.

By early 1941, he had completed his studies at the Kazan School of Justice and was appointed a public detective in the Prosecutor's Office in one of the rural areas.

I remember my father telling me that, at that time, he had had a very strange dream. He had seen huge metal birds swooping down from a leaden sky, grabbing at people, dismembering and eating them. In this Armageddon were steel monsters crushing people into the earth, creating rivers of blood and piles of broken bones. There was no escape, either on land or in the air. He said he'd tried to run and, just as he was about to be caught by one of the fantastic metal monsters, he had woken with a feeling of tremendous relief at his lucky escape.

The nightmare left such an impression on him that he went to a gypsy fortune-teller, reputed to be able to interpret such things. She listened quietly, sighed heavily and announced that soon the population should expect terrible grief, but that he personally would survive.

She was correct. Just six months later, on 22 June 1941, Germany invaded Russia. Twenty-eight-year-old Daniel volunteered to join up immediately, but was refused duty because of his status and consigned to the reservists. Out of a sense of patriotism, he applied to join the Communist Party, feeling this to be the best way to defend his motherland. He was among many to take that action in solidarity with his fellow countrymen at that time.

The fighting was to last much longer than initially anticipated. Daniel lost his elder brother, Yephim, soon after the invasion, and his second brother, Vasili, returned crippled for life. It wasn't long before the Soviet government called up even those designated invalid, for service in non-combatant capacities. Daniel was mobilised in 1942.

After a brief training period in counter-intelligence, he was sent to Kalinin to train female radio and field telephone operators. After that, he was assigned to a position in security, escorting loaded trucks.

In 1944, in Kalinin, he met my mother, Antonina. They married two months later. There was no proper wedding; neither were there rings or a wedding dress. The war was still raging and circumstances did not permit such frivolities. The ceremony was a brief affair in a municipal office, with just a few friends and relatives to congratulate the happy young couple.

Soon after their marriage, Daniel was posted to Rzhev, a town in southwest Kalinin province. Antonina accompanied him, and Victor, their first child, was born there in 1945. They continued to work in Rzhev until he was demobilised in 1948, again because of his invalid status, and they returned to Kalinin.

There were three categories of invalid. The first was unable to work at all and was given a pension; the second could work at certain light duties and was given a smaller pension; and the third, which was my father's category, was designated as able to do 'suitable work' and received no pension at all.

With no income, a family, as well as a son from his first marriage to feed, it was essential for Daniel to find a job. The city of Kalinin had suffered badly during the invasion. Accommodation was almost impossible to find and food was severely rationed.

In those circumstances, Daniel and Antonina decided to leave the devastation of Kalinin and head southeast, near to the border with Kazakhstan. (The Germans had been stopped at Stalingrad, formerly Tsaritsyn, so never reached that area.) They settled in Orenburg province on the Great Russian steppe, breadbasket of the nation.

The young family lived in a typical Russian wooden country house in a large village. Daniel was able to return to his chosen career as a detective and Antonina became a primary school teacher. Soon they bought a calf, then lambs, some piglets, geese, ducks and chickens. There was enough food, so Daniel was able to invite his mother, Elena, to come to stay with them and assist in the upbringing of her grandson, Victor. Two years after arriving in Orenburg, they had another son, Evgueni, and, in 1955, I was born.

Unfortunately, Elena died before I was born, but my grandmother, Katerina, came to stay with us. The whole family was happy in the area and would have been satisfied to live there forever. However, young Victor became very ill with bronchitis, which turned into bad asthma, adversely affected by proximity to certain farm animals. His condition was serious and the doctor said it was essential that he be moved to town, where his allergies would be less stressful. So, in 1958, the family moved back to Kalinin.

My father was unable to get work as a detective there, because they had a full complement of staff and he was now recognised as an invalid, which had not happened in the rural area of Orenburg, where nobody appeared to care too much. He was obliged to take whatever jobs he was offered appropriate to his medical condition, and the jobs never lasted more than about five years.

When I was five, the whole family was at home one Sunday when there was an unexpected knock on the door. A young, good-looking man of about 25 presented himself, claiming to be the son of my father. Naturally, this was a shock to us all, until we realised that it was true and this young fellow had come to find his real father. He had known only his stepfather throughout his growing years.

When I realised he was my half brother, I was most unimpressed. I already had two brothers, five and ten years my senior. They displayed scant interest in me, would never play with me and, furthermore, chased me away if I tried to get involved with anything they were doing. All I wanted was a sister, so what use was another elder brother to me?

'Okay,' I said, 'but I have enough brothers, can't you find a sister for me?' Everybody laughed – I had inadvertently relieved the tension.

From that point on, we were all more relaxed and my newly arrived half-brother spent the rest of the day with us. Having satisfied his curiosity, he decided to leave, but before doing so he thanked Father sincerely for having always sent money to his mother to pay for his upbringing. He said he was pleased to find his father a normal family man, happy and surrounded by a loving wife and three children.

It was strange to me that my father sometimes talked of his first son, but never mentioned his first wife. I guess she must have hurt him deeply, but it didn't affect his love for our mother, whom he always respected and adored.

In 1963, my mother turned 40. Early that morning I remember Father presenting her with a little jewellery box. As Mother opened it, we all craned our necks in curiosity. With gasps of surprise we saw a delicate, beautiful lady's gold watch.

Father said, 'For all of your life you have never had anything precious, not even a wedding ring. Now it's too late to give you a ring, but you can wear this watch forever as a token of my love for you.'

We children could not take our eyes off the magnificent present. Mother was touched by the expensive gift, but could not understand where Father had found the money to buy it. He explained that he had thought about it years before and saved a little every month in order to be able to buy it for her.

Despite the fact that my parents had little and lived a spartan existence, I will always respect and appreciate the way they treated each other and us, their children. Father suffered bad headaches all of his life as a result of his accident in the army. Mother always tried her best to keep us from disturbing him, which was exceedingly difficult in the confined spaces in which we had to live. He never complained, even when it got so bad that he had to be admitted to hospital for treatment.

Because he was never able to get promotion in his mostly short-lived jobs, mother always earned more than he did, although she never mentioned it or derided him for it. There was no competition; they were husband and wife and that was all that mattered. I never saw them have a serious argument and we, their children, grew up in a warm, loving environment, expecting our lives to be the same.

Father finally decided to retire at 62. He gathered my brothers and me around him and told us that he had worked most of his life and was now entitled to a State pension. He said he had seen us all through a higher education and knew that, from that point, it didn't matter if he worked or not. He would certainly not be able to support us, so it was up to us to earn our own livings. He thought his pension would be sufficient for him, even if it were miserable. He was tired of battling his injury and thought it best to rest. We realised then that we would have to be responsible, not just for ourselves, but also for our parents.

4

Antonina, my mother

B ORN IN 1923, AFTER THE REVOLUTION, ANTONINA'S childhood took place during the development of the new Soviet State and the establishment of a strong Communist Party. She was, and still is, a child of her times. The beliefs inculcated in her at a very young age remain strong.

Antonina has always believed in the merit of the revolutionary, fairer State that was established, where all people would enjoy a better standard of living through Communism. She is fanatical, but devoid of aggression. Her early experiences of Communist propaganda have permanently set her thinking in this particular way. In any event, she has shared her life exclusively with other Russian people, never having had the opportunity to travel or communicate with different nationalities.

Antonina's childhood in Bortnikovo was typical of any country girl's. Children were expected to do their share of household chores, such as feeding the chickens and geese, weeding in summer and generally doing whatever they were capable of around the home. As they grew older they would take care of the younger family members and, in season, assist their parents in the fields.

Because of my grandmother Katerina's earlier injury, resulting in her being unable to lift anything that weighed much at all, my mother, Antonina, her eldest child, had to help her carry everything, from her younger siblings to buckets of milk, and assist at home in many ways.

For recreation, children would swim in the river, go to the oil mills to see what they could scrounge in the form of oilcake (which, to them, was like candy), and, with the curiosity of the uninitiated, watch the teenagers' tentative socialising. Mother was lucky because her paternal grandparents had a rare apple orchard, where her kindly grandfather, Osip, loved to spoil her with a blouse full of delicious fruit. Antonina's grandmother, Avdotja, who was a very strong disciplinarian, disapproved of the practice because she was the one who took the crop to town to sell at the market, and thought the old man foolish to waste profits on his young granddaughter.

The school year would always start in September, but pupils had to have turned nine to gain entrance. Because she was born in January, Antonina had to wait until the following year to begin her schooling. Most of her friends had already started, which left her behind, feeling very frustrated at having to wait another whole year. Every day she would find out what her friends had learned and, when she first attended school, her teachers were amazed that she already knew everything they intended teaching her. And so they decided to promote her immediately to the second class.

Rural social life was lively and kept teenagers safely occupied (as explained to me by my mother). In summer, gatherings often took place in the street – what might now be called an open-air discotheque. Teenagers had their own society, divided into age groups: 15- and 16-year-olds, 17- and 18-year-olds, and 19- and 20-year-olds, who were expected to marry in the near future. Since there were no radios, television, electricity or newspapers, all their fun revolved around meeting each other at weekends, bringing together any musical instruments they had, such as balalaikas, harmonicas and wooden spoons for percussion, to dance, sing, joke and meet contemporaries from other villages.

This meant that people from surrounding villages would meet, thus decreasing the chance of inbreeding. Parents would visit the meeting places to scout for future partners for their offspring. Social discourse at these gatherings kept everyone abreast of what was happening in the region.

In winter, when the countryside was blanketed in snow, teenagers would gather in their age groups in different houses. Girls were not allowed to go to boys' houses, so it was up to the parents of girls to host the parties. Girls would gather in one of the houses, usually occupying themselves with some form of home craft, while singing and chatting. They did less work and a lot more talking than singing when the boys arrived.

In 1930, collectivisation hit their area. Antonina, at the tender age of seven, attended political meetings with her mother, Katerina, and accepted with enthusiasm the Communist propaganda about a better life under the new system. She embraced the ideology, not realising how difficult it might be for her elders to contemplate giving up what they owned for some 'pie in the sky', new-fangled idea.

Antonina remembers how the village women, then known collectively by the new name of *kolkhoznitsa*, would gather on their way to the collective fields to cut hay. One woman from the far end of the village would leave her house carrying a sickle, to be joined almost ritualistically, one by one, by other women whose houses she passed. She would sing and, as the crowd grew, the singing would become louder, much to the delight and amusement of the children who would follow them, trying to sing along.

One day, news passed quickly through the village that a tractor was on its way to the *kolkhoz*. It was the source of tremendous excitement, since few, if any, of the local people had ever seen one of these wonderful labour-saving inventions. Antonina, together with the village children, ran some distance up the road. They were shouting in wild anticipation, all wishing to have first sight of the great innovation.

When they saw it for the first time they were stunned into momentary silence, but when the driver offered to take some of their number for a ride on the huge metal monster, pandemonium broke out. A few were brave and lucky enough to be hoisted up for the first ride, while the others walked alongside the slow-moving machine, arguing about who would be next to display their courage on the big iron ox.

All of the inhabitants gathered at the entrance to the village to welcome the driver and celebrate the arrival of the machine, which would be of such benefit to them. There was exultation among the adults who, after collectivisation, had found that the lands they were expected to work were bigger than they had envisaged. The government had added ground to their expropriated acres with the intention of getting them, in yet to be established patriotic zeal, to produce more for the benefit of the motherland. It had been for the dual purpose of motivating such zeal and increasing production that the tractor had been delivered.

At the end of that summer there was further elation when the first threshing machine arrived at the *kolkhoz*. It was a cumbersome, unwieldy machine that, after delivery, remained stationary in a shed that had been specially constructed to house it. Wheat would be harvested manually, loaded in sheaves onto horse-drawn wagons and taken to the thresher for processing.

A winnowing machine was later added to the collection of modernising marvels. Having these was a boon to the workers, but working in close proximity to them was another matter. The dust and noise created in the shed were untenable. The machines choked those obliged to tend them, and covered them with fine dust that itched and nearly drove them demented in the heat and humidity that sometimes occurs at that time of year. When they emerged from the shed they found their hearing impaired. It took hours to return to normal.

Despite the drawbacks, everyone was excited and delighted to have these wonderful labour savers. Even the oldest and most conservative farmers among them tried to get into the shed to witness the revolutionary process, for which there was universal approval.

The people were given to understand that the machines had kindly been loaned by the Soviet government, with Stalin at the forefront. They did, however, have to move from one *kolkhoz* to another, to assist all; there were not yet enough machines to allocate one to each newly established *kolkhoz*, although that was planned for the future.

Factories for the manufacture of farming machinery had only just been established and time would be needed to enable them to produce sufficient for the entire country's requirements. The *kolkhoz* was later to learn that the machines had merely been loaned them on a temporary basis. They were expected to buy their own equipment out of 'profits' made on the sale of produce. Of course, there was only one customer for their produce and that was the government, which fixed prices in order to comply with a system visible only to those privileged enough to see the 'big picture'.

As time went by, people slowly began to realise that their miserable salaries were still insufficient for them to buy anything other than the bare necessities of life, such as winter clothing for their families or essential repairs to their humble houses. They would still be obliged to grow their own food in order to subsist, as they had always done, except that they had only tiny plots of land now on which to do it. The large acreages they had previously farmed for their own benefit had been forfeited to the collective.

Against this background, in 1933, the family packed their worldly possessions on a wagon and moved to the city of Kalinin. The decision to move to town had been forced on them by Katerina's injury and consequent inability to carry on working on the collective, or to manage the family plot. As it turned out, the move would be of benefit to Antonina, as she would now not have to spend the rest of her life as a *kolkhoznitsa*. It was initially exciting for the children, who expected life to be much improved in the city, until they found out that the city was really nothing but an oversized village, with a few more streets and some big stone buildings.

Most people still lived in wooden houses, and those on the periphery of the city even kept animals, as if they were living in the countryside. Because the family was unable to find a flat to rent, they moved into a room in the house of a distant relative. It measured about 12 square metres, with two windows facing onto the backyard. In the centre of the room was a brick oven, used for both cooking and warmth. A fire was lit every morning and food was prepared for the family for the day, so that by nightfall the oven had cooled and, in winter, would be covered with thick mattresses and used as a bed. Under the windows was a large metal trunk that, when covered with a mattress, served as a bed for children.

Although Katerina's health was failing, she and Ivan had to continue working. They both found menial employment – Ivan as a construction site worker and Katerina as a cleaner in a clinic. Antonina was 10 years old and attending school. Her brother Alex, aged seven, had to stay home with his grandmother, Avdotja, while his two younger sisters, Nina and Lydia, at three and one-and-a-half respectively, went to kindergarten.

After school, Antonina would go home, fetch her brother and, together, they would go to the kindergarten to bring the two young children back. Alex would take Nina by the hand and Antonina would carry Lydia. Antonina and Alex's primary responsibility was to care for the younger ones, keep the house in order and go shopping when necessary.

The family lived in that 12 square metre room for a year, while looking for better accommodation. Katerina eventually found a better room to rent, at an affordable price. It was a big improvement on their previous home; it was larger, it also had a brick oven in the centre, and it featured a door allowing them direct access to the street.

It afforded them a degree of independence not previously enjoyed while living in the house belonging to relatives, who had felt at liberty, at any time, to make social visits. The only drawback was the fact that the new room possessed just two small windows, not really letting in sufficient natural light, even at midday. Antonina battled to do her homework without the aid of electricity, which the family avoided using because it cost money that they needed for other necessities. They remained in this house until 1936.

In 1935, Katerina was lucky enough to get a better job in a newly constructed chemical plant that, after a year, offered employees purpose-built accommodation.

At this windfall, their joy was boundless. They secured a 20 square metre room on the third floor of a brand new brick building in the centre of town. There were another two rooms on the same floor that were occupied by two other families, and all shared common kitchen and ablution facilities.

Whereas previously, bathroom facilities had been outside the wooden buildings in which their rooms were situated, they were now inside and on the same floor. That was comparative luxury. While the old accommodation had featured brick ovens in the centre of the room, the new building had fireplaces against the walls. Each family was allocated a wooden shed outside the building, in which they dug cellars to enlarge the capacity for storing vegetables below ground level for the winters. It also housed their supplies of firewood.

As the children grew, Katerina had to find extra work to earn money needed to provide for them. She would wash and clean house for anyone who had the money to pay, and the children helped her carry any weights beyond her capacity. There were few families with any extra cash, so providing food throughout the winters was a real struggle.

In 1938, the Communist Party Congress adopted the third of many Five-Year Plans. Their main aim was to catch up to and overtake the West in terms of productivity per capita of population. But the reality on the ground was far removed from such theorising in Moscow.

Most families with origins in the countryside looked for nearby plots of unused ground on which to cultivate potatoes and other nutritious vegetables. Past experience had taught them that this would be the only way to survive. Of course, the practice was not strictly legal as the government owned all land. At any time the authorities could intervene and decide to allocate the site for other purposes. And there was a further risk involved: a great deal of hard work had to be put into plots that could not be defended against robbery, as fencing the sites was not permitted. The government generally turned a blind eye to such cultivation, probably because they knew that, without the extra food provided in this way, the people could not sustain themselves.

Katerina and her children sought out a little piece of ground and began to cultivate it. Tending this patch daily was the responsibility of the children. They had to dig, plant, water and weed, which they managed well and the venture returned essentials for survival through the winters. However, the produce was still not sufficient for the growing youngsters, and Katerina decided it would help if she kept chickens and rabbits in the storage shed to supplement the vegetables grown on the plot. This suited Alex, who took it upon himself to make the animals his department, as he disliked growing vegetables.

Despite all of these activities, it was still difficult for Katerina to make ends meet. Her husband had become increasingly unreliable and there were months when he did not contribute a rouble. Clothing the growing children was getting more expensive by the season, and even potential hand-me-downs between the two little girls were often worn out before they could be passed on. Sporadic help came in the form of the newly created Trade Union at the chemical plant. They had decided to try to assist workers with large families in the form of clothing vouchers for essential items and shoes, even though they were of the 'bottom of the range' variety.

Antonina was the eldest daughter and had been obliged to take on the most responsibility. She nevertheless began to dream of a time when she would find some relief from the drudgery and anxiety of daily life, but could never consider letting down her mother, brother and little sisters. The best solution was for her to find a way of making a more meaningful contribution to the family budget. She had always been a bright, active pupil and her teachers had decided that she was definitely university material. In her final school year, Antonina chose a Moscow university that offered courses in communications, and applied herself to studying for the necessary entry examinations.

Katerina was delighted at the progress made by her eldest child, who would soon leave home to further her studies. Her younger children were now old enough to be of considerable help; for the first time in many years she felt some relief from the heavy burden she had carried for so long. There was even time for her to make a dress on her Singer sewing machine for Antonina's final-year school party.

It was Saturday, 21 June 1941, the day of the party. Antonina had been preparing herself all day for the event that evening. Her mother had been occupied at work for the day and arrived home eager to see her 18-year-old daughter dressed for the occasion. At the sight of Antonina in her evening dress and fully made up, it struck Katerina that she had failed to notice that her little girl was little no longer. She was stunningly beautiful in her simple hand-cut, white silk dress and low-heeled white shoes, bought new for the occasion.

At school, Antonina had been one of the best in physical exercises, which had provided her with an exceptional figure, strong but shapely. Her hair was auburn, fashionably cut in the *komsomol* style (approved by the Communist youth league) – straight and worn just below the ear. Her dark brown eyes shone in anticipation of a wonderful night. Her flawless olive skin prompted a sigh from Katerina, who remembered her own eighteenth year that had been spoiled by the Revolution in Petrograd.

At that moment, she was confident that her daughter would enjoy a happier and more fruitful life than she herself had been allowed. The Soviet government was promising a bright future in the new State and Katerina had begun to believe it, mostly because her own life had started showing some small improvements.

Her motherly emotions were to keep Katerina awake until Antonina returned home from the party. Then they sat up all night until sunrise, chatting about her wonderful celebration. They talked about the first real party in Antonina's life, the sadness of saying goodbye to her schoolmates, her anticipated departure for university in Moscow, and generally reminisced about their lives. Never could they have imagined that it was to be the last happy and peaceful night they would enjoy together for a long time to come.

The following day war was declared. It was Sunday, 22 June 1941. The German fascists had invaded the Soviet Union.

5

Wartime

O N THE MONDAY AFTER THE DANCE, THE SCHOOL LEAVERS gathered in the central city park, as was their custom when they needed to meet. Their discussion centred around the invasion and what they, as patriots, could do to assist in the defence of their motherland.

Recruitment for men had already been announced and some of the male school leavers had by now been called up. The girls found it hard to believe that, just three days earlier, they had all been sitting behind school desks together. Now their friends were soldiers.

It was 25 June 1941, and Katerina's husband, Ivan, had been recruited. He said his farewells to his wife and youngest children early that morning. Katerina was employed in security at the chemical plant and was obliged to go to work because of the State of Emergency, so she was unable to accompany him to the railway station as most other wives and families were doing. Everything had happened so quickly, and it was really only at the last moment of his impending departure that she realised she might never see her husband and the father of her children again.

Antonina was the only one who went to the station and was with her father until the train pulled slowly away from the platform. She never imagined that it would be the last time she would see him.

By the following day, patriotism had become the prevailing emotion and, at the usual meeting place in the park, the girls decided that they should volunteer their services to their country. It was agreed that they would go *en masse* to the military registration and enlistment offices and demand to be sent to the front.

The military commissar met the excited crowd of teenage girls. He directed them to the *Komsomol* Committee offices in the city, where they were instructed to go on military nursing courses, which, by coincidence, were taking place at the chemical plant where Antonina's mother worked. The authorities had already decided that the plant was to be transformed from the manufacture of peace-time products to an armaments factory producing artillery shells and rifle bullets. Equipment for that purpose was already on the way, so 400 school leavers, including Antonina, were immediately employed in the armaments factory and attended their nursing courses in the evenings.

It wasn't long before the government was forced to review its decision to install the munitions factory in Kalinin, as the Germans were already making headway in their approach towards the area. Consequently, the equipment was packed, with the assistance of the school leavers, and loaded onto trains for transportation to the Urals.

After eight days, everything was prepared. On 1 July, the select group of people and equipment, including Antonina and her former classmates, departed for the industrial city of Chelyabinsk, across the Urals.

The trip took 10 days on the single track. Considering the vast movement of men and material towards the front, in the opposite direction, 10 days was very quick indeed. Their echelon had been given priority of movement due to the urgent necessity of producing armaments. Many other factories, institutes and hospitals, as well as cultural treasures, agricultural and industrial equipment and livestock were also moved east in preparation for the anticipated occupation of the Kalinin area by the Germans.

A vast number of ordinary people also evacuated the Kalinin area to avoid the approaching conflict. The *blitzkrieg* had caught the Russians unprepared and unable to defend all areas under attack. Priorities were considered, and the most obvious area to defend was Moscow.

On arrival at Chelyabinsk, Antonina, together with other personnel, was housed in the student hostel buildings of a teachers' training institute. The four-storey main building was to be turned into a munitions factory, and an immediate start was made on the installation of the necessary heavy engineering equipment, some of which weighed more than two tons.

There were no lifts in the building, so machinery had to be manhandled up narrow stairways on wooden planks. With great effort it was finally achieved and, within days, more young women from Kalinin and other towns arrived to assist at the factory.

Engineers from the city of Tula, south-southeast of Moscow, where the munitions manufacturing equipment had been made, came to teach the workers how to use and repair the machines. After one month the factory was producing machine gun and automatic rifle bullets. The Russian Commander-in-Chief, Marshall Voroshilov, arrived at the factory personally to check the progress made and to motivate the workers to increase production to maximum capacity.

The gunpowder used was produced in the Soviet Union, but the brass needed for casings had to be flown in from America. The Russian brass factories were in the process of being moved from Tula to the Urals. Time was required to get them up and running. When consignments of brass arrived, workers had to remain at their stations and work until all of it had been used. While one worked, another would sleep behind the machine. A catering division brought food for them.

Between processing consignments of brass, the girls, by now qualified nurse aids, would go to the hospital to help the wounded off trains arriving from the front. They would take down the personal details of incoming soldiers and list all the items they carried. The soldiers would then be undressed, washed and, in most cases, prepared for surgery, in which the young girls also assisted.

As the war progressed, not only wounded soldiers were arriving for treatment; numbers of civilians suffering as a result of the blockade of Leningrad (formerly Petrograd) were also arriving. When it became evident that that city would come under attack by the Germans, doctors and staff fled to the Urals, and their hospital equipment was relocated there.

The majority of those evacuated from the blockade were suffering frostbite of their extremities. People had been starving and, in their desperate quest to find food, water or fuel, had been forced to leave whatever shelter they may have been lucky enough to find, to venture out into the freezing winter weather.

Lack of nutrition had slowed their movements, making frostbite all the more likely. Large numbers of amputations were necessary. Because there was a shortage of anaesthetics, many operations had to be performed on patients who had simply been given a large quantity of vodka. In most cases this was no substitute for an anaesthetic.

When the surgeon started to saw through the leg or arm of a patient, it was too much for Antonina – she would burst into tears. The doctors soon realised that she would never be able to cope with theatre work and she was re-assigned to offloading incoming trains.

The Stalingrad Mechanical University, an institution of some importance, had been relocated to buildings adjacent to the munitions factory. Antonina's main occupation was in the factory, producing munitions, but when she was not busy there or at the train station, she would look at the university and dream of being a student. Having been a good scholar, she hoped the war would end soon, allowing her to gain a tertiary education.

To that end, she decided to study for the entrance examination at night, before going to sleep. She passed at her first attempt and was accepted to study mechanical engineering. Wartime had changed all the rules. Schedules were flexible and dictated by circumstances. Factories were working three eight-hour shifts on a rotational basis. The hospital called for help whenever it was needed, so, somehow, study time had to be found in between other activities. It resulted in her having little time to sleep, but she was young and strong. Her life continued in this way until May 1943.

Then a call came from the authorities in Kalinin. Antonina was told that her mother was dying and that her two younger sisters were likely to be orphaned in the near future. On receipt of this frightening information, the factory authorities immediately released her on compassionate grounds, sending her home.

Once there, she found Katerina lying motionless on her bed and her two young sisters sitting close by, silently watching their mother. They were all incredibly thin, with lifeless complexions. Her mother's appearance was shocking. She was emaciated, but her head and face had swollen out of proportion to the rest of her body. Antonina waited for a reaction to her presence, but there was not a glimmer of life from Katerina.

Antonina began crying aloud, 'Mother is dead! Mother is dead!'

There was the slightest movement and Katerina, barely audible, whispered, 'Not yet, my daughter.'

Antonina's reaction was immediate. She fled the house in search of a doctor. She was told to give her mother certain prescribed pills, and white bread and butter. At once, she spent her accumulated savings to acquire the necessary food and medication. Then she set about feeding her mother, trying to get Katerina to regain some strength. But her sisters were also starving and there was not enough food to go around.

Nor was there any money left. So she decided to exchange her best clothes and shoes for food; her favourite georgette dresses and new, unworn suede shoes, originally bought for her anticipated student days. She was just 20 years old, but had never had the opportunity to wear any of the treasured items.

Her neighbours planned a trip to exchange clothing for food in the country town of Bezhetsk, about 120 kilometres from Kalinin. The Germans had not reached that area and the farmers were still able to accumulate food to exchange for whatever they wanted. Antonina went with them and managed to procure a kilogram of butter, a few kilograms of refined flour and some other items, such as cheese and vegetables.

Her mother and sisters started to recover slowly, and soon Antonina was able to find work and earn just enough to buy food. When Katerina was able to talk again, she told Antonina that there had been serious starvation in Kalinin after the city's liberation. Food had been rationed and the little they received had been insufficient. She had tried, with little success, to beg for potato peels and leftover bread at the local hospital and army barracks. After the long winter, with minimal nourishment, Katerina had finally collapsed.

Later, she told Antonina the full story of what had happened to the family. Both Ivan and Antonina had left home not long before the Germans began bombing the city and its surrounds. The citizens tried to find places as close as possible to their homes to dig trenches or make bomb shelters to escape the daily pounding. As soon as the air-raid sirens were heard, everyone rushed for cover. Katerina made rucksacks for each family member in which she stored their identification documents, some extra clothing, dry bread and food that would nourish them in the event of an attack lasting a long time. At the first hint of a bombing raid, old Avdotja and the children were drilled into grabbing their rucksacks and running for the shelter. The fascists' *blitzkrieg* had been so fast that it seemed inevitable that Kalinin would be overrun.

On 13 October 1941, Katerina had left for work as usual, but she was filled with dread at the thought of her city being captured and her beloved family being taken prisoner. Rumours were circulating that the Germans were already on the outskirts of the city. The security detail at the chemical plant knew that they were not allowed to desert their posts, but by lunchtime the tension was overwhelming and, at their breaks, some workers ran home to see what was happening.

When Katerina got her break she immediately made for home, only to find that it was like swimming upstream. Hundreds of people were running in the direction of the road to Moscow. That was in the opposite direction to Katerina's home and her progress was slowed by the panicked crowd, who were carrying small children, helping old people, dragging suitcases or pulling domestic animals. After an enormous struggle, she finally arrived, trembling, at their shelter, amid a cacophony of falling bombs and screaming citizens. She reckoned that the chemical plant was certain to be captured and that their only chance now was to escape from Kalinin. She told her family to hold hands tightly, so as not to be split up in the chaos, and pointed out the direction towards

Moscow in which they should try to escape.

Meanwhile, the bombing was intensifying, adding to the panic and swelling the crowds attempting to flee. Among those trying to escape were a few cars with hooters blaring, frightening horses that were part of the exodus. Everyone was trying to reach the road to Moscow, which was built on a flat area, making it devoid of any natural topographical protection.

At this point, Katerina realised that her family could not walk the 160 kilometres south to Moscow and that, even if they did, they might not find shelter. They had no relatives or friends in that city.

She decided, therefore, to change course and head for her sister, Sasha, in Rozhdestvenno, east of the Volga. She had relatives there, and at least a chance of finding a roof and perhaps some support. She indicated a change of direction to her family and they tried to leave the panicked throng to head for the banks of the river.

Somehow, in the chaos, the two girls became separated and disappeared in the crowd. Desperately, Katerina shouted their names, frantically elbowing her way in and begging people in the mob to help find them. The shock of their loss stopped the war for her. Nothing mattered to her other than finding her children.

She was never able to recall how much time passed while her desperate search continued. Meanwhile, though they were only nine and eleven, her daughters did have an idea of the direction that their mother had chosen. Finally, managing to push through the crowd, they emerged on the eastern side of the road, some distance from their frantic family. The reunion was very emotional, but brief.

When they arrived at the western riverbank, they were lucky to find a man in a boat about to leave for the opposite side. They implored the boatman to take them across the 400 metres and, with shells raining down around them, Katerina prayed that she had made the right decision. If the Germans managed somehow to cross the river, they would easily outrun the slow-moving family, or perhaps capture the village of Rozhdestvenno before they even arrived there.

As soon as they landed on the eastern bank, they hid themselves in bushes to await a possible lull in the bombing. From there, as they looked back at the Moscow road on the western side to see what was happening, more chaos erupted. Tanks were following and firing machine guns at the refugees fleeing Kalinin, and German paratroopers had landed further down the road to Moscow and opened fire with small arms on the people coming in their direction.

The crowds were sandwiched between two fronts of attack, and a great melée ensued. To add to the disaster, German mortars found their range and opened up, shelling the terrified crowds which, by then, had no idea of where to escape.

It was like watching a horror movie for Katerina and her family. Had she not taken the decision to head east, the family would most certainly have been caught up in that ghastly annihilation. They could not avoid the sight of their fellow townsfolk being blown to pieces by the Germans attackers. As they wept for their compatriots, shells began to fall closer to their position. Avdotja, who was not well, lifted herself to a sitting position and a bullet took part of her right ear away. They were frozen in fear. It seemed like an interminable time before darkness fell. The firing began to abate somewhat, so they decided it was time to move on as quickly as they could.

The following day, 14 October 1941, the Germans announced that they had occupied the city of Kalinin and the town of Rzhev, about 120 kilometres away. Of the 69 districts that make up the province of Kalinin, the German invaders eventually took 38. Unbeknown to the Germans, before they arrived at the Volga, the Russian Army had destroyed bridges that would have enabled them to cross quickly, and had positioned their not very strong defences on the eastern side of the river, with most of the Russian Army strength being held in reserve for the defence of the capital. The Russians had guessed, correctly, that the Germans would head south in a bid to take Moscow.

Katerina and her forlorn little family walked with as much speed as they could muster, but, with old Avdotja being so weak, it took two days to cover the 40 kilometres to the village. In their state of desperation, they had made the journey relatively quickly.

On their arrival, they met with Katerina's sister who pointed out an unoccupied wooden house. They found a supply of wood there, but no food. Some of Katerina's relatives who had not fled tried to help by bringing them a little food from their meagre stores.

It was October, so before the winter set in, the children and Katerina combed the forest for mushrooms and cranberries. Alex occupied himself with trying to snare rabbits and catch birds. By very strictly rationing their food resources, they survived until mid-January 1942.

On 16 December 1941, they learned that Kalinin had been the first provincial capital to be liberated by the Russian Army. In doing so, the Russians had suffered 50 000 men dead or wounded. A special 'Kalinin Front' had been set up and headed by General Ivan Konev, with the express purpose of forcing the Germans to retreat from the Moscow area.

Word now reached the refugees that, despite the ongoing blockade of Leningrad and the proximity of the Germans to Moscow, it was unlikely that the Germans would return to Kalinin, since it had now been strongly reinforced as part of the larger plan to defend Moscow.

For a variety of reasons, Katerina felt she should go back home. She had left stores of food hidden in the cellar, they needed winter clothing to enable them to return those kindly lent to them by relatives, she wanted her children to return to school, and she needed to get back to work to earn money for them all.

Avdotja had become too sick to make the journey back to town. What she had witnessed recently, near the end of her life, had broken her spirit and gone a long way towards destroying her will to live. The flight to freedom had sapped her of strength and she decided to remain where she was, to die with her country relatives who had shown her sympathy and kindness. It was obvious that her life was drawing to a close. Parting from her was very traumatic. She had been with the children all their lives, and had cared for and spoiled them as much as she had been able.

As the family were preparing to leave, Avdotja took off her

wedding ring and gold crucifix, handed them to Katerina and said, 'I won't be needing these and maybe they will help you in town.'

For the brief time she had them, these were to be Katerina's most treasured possessions. Leaving the old lady behind felt like a heavy blanket of sorrow being thrown over the family; they understood that, on account of her weak condition, they were unlikely ever to see her again. Six months later, at age 75, Avdotja quietly passed away. Her death certificate noted that she had died of 'natural causes'.

When Katerina reached Kalinin, she could hardly recognise the city. Bombing had flattened hospitals, public buildings, houses and railway stations, and destroyed roads. Rubble was everywhere, making progress through the streets difficult. Dead bodies were buried in the destroyed buildings or lay covered in snow, waiting to be found and given a proper burial.

She was relieved to find that her flat was still intact, although much of the building had been destroyed. Her cellar was still there too, but both had been ransacked and not a scrap of food was to be found, nor anything else of value. Only her Singer sewing machine was left, although the precious silver attachments had been stolen from it. It had obviously been too heavy for the thieves to carry.

She found in her cellar a small bag belonging to one of her neighbours. It contained his personal documents and had obviously been dropped when he removed her supply of 20 sacks of potatoes and vegetables. Twenty sacks of potatoes represented the difference between the survival of her family and the probability of slow death by starvation.

When she tried to find the man who had stolen her food, she was told the Germans had executed him. Witnesses said that he had been drunk, lost control and had sworn at the occupiers. He had been shot on the spot.

The town's population appeared far smaller than she remembered, and she learned, to her horror, that many who had not managed to escape the German advance had been captured and sent off to Germany in cattle trucks, to an unknown fate. Anyone displaying any kind of resistance had been executed.

The chemical plant at which she had been employed had been bombed so badly that there was nothing left to guard.

One of her first priorities was to look for another job, preferably close to a source of food. A bakery, food shop or any place where food was supplied, such as an army canteen, would be ideal. However, all sources of food had been plundered. The Germans, who had been too busy with their war, were not the main culprits. The minute the German army had retreated from Kalinin, local people who had somehow evaded capture had looted all the food left in the city – and in fact, anything considered of value. Who could blame them for helping themselves at a time when they were unlikely to get help from anyone else?

Those who had stayed in the town and been lucky enough to survive the brutal occupation had been first to apply for jobs. Anyone who had been absent from the city, returning after its liberation, could expect only the leftovers.

Katerina had to take the only employment on offer: clearing the ruins and cleaning up the streets. Her immediate responsibility was collecting dead bodies on a horse-drawn cart that she drove while others loaded it. The bodies were taken for burial in common graves since most were unidentifiable and, in any event, it was necessary to bury them as quickly as possible to avoid health risks.

Once the schools had been re-established in any available buildings and cellars, the children could begin studying again. The authorities applied strict rationing of food, but students were given one meal daily. That usually consisted of a small piece of poor quality bread and a cup of thin vegetable soup.

Katerina was unable to provide sufficient nourishment for the children. On their meagre rations, she watched helplessly as they became progressively more emaciated. Her mother-in-law's treasures, together with everything of any value that she owned, were exchanged for food at the market. They managed to survive the winter that way and, when spring finally arrived, she was able to collect wild herbs, stinging nettles and sorrel, which she added to whatever else she received in rations to make a soup with a little more nutrition.

Prior to the war, citizens had taken over small patches of land anywhere they could find an unused piece, where they grew potatoes and other vegetables. Katerina was unable to do this now; all of her seed had been stolen and there was none available anywhere in the area. During summer she went, together with the children, to the nearby forests to collect mushrooms and berries, but such excursions were very dangerous on account of unexploded bombs lying about, and the possibility of mines having been laid. The ravenous children immediately ate the little they were able to gather, so none could be kept or preserved for winter.

Meanwhile, her son, Alex, had turned 16 and completed his short course at the technical college. He could not officially join the army because he was under age but, together with his friends, formed a civilian unit and volunteered for attachment to an armoured repair unit. Their job was to follow and repair tanks. At 17, Alex was decorated with a medal for bravery and, in recognition, allowed leave of absence for 10 days.

Until his official conscription at 18, Alex was paid as a civilian and earned 1 000 roubles a month, most of which was sent directly to his mother. Antonina, still employed at a munitions factory in the Urals, also sent most of her 600 roubles monthly salary to Katerina. The sum total of this money was sufficient to buy just two to three loaves of bread.

Alex and his young colleagues worked tirelessly following the armoured conflicts, in most cases finding the early model Russian tanks no match for the more powerful German panzers. However, the introduction of the superior Russian Model T34 tank, which rolled off the hurriedly constructed Siberian production lines in ever-increasing numbers, finally swung the balance of armoured strength in Russia's favour. By the end of the war, Alex's group alone had repaired some 3 000 Russian tanks. He survived and was in Latvia when the Germans finally surrendered.

Profiteering was rife in Kalinin and the only food available, besides that rationed by the government, was at the market. It was being exchanged at exorbitant rates. You could swap a pair of diamond earrings for a loaf of bread.

Starvation among the town's civilian population continued unabated. Fighting with the Germans still raged 100 kilometres southwest of the city, around the town of Rzhev, and the government, which was in control of food supplies, always gave preference to those fighting and their support units.

Katerina felt powerless to provide for her girls. She would forego eating, pretending that she had eaten earlier, and divide her portion between them. They didn't always fall for this and often resisted, insisting that their mother should eat more, but their faces were all beginning to swell.

By May 1943, at 44 years of age, Katerina's condition had deteriorated badly, reducing her to an emaciated skeleton with a severely swollen face and with insufficient strength to lift herself off the bed. That was the sight that greeted Antonina when she arrived home.

Once she was back in Kalinin and had attended to her mother's and sisters' plight, Antonina reported to the military registration and enlistment office, then to the internal passport office. Desperate to find a job and get ration cards, she applied at a newly opened military food storage depot. The colonel in charge checked her papers carefully and offered her a clerical job. She was overwhelmed at her good fortune.

For the next year, her routine varied little. She went to work, went home to check on her mother and sisters, then left to help clean up the city. Most of the trees in the park that she had frequented as a teenager were lying askew with their roots exposed. There were bomb craters everywhere. Ruins stood as stark reminders of the buildings she had known just a few years before. Antonina was given a graphic description of how the Germans had hanged partisans, Communist officials and *Komsomol* members from the few trees left standing in the park. That park would never again be the same for her.

It took in excess of two years after the liberation of the city to clean up and rid the place of unexploded bombs and other debris. Once a brick factory had been opened, an all-out effort was made by volunteers to rebuild the city. Paid workers joined them after the war ended, but it took nearly 10 years to return the city to normality.

Trucks from outlying military divisions arrived daily to collect food at the military food storage depot where Antonina worked. The soldiers were friendly and often flirted with the women employed there.

In June 1944, two officers came into the depot. One was from the security service, as loaded food trucks always carried security guards at the time. He asked permission to use the telephone, which was on Antonina's desk. As soon as their eyes met it was all over. The handsome, wavy-haired officer thanked her and left without saying more. Her heart was pounding. It was the first time in her life that any man had made such an impression on her.

Two weeks passed without his reappearing. Then, one day, she opened the office door to go home and he was waiting outside. He introduced himself as Daniel Devjatkin and offered to walk her home. A few days later he was back and they began a friendly relationship.

Granny Katerina and Antonina's sisters took to Daniel. He began taking care of them as if they were his own family, bringing medicine for Katerina and sharing his superior officer's food rations with them.

Two weeks later, he asked Antonina to marry him. She would not accept his proposal at first; she felt it had come too soon. There was a war still raging in the country and she could not leave her mother and sisters. They continued meeting daily and Daniel persisted. He swore he would not leave her and her family without help.

Antonina loved him, felt that he loved her and, after a few weeks, capitulated. They married on 2 August 1944. The wedding table held half a litre of army-issue vodka, a two-pound tin of American sausages and a loaf of bread, all brought by Daniel. Katerina made boiled potatoes and pickled cabbage.

In mid-winter 1944/1945, Daniel was transferred, together with his unit, to the town of Rzhev. Antonina, who accompanied him, was expecting their first child. When they arrived at the town, they were astounded to find it a name only – the town had been all but obliterated. It had been overrun at the same time as Kalinin, in October 1941, but had taken more than a year longer to liberate because of the stiffer resistance offered there by the Germans. Fighting at Rzhev had been particularly fierce, and in the bloody, uncompromising battles for the town, many had been lost on both sides. Of the population of 55 000 that had inhabited the place before the war, only 362 were left after its liberation. The Soviet army lost an estimated 72 000 men in the battles for Rzhev and, to this day, it is known as 'A Town of Heroes'. In 1978, it was accorded the 'Order of the Great Patriotic War, First Class'.

At the age of 21, Antonina had witnessed many deaths first-hand. There were the mortally wounded soldiers at the hospital in Chelyabinsk, girls in the munitions factory killed by accidental firings of the bullets they were producing, corpses found among the ruins of Kalinin, not to mention the deathly first sight of her own mother when she had arrived back home. But nothing could have prepared her for what she was to encounter in Rzhev.

The town, with the miraculous exception of two wooden houses, was a vast, grotesque field, with odd-shaped pieces of jagged, charred wood protruding, stark and surreal, from the uneven blanket of snow. It looked to her like a huge cemetery designed by a demented artist.

The two houses left standing were the only visible reminders of the town that had existed before the war. After the fierce battles for Rzhev, the Soviet army had relentlessly pursued the remnants of the German forces fleeing the area, not stopping even momentarily to bury the dead or to make any effort to clean up. It was expected of the local citizens to do that, but the survivors were just too few in number and were mostly old people and children, all of whom were weak from hunger and badly traumatised by their experiences. It was going to take at least six months for the authorities to get around to sending clean-up and reconstruction teams to the area.

All survivors and the military detachment to which Daniel and Antonina belonged lived underground in the cellars of the destroyed buildings. As the young, pregnant Antonina walked in deafening silence through the spring mists over the desolate, snow-covered devastation, people would rise eerily out of the ruins like ghosts from nowhere, and sometimes disappear, as if being swallowed by the earth. She knew these were survivors, not ghosts, but she always found herself inhaling sharply at these ghoulish visions.

If those sights had been frightening, they were to prove nothing compared to those that would confront citizens as the snow melted. Thousands upon thousands of bodies of Russian and German soldiers, civilians and animals, lay about. Some had been there for more than two years, but constant fighting had made their removal impossible.

As the weather warmed, the stench of putrescent flesh became overwhelming and the risk of disease escalated. Special teams were finally brought in to identify the bodies, where possible. All able-bodied people in the area were encouraged to assist, but pregnant Antonina could not do heavy physical work, so gave of her time in various clerical capacities.

Hasty burials were called for; consequently, the corpses had to be consigned to common mass graves, without the niceties of headstones or any other form of identification. Later, public places of remembrance were constructed and the names of those identified as having died in the town were commemorated on plinths. Future generations were to remember them by regularly placing fresh flowers at the monuments, but the town would never fully recover. In the 1994 census, just 17 200 residents were counted, compared to the 55 000 that had lived there before the war.

Daniel and Antonina were still at Rzhev when victory was declared on 9 May 1945. It happened at 4 a.m. The duty radio operator picked up the announcement of the capitulation of the enemy and the glorious victory of the Soviets over the German fascists. The war had ended. He ran to report the good news to his commanding officer, an old colonel brought out of retirement to bolster the ever-dwindling number of officers. The radio operator's excitement was overwhelming, making him shout the news at the top of his voice all the way to the colonel's billet.

Most within earshot awoke immediately to the best news they had received in years. They leapt from their beds to spread the news of victory to those who may not have heard. They ran around in a state of euphoria, shouting. Some, overcome with emotion, were crying, others laughing, and all were hugging and kissing each other.

The crowds naturally gravitated towards the colonel's billet where a rostrum was hastily constructed from planks and chairs. The old colonel, who had by then emerged, hoisted himself with difficulty onto the rostrum and prepared to address the crowd from his elevated position.

Never, in his entire career, had he been lost for words. Commanding had been his forté for decades, but on this occasion he appeared unable to utter a sentence. Overcome with emotion, he stood in front of the crowd with tears streaming down his face. Eventually he managed to achieve a modicum of control and said in a broken, husky voice, 'My dear friends! It is a victory! Finally, victory! We have waited for this for such a long time!'

He was right. It had taken the German army just four months to get to the outskirts of Moscow and nearly four long years for the Russians to rid themselves of the invaders.

Suddenly someone shouted, 'Look, our colonel's in his drawers!' Gripped by feverish exaltation, the crowd had neglected to notice that he had not dressed for the occasion.

Now laughter erupted. The old man was standing there in his long johns, a hole at the left knee. His salt-and-pepper moustache, modelled on a proud Cossack commander in one of his treasured paintings, was dishevelled and his hair unbrushed. They laughed even more when they noticed that they themselves were in their nightclothes – pyjamas, underwear, or naked but for the blankets they had hurriedly thrown over their shoulders. For the first time in years tensions vanished and they rejoiced in the euphoria of the moment.

On 18 July 1945, a son was born to Daniel and Antonina. It wasn't difficult to find a name; he was called Victor. All at Rzhev congratulated the young parents. Without exception, they expressed the wish that the boy would never experience war in his lifetime.

The Germans took an estimated four million Russians to use as slave labour, including women and children. In the process, they destroyed 1 710 towns and more than 70 000 country villages in which more than six million buildings were rendered uninhabitable.

As a consequence, more than 25 million people were left homeless. The destruction of industry was enormous. The country lost an estimated 30 per cent of its national assets. And I vividly recall that, in my youth, there were many amputees in our community.

Russian children born after 1945 grew up on war stories told by survivors. At school, a considerable part of our curriculum revolved around the history of the conflict. Partisans, survivors of the concentration camps, parents of people who had died heroes and witnesses of important events were brought to our schools to lecture us on their experiences.

As children, we wore uniforms, marched and sang patriotic songs. Many of our films and television programmes were based on the subject. When we played children's war games, nobody wanted to be on the side of the fascists, everyone wanted to be the commander of the Soviet soldiers so that they could shoot the fascists and achieve victory.

Practically every town and village in the USSR has a museum and a memorial about the Great Patriotic War, as it became known. No-one in Russia was untouched by the conflict; not those who lived through the hostilities, nor the generations to come. The constant reminders of WWII in Russia, the graveyards, anniversaries, ceremonies and memories handed down through the generations have, over the years, engendered a powerful yearning for peace.

In 1974, at the age of 19, I was part of a group that toured East Germany and Czechoslovakia. The tour featured a visit to Buchenwald, a Nazi concentration camp. The gas chambers, ovens, photographs and documents made a devastating impression on us. On the way back to town, we drove by bus on a good concrete road. Our guide told us that the road had been constructed especially for the concentration camp and the thought occurred to me that, only 30 years before, we might have been travelling in the other direction, on our way to a frightening fate.

6

Homes

LIVING SPACE IS STILL A PROBLEM FOR RUSSIAN PEOPLE. RUSSIAN families have, historically, been big. Frequently, children remained with their parents until they were married, and often thereafter, because they either could not afford or could not obtain a place of their own. It was simply that they had no choice, both during the Socialist era and right up to the present day.

For centuries, different generations of Russian families have lived under one roof. As a rule, the house belonged to the oldest generation who may have been the grand- or even great-grandparents. In many instances, the arrangement was practical, enabling the grandparents to look after their grandchildren while the parents went out to work.

After the Revolution, the Bolsheviks expropriated the mansions of the wealthy and allowed the proletariat to occupy them. This had the effect of encouraging village farmers and others, whose land had been collectivised, to migrate to the cities, in the hope of finding accommodation. In time, the cities became too crowded and accommodation was very difficult to find. People occupied every available space. They lived in cellars, lofts and in rooms divided by sheets of fabric, separating the living spaces of as many as three families. In what had previously been a large house or apartment, there could now be a total of perhaps 20 families, putting tremendous strain on kitchen and ablution facilities. Anything could happen in those circumstances, ranging from amicable relationships to murder over some mundane disagreement.

A few years before WWII, the Communist government began a programme of constructing blocks of basic flats, intended to alleviate the housing shortage. Although this spate of construction helped house people, many of the new buildings were flattened in the war, setting back the whole programme.

Consequently, after the war there was even less accommodation than had existed prior to it, despite the loss of so many lives. Desperate people even dug holes to live in, covered them with wood and piled earth over the top. A generation of millions of children grew up in adverse circumstances, never having their own bed, let alone their own room. There were those, mainly in government, who may have lived in relative comfort in their own flats, but my family did not number among them. Accomodation was in such short supply that the government even turned a blind eye to people letting property, although it wasn't legal.

In 1958, my parents took the decision to leave Orenburg province, where I was born, and return to Kalinin. We stayed for two months with my aunt, her husband and daughter while my parents hunted for accommodation. We were six, so there were nine in total living in a 20 square metre room, sharing cooking and bathroom facilities with two other families living on the same floor.

Finding a place to live proved extremely difficult for my father. Whenever he entered into a discussion with someone able to let a property, he would be asked his surname. As soon as that person heard that he was a Devjatkin, they closed the door on him. He could not understand the outraged expressions until he found out that the first Communist Party Secretary of the Kalinin region had gone by the same name. A few years before, when Stalin had still been alive, the man had been denounced as an 'Enemy of the State', had been arrested and had then vanished. Much publicity surrounded his denunciation and everyone in the province was conversant with 'the facts'. Even though some years had passed, nobody was prepared to associate in any way with an 'Enemy of the State'.

When Daniel finally understood the reason for his perceived pariah status, he was able to explain that he was unrelated to the disgraced man and managed to find a small room in a wooden house on the outskirts of the city. It was relatively expensive for its size, but he was obliged to take it until something better could be found.

Meanwhile, someone advised Antonina to seek employment at the same chemical plant at which her mother had worked before the war. The plant had been rebuilt and, as an employee, one could apply for a room in flats under their control. Luckily she was given employment and, in little more than a year, was able to get a room.

It was in a relatively new brick block of flats, built by German prisoners of war, close to the centre of town. It comprised eight flats, some with two rooms, others three, with every room occupied by a family. The three double-storey buildings that surrounded the courtyard contained 40 flats that comprised, in all, 100 rooms inhabited by nearly 100 families. Only three or four very senior factory directors were allowed the privilege of a full flat to themselves. My parents were ecstatic about sharing the kitchen and ablution facilities with just one other family.

As a child, I was delighted to be able to play with the many other children in our courtyard, the arrangement of which was conducive to our socialising. Our flat consisted of two rooms measuring 14 and 12 square metres. We occupied the larger room, and the smaller housed a young couple and their son. The shared kitchen measured six square metres. It contained a brick oven, fired by wood or coal, when available, and an enamel sink with a cold water tap, which was the sole source of water in the flat. Each family had its own small kitchen table with cupboards above for storing pots, pans and dishes. The two families had to take turns to cook and eat. Leading off a short corridor inside the front door were two tiny storerooms measuring two and one-and-a-half square metres respectively. The courtyard had small wooden sheds, one for each family, which stored our wood and coal, among other items too inconvenient to keep in the flat.

I often wonder how our family managed to store the clothing required for four distinctly different seasons in such confined circumstances, even though we owned little. Just like the families around us, we could afford only what was essential, but even that was quite voluminous for six people.

Adjacent to the kitchen was a toilet, small and torturously uncomfortable, that invariably had a queue of people outside it each morning, all trying to retain a sense of humour.

The communal style of co-existence had evolved its own rules. Each family shared responsibility for the cleaning of common areas such as the entrance hall, stairs and landings. A roster was drawn up and one duty week allocated to each family member. Consequently, my family cleaned for six weeks at a stretch.

Both 'living rooms' in the flat had fireplaces for winter warmth. The floor space in our family's room was taken up by a metal bed for our parents; a sofa on which my two brothers slept head to toe; a general-purpose small table with two chairs; and a small wardrobe. Each night my grandmother and I shared a fold-up bed that was put away against the wall in the morning. All in all, there was little space to manoeuvre when everyone was home. The only way to wash oneself was by heating water on the stove, chasing everybody out of the 'living room' and performing contorted ablutions.

Every weekend, the family made a ritual of visiting the sauna/bathhouse provided close to our building by the State-owned chemical plant that was within walking distance of our flat. The entire district, including shops, the cinema and the clinic, belonged to them. Only the smell of carbon bisulphide that it emitted belonged to us. Whenever I make the annual pilgrimage to visit my parents, I get a whiff of the chemical that immediately brings back vivid memories of my childhood.

I don't know how the other members of my family felt about our living conditions, but they didn't bother me between the ages of four and nine. Sleeping on a single bed with my much-loved grandmother never troubled me. Somehow, I always managed to find a corner to play with my only toy, a fabric doll made for me by my grandmother.

When I was nine, we got lucky. Our neighbours moved to another town and the chemical plant authorities allowed us the luxury of having their room too – on account of being a family of six and, therefore, entitled to another room if one became available. To have a complete flat to ourselves was pure bliss and surrounding neighbours were jealous. At that time, my father was 51, my mother

42, my brothers 19 and 14, and my grandmother 65. The two boys were given the privilege of sharing the new room, leaving the rest of us in the old room with a bit of extra space.

In 1972, the flat was renovated and central heating was installed, delivering hot water. A gas stove was put in and the bigger storeroom was converted to a small bathroom. That made our living conditions comparatively luxurious. After all these years (43 years at the time of writing), the rest of us having left long ago, my parents still occupy their two-roomed flat, which they now consider spacious – and which holds memories of their younger years and their children.

During Stalin's rule, solid buildings containing relatively spacious flats were constructed. They are much sought after today, because they feature high ceilings, wide passages, large rooms and relatively big kitchens, bathrooms and toilets. They were mostly occupied by senior bureaucrats, military and KGB chiefs, or recognised celebrities. These 'Stalin-type' buildings ultimately became too expensive to continue building.

When Nikita Khrushchev inherited the housing problem, the situation was very bad. So much had been destroyed in WWII, that a faster, cheaper way had to be found to satisfy the ever-increasing demand of the proletariat. The Communist Party decided to build huge plants for the manufacture of precast concrete panels. Massive, uninteresting blocks of claustrophobically small flats were built. Once those blocks became habitable, the queues of families waiting for housing became shorter. Even though the flats were pathetically small, people were happy to have the privacy they afforded. They were finally able to close their own front doors and not see their neighbours.

A formula was arrived at for determining the size of flat issued to each family. Every flat had identical kitchen, bathroom and toilet facilities that were excluded from the calculation. Six square metres of space per person, plus an extra six for the whole family, was the standard. For example, a family of four was allowed a maximum of 30 square metres. It meant that they could occupy a flat with two rooms measuring, say, 12 and 15 square metres respectively – as long as the total was less than 30 square metres. This went a long way towards alleviating the housing shortage as millions of people were able to come out of their cellars and overcrowded flats. But the problem was not completely resolved and persists to this day.

Between 1960 and 1975 there was little innovation. Thousands of the same types of buildings were constructed. When Leonid Brezhnev had been in power for about half of his 18-year term of office, demand started rising for an improvement in the quality of flats. The precast concrete structures were considered unhealthy and people complained that they found it difficult to breathe in them.

A bigger and better design was approved, in most cases featuring a small covered balcony, and the formula determining the issuance was revised. A family of four were now allowed 42 square metres. That meant the comparative 'luxury' of a three-roomed flat of 10, 12 and 20 square metre rooms.

If anyone, for any reason, had square metres in excess of what was allowed, the rental for the excess was very high, forcing people to exchange their flats for smaller units. The intention was that everyone should have 'the same'. Shortly before *perestroika*, an increase to 12 square metres per person was introduced.

A visitor to Russia could not be blamed for thinking that the towns were all cloned. The ubiquitous blocks of compact flats also gave rise to the necessity for compact furniture. Suspended wall units with fold-up divans and tables were standard, with the colour of the rug on the floor or the wallpaper offering the only scope for variation.

The Communist government succeeded, to some extent, in making everyone equal, although, as George Orwell noted in his writings, 'some were more equal than others'. A local joke was that, since everything looked the same, inebriated Russian husbands, if caught in another woman's flat, could claim to think they were at home.

In some instances, flats were issued to employees by the factories for which they worked. They were known as 'departmental' and issued subject to the person remaining in the employ of the factory. In the event of the person resigning, he or she would forfeit the flat. But if they continued working there until retirement age, 60 in the case of men and 55 for women, the flat remained 'theirs'. However, it could not be inherited by anyone else and reverted to the employer on the death of the retiree and spouse. That is the type of flat my mother was given and in which my parents still live.

The vast majority of flats were not 'departmental'. Factories issued them to employees, often after a long waiting period, sometimes up to 25 years, but the occupants were not then tied to the factories that had issued them. Because the bigger factories were able to offer more flats, it was often a case of people preferring menial work there, in the hope of getting accommodation, rather than a job of their choice elsewhere.

My uncle Alex and his wife worked in a toxic area of the same chemical plant for 25 years before they were given their own flat. There was supposed to be an eight-year limit for employment in the toxic area, but they continued working there because they were scared of losing their place in the queue for accommodation. On account of the years spent in the toxic area, they were invalids when their flat was eventually issued.

At the age of 17, all I wanted to be was a fashion designer. My mother was totally opposed to this, because she knew that there were certain occupations, such as doctors, teachers and artists, that offered no chance of securing a flat. Fashion design fell into that category. She insisted on my becoming a civil engineer because those involved in construction were often more successful in getting their own flats, ahead of the queue.

Not only did the State control housing, but the police controlled the movement of people inside the country and knew what everyone was supposed to be doing – studying, working, serving in the army, travelling, whatever. The government was opposed to anybody being unemployed and considered them parasites or society's spongers.

The law dictated that everyone, at the age of 16, should have an internal passport or identity document with their domicile specified. It was not permissible to live anywhere other than at the address denoted, and only one address was allowed. That determined your life, to some extent; it dictated where you would attend school, which clinic you would be able to visit, and under which police precinct you fell.

There was another odd law stating that if one's domicile were listed in a particular town, one was not allowed to book into a hotel in the same town. That was fine as far as travellers were concerned, but not convenient for locals needing to evacuate their domicile for any reason. In the event of an argument occurring between spouses, the offended party would be obliged to seek refuge with relatives or sympathetic friends – or adapt to a cold park bench.

Changes have come about in Russia in the last decade, and the circumstances I have described existed mainly prior to 1991, but the internal passport system is still in effect, without being so rigidly applied. People are able to travel more easily inside the country now, choose which clinic they visit, and choose where they want to live and work.

With the introduction of privatisation, properties became saleable or could be inherited. Formulae determining permissible 'living room' no longer apply and 'new Russians', a generation of new businessmen and women, are able to make money and build mansions.

However, although we have moved into a new millennium, accommodation is still difficult to find and many flats continue to be shared by more than one family.

Over the past 10 years, the mentality of the previously Communist society has had to change. People are learning fast that money makes most things possible, but chronology has not been kind to the older generations, precluded from entrepreneurial activities. Young people are finding that, as always, timing in life is most important. In the rush to enrich themselves, it is hoped they will remember the struggles and deprivations forced upon their elders by wars, misguided politicians and avaricious bureaucrats.

7

A young Communist's education

THE YOUNGEST IN A FAMILY OF THREE CHILDREN, I WAS BORN on 17 April 1955. My elder siblings were both boys and my parents had not planned a third child. When my mother was carrying me, my parents were convinced that I would be another boy. They had prepared to name me Vladimir, after Vladimir Lenin, whose birthday was 22 April. My birth as a girl upset their plan, so they named me after one of Lenin's sisters, Olga.

As a child, I was proud to have been named after Lenin's sister. Later at school, doing the obligatory study of the lives of Lenin's family, I learned that Olga had died at the age of 24 from typhoid, presumably without deserving a place in history for anything other than being Vladimir's sister. The other children in the Lenin family had all managed to distinguish themselves by preparing or participating in revolutionary acts. It was a disappointment to me, personally, and I wondered why my parents had chosen to name me after such an unremarkable figure. I was even frightened that I might die at a similarly young age. But I have managed to learn and do a lot more in my lifetime than the unfortunate sister of Lenin.

Under the care of my grandmother, my early pre-school years were happily uneventful. When I was five, my parents began preparing me for school. Questions inconvenient for them were always fielded by the same answer, 'You'll learn about that at school.'

If I misbehaved, they would frighten me with comments like, 'Olga, stop that or you won't be able to go to school.' Often my father would take my thin arm tenderly in his hand and say, 'Look at her, she's not strong enough to go to school yet.' That resulted in my being very curious as to what 'school' had to offer.

When I turned six, it was decided that kindergarten would help prepare me for real school; and summer camp, attended by all kindergarten children, would strengthen me physically.

From that point, my part in Socialist life began. I learned quickly about organised collective action that brought my relatively unregulated life at home to an end. From eight in the morning until five in the afternoon, everything we did in kindergarten was regimented. We all ate, slept, walked in line, played, ran and went to the toilet on instructions from our teacher.

Kindergartens, for the convenience of working parents, had begun developing in Russia after the Revolution. The intention was to care for the children of the workers if there was nobody in the home to do so, such as a grandparent. According to the Constitution, everyone was obliged to work for the State, including mothers, as early as two months after giving birth. That rule applied until 1959, after which it was relaxed progressively so that a woman was allowed to care for her child for up to three years without losing her job.

The pre-school system of kindergartens was made up of two divisions: children from the age of two months to three years, and from three to seven years. In 1936, in the province of Kalinin there were 700 kindergartens that cared for around 23 000 children. World War II destroyed most of the infrastructure. When the province was finally liberated from the Germans, priority was given to rebuilding kindergarens in order to free up parents for the vital task of reconstructing everything else that had been destroyed. By 1950, all of the USSR had kindergartens, all designed in the same way. Typically, the modules would accommodate either 140 or 280 children, depending on the requirements of the region.

By 1959, a common education system had been put in place by the Soviet government for pre-school children throughout the country. Regardless of ethnic origin, all children were taught in Russian, the main language of instruction, in addition to their mother tongue, sang the same patriotic songs and recited the same poems.

According to 1989 official statistics, 73.9 per cent of all children attending their first school class had come through the kindergarten system. More than 10 000 teachers in Kalinin province alone were responsible for educating the very young in ways approved by the Soviet State. There was little choice. My parents had to send me to one of the 18 kindergartens, all much the same, belonging to the chemical plant at which my mother worked. At the age of six, I naturally had no idea what to expect.

Once I started, I enjoyed being part of the system. The process had begun to prepare me for 'collective candidacy'. On every celebratory occasion our teachers would prepare us to take part in concerts that our parents would attend. We were taught to sing and recite stories of our glorious Revolution, our wonderful State, our happy childhood and the kindness of our 'grandfather' Lenin, whom we were encouraged to regard with great love.

At least we could understand who Lenin was, because his picture was everywhere, although it was a mystery how one man could have so many grandchildren. But at six years of age we had no idea of what a 'State' was, much less how we were supposed to get our arms around it to love. We learned with enthusiasm the songs of praise about our heroes, and about Red Square, and ruby stars on the Kremlin walls. It really didn't matter what the occasion was, it always began with a display of Socialist patriotism, as was customary then everywhere in Russia.

Almost daily my father would check the thickness of my arms. He was upset to note that the condition was not improving and I had to swear that I was eating all my food at the kindergarten. I even asked for more sometimes. Despite my fragile body, I was very active and strong enough to keep up with the other children. My parents' hope of turning me into some kind of pocket Amazon rested on the coming summer camp.

That particular camp was situated in a pine forest on the banks of the Volga River, 30 kilometres outside of our city. Children of various age groups up to about 15 used other camps in the vicinity. They belonged to different organisations, often large factories, and my camp, as with my kindergarten, belonged to the chemical plant.

If they wanted their children to be able to participate, it was important for parents to be employed by an organisation that had such facilities. Workers in those factories had the privilege of being able to send their children on camp holidays.

We were housed in big wooden buildings made up of dormitories accommodating 20 boys or girls, leading off a large dining room, kitchen and playroom with many toys and games for our amusement. There was a duty roster for laying tables at mealtimes and clearing away afterwards. It was the first time that I experienced being separated from my family and I learned fast about taking care of myself, being tidy and hygienic.

Almost every day, weather permitting, we walked in squads to the same 200 square metre clearing in the pine forest. There we swept away the needles and pine cones, and picked up twigs and anything else lying about until the whole clearing was pristine.

Cleaning up the clearing was supervised by our tutors and anyone slacking was given a lecture on the necessity for tidiness and cleanliness. The following day would require the same effort after wind had blown the needles, cones, twigs and branches all over the ground again.

Then we were taught our patriotic songs and poems, standing in that tidy area. I didn't understand why our tutors made us clean the place repeatedly. Surely we could have stood on the needles and learned songs and poems? Maybe they intended to teach us to be disciplined and industrious, or perhaps they thought that cleaning the ground would lend more dignity and importance to their lessons? Who knows what was going on in their Socialist heads.

In order to swim in the river, we had to have the permission of the camp doctor. Temperatures of both air and water had to be right and the sun had to be shining, because the doctor was reluctant to take responsibility for our health. An outbreak of some malady might result in his losing his job, so he nearly always found some reason to withhold permission to swim. We were lucky, during the two-month duration of our camp, if there were two days when we were allowed to swim.

There was a wooden enclosure in the shallows of the river

measuring approximately 25 square metres, with a water depth around 80 or 90 centimetres. On those occasions when we were allowed to swim, we were divided into groups of five and each group allowed to enter the water for about 10 minutes. At first the water seemed very cold, but no sooner had we acclimatised to it than we were told to get out to allow the next group in. Every group resisted the instruction to get out, which drove the tutors mad.

At that time, there was not one swimming pool in the city of Kalinin, so none of us had learned to swim. Swimming in the river was the highlight of our camping days and the first thing we told our parents about when they visited. They were allowed to see us on three Sundays during the two-month camp. These were known as 'parents' days'. The authorities considered more frequent visits disruptive, or even traumatic for the children, which they certainly were.

Parents' days were, for us, very exciting. Our parents brought sweets, which armed us to eat less of the unpalatable camp food. We were happy all day until the moment of their departure, when a general wailing could be heard throughout the camp.

Anyhow, fresh air, physical activity and regular meals were good for us. When I arrived home at the end of summer, my father thought my arms were bigger and I was stronger for having attended. It meant I was ready for school.

After the Revolution, the Ministry of Public Education of the Soviet State had taken over the entire educational system, including the tertiary grades. A completely revised common educational curriculum was introduced, applicable to all centres of learning. The intention had been to eliminate illiteracy, particularly among the adult population. More schools were constructed throughout the country and, while children attended classes during the day, adults were encouraged to attend free night classes.

In 1925, 84.4 per cent of children in Russia were attending school. By 1930, a law had been passed to make education compulsory for all children. World War II caused great disruptions in the educational process, but, by 1949, seven years of free child education was mandatory. Higher education was not entirely free at that point, but, from 1956, education at all levels was given free of charge.

In 1959, eight classes of education were made compulsory for all children and, in 1984, 99.8 per cent of all eighth-class school leavers continued studying. They had the option of attending classes nine and ten, which qualified them for a university education, or going to a technical college where they would complete classes nine and ten, and, in addition, qualify for lower technical certificates, some of which required an extra year's study.

Every aspect of education was strictly controlled. All examinations had to be passed and the necessary official stamps obtained if further lessons were sought. Teachers were given a curriculum from which they were not to deviate.

The first of September is a special day in Russia. On that day, all educational establishments open for the year. It used to be an unwritten rule that all children took flowers to their teachers and every classroom was filled with buckets of floral tributes, creating a happy, celebratory atmosphere. On the first day of the school year we also wore a smart uniform, not used otherwise. For girls it consisted of a brown dress with a white collar, a white apron, white hair ribbons and white stockings. Usually, parents took their children to school for the first day or two, to show them the way, but thereafter they were on their own. Although parents had to work, they were allowed a few hours off in the first days of September.

My school was half an hour's walk from home and there was no transport available. Every day, my friend Valya and I carried our heavy school satchels there and back. We were often late for school, no matter what time we were told to leave home, because on the way we invariably found something new and exciting to absorb our interest. That gave rise to our being woken progressively earlier each morning. I have vivid recollections of measuring the depth, with our rubber boots, of every puddle that we encountered in spring or autumn, and in winter we made snowballs to throw at each other.

There were 44 children in my class, seated at three rows of double desks. Each desk usually had a boy and a girl seated next to one another, our positions decided by the teacher. I enjoyed school because it was relatively easy for me. I suppose I was lucky because my grandmother had taught me to read and count before I started. In my first year, I was given a prize for the best reader in the class, thanks to her.

We didn't like parents' day at school; in fact we were scared of it because the Russian educational system appeared to be designed to find fault in each child and point this out to parents. Perhaps it was part of the regimentation process, to break us down so that we could be remoulded in the desired form.

I would imagine that some of the subjects we studied were much the same as those taught in Western European schools, but there were differences in our history and political education, as well as the lamentable quality of our foreign language teaching.

Children studied foreign languages in 45-minute lessons twice a week from the age of 12; in most cases, English. Conversational language was not taught. Listening to foreign radio broadcasts was illegal and communicating verbally with foreigners, strongly discouraged by the KGB. It made practising our limited knowledge of a foreign language virtually impossible. Even students graduating from their final year at university were given a diploma stating that they were 'able to read and translate with a dictionary' only. Those who studied a language in order to teach it may have been exceptions, as they became fairly proficient, but certainly not fluent. The impression I have is that the foreign language curriculum was designed to render us unable to communicate effectively, and to keep us isolated from the rest of world society.

As bad as the foreign language education was, our political and history education was, conversely, thorough – and distinctively Soviet. While subjects such as Mathematics, Science, Geography and Botany continued to be taught from textbooks that had been modernised, but not affected by, the Revolution, History and Politics was another story entirely. Post Revolution, the books had been completely rewritten to reflect solely that which the

Soviet government considered appropriate.

From the age of 12, school children were obliged to study a variety of historical subjects, such as History of the October 1917 Revolution, History of the Communist Party, History of Socialism and Communism, History of the Soviet Union, and History of Foreign Countries.

In addition, documents from the congresses of the Communist Party had to be studied, and the speeches of Lenin and Stalin, together with their writings and those of Marx and Engels. More senior classes studied Philosophy, Political Economy, Social Science and Dialectical and Philosophical Materialism (a philosophical approach to reality derived from the teachings of Marx and Engels).

For children and teenagers, extracurricular activities such as belonging to the *Oktyabryonoks*, Pioneers, and *Komsomols* were regular features of our lifestyle. The organisations were rigidly controlled by the Central Committee of the Communist Party and were overseen by the *Komsomol* Central Committee. Every child in the Soviet Union was expected to pass through these organisations; it was seen as an honour to belong to such organisations, and the few who did not join were ostracised.

Children of seven years of age and upward, preparing for entry into the Pioneers, began as *Oktyabryonoks*. We were the 'grandchildren of Lenin and descendents of Red October'. Every October, there was a big celebration at our schools with music and patriotic songs. We wore a special black-and-white parade uniform and, as a rule, one of the heroes of the Revolution or WWII would give out red star badges, with the face of Lenin as a child, before making a stirring patriotic speech.

We would proudly swear a five-part oath of loyalty to the country and later, in class, be divided into five groups, each representing a point of the red star. Each group was expected to compete against the others by earning good marks at school, and doing good deeds such as helping old or sick people. Groups were given credits for their achievements. It was the beginning of a long process of political indoctrination and we accepted it happily with the innocence of children. Ultimately, we were equipped to discuss Lenin's childhood and family, the October Revolution, the Red and White Armies, plus the good Bolsheviks who fought against the evil Tsar and the capitalists.

In April (the month of Lenin's birth) of the year in which we attained the age of 10, we joined the Young Pioneers, until the age of 14. A solemn ceremony was held, usually around the Lenin Monument in the city centre. Again, a Communist hero would make a speech, tie red scarves around our necks and present us with badges after we had sworn loyalty to the Communist Party.

Our oath was, 'I, Olga Devjatkina, join the All-Union of the Pioneer Organisation by V.I. Lenin, in front of my comrades, and solemnly promise to love my motherland fully, to live, study and struggle as Great Lenin bequeathed and as the Communist Party teaches. I promise always to obey the Soviet Union Pioneer Laws.'

The first Pioneer detachment was established in my home province in 1922. It was created for the children of workers in the Proletarka Weaving Factory. By 1926, it had expanded to 625 detachments of some 21 000 Pioneers. One of their main aims then was, with the help of child teachers, to assist in the eradication of illiteracy among the adult population.

Another of their tasks was to help the All-Russian Special Commission for Combating Counter-Revolution and Sabotage Division of the Cheka (later the KGB) to find homeless children and ensure they were given the assistance needed. Pioneer children also served as conduits between the Party and the proletariat by forming themselves into teams of agitators, holding concerts, plays and lectures to attract crowds. While helping the Communist authorities to further their aims, they also assisted in improving amenities in the towns and countryside, creating a good impression on behalf of their Communist leaders.

Before WWII, Pioneers were put through a course of civil defence and a regime of physical training. The best among them were awarded special 'Ready to Work and Defend' badges. At the beginning of 1940 there were 7 955 detachments made up of 232 000 Pioneers in Kalinin province alone. Their childhood was cut short by the the war because they were used as substitutes for adults who had gone off to fight. They worked in manufacturing plants, on farms and, in fact, anywhere that their age permitted. Many of them became heroes as partisans, spies and messengers.

At the end of the war, teenage Pioneer survivors occupied themselves by assisting in the reconstruction of the country. They collected scrap metal and waste paper for recycling in special factories built for the purpose, and everything they did was noted for report at Communist Party congresses, which sometimes awarded National Pioneer Organisation honours in the form of special medals.

A Pioneer detachment was usually made up of one class of schoolchildren, totalling approximately 40 people. When we marched, a drummer led the way, followed by a bugler, then the flag carrier and after him the detachment commander, with the rest behind him in three columns. We kept time with the drumbeat, singing or reciting patriotic songs.

Usually, there would be a person representing the *Komsomol* movement, who would call out, 'Pioneers of the Soviet Union, be ready to battle for Communism.'

We would answer in unison, giving the special Pioneer salute, 'We are always ready.'

Competition was used to motivate us. After being divided into three groups, we would compete against the others by trying to outdo them, get better marks at school, collect more waste paper and scrap metal, look after old people and generally be active in a positive way.

Simultaneously, we competed against other detachments; the prize for the best detachment was to be named after one of the Communist or Pioneer heroes. With hindsight, I can see that the State wanted to prepare us for acceptance of the battle for survival and faithfully embrace the accompanying hardships that were unavoidable under the system.

Our heroes were people who had struggled for Communism, sometimes giving their lives for the cause. We didn't choose them; they were thrust upon us and we were expected to try to emulate their heroism. A nice comfortable life was portrayed as being morally bad and we were encouraged to battle for everything. We were proud though, oh yes! When I wore the red scarf of the Pioneers, I believed that our State was the best, our Russian people were the greatest in the world, and our childhood the happiest, because our State cared for us.

My detachment once won the competition and was named, 'Pioneer Hero Pavlik Morozov Detachment'. It was supposed to be a great honour because Pavlik Morozov was recognised as a hero of collectivisation. Everyone knew his story. At the age of 10 he had overheard an adult conversation between Kulaks and *Serednjaks* opposed to collectivisation and planning resistance. When he reported the 'plot' to a Red Commissar, the people involved were arrested and punished. Supporters of those punished later killed Pavlik Morozov, which instantly elevated him to martyr status and he was posthumously awarded the title of 'Communist Hero'.

We were told that he had given his young life for Communist ideals. Thousands of Pioneer detachments competed over the next 60 years to be named after him. I was so proud when we were given his name and never doubted what we were told of his heroism.

Years later, after *glasnost* was announced by Gorbachev, an article was published about Pavlik Morozov. It transpired that his father had been chairman of the *kolkhoz*. To give rebellious *Kolkhozniks* the opportunity to flee, the chairman had warned those who were being investigated of their imminent arrest – not that they had committed any heinous crime; they had simply resisted certain dictates of the State. The son eavesdropped and reported what he heard. As a consequence, his father and the 'offenders' were arrested and shot. It came as a horrible shock to me – I had considered him a hero, when, in fact, he had caused the death of his own father and other innocents.

A flood of information was released at that time, often resulting in those who had been accorded hero status being knocked off their pedestals. I realised then that, despite my happy childhood, we had been brainwashed, lied to and fed half-truths, to provide the

State with the advantages it sought.

From age 12 we took part in the Soviet Union Pioneer game called *Zarnitsa* (summer lightning). The 'game' originated in 1966 and revolved around military exercises designed to prepare children for defence of the motherland. The Communist Party, supported by the Soviet Union ministries of Defence, Education and Sport, dreamt up the idea, then delegated it to the Central Committee of the *Komsomol* for implementation.

A hero of the Soviet Union, Artillery Marshall V Kazakov, was the commander of the exercise. As *junarmeetz* (junior soldiers), we had to respond to orders from the Marshall. All children from the Baltic to the Russian Far East took part. Every school became a battalion and classes were squads. We had to buy special green uniforms with epaulettes designating rank.

Our military education involved map reading, stripping and assembling AK47s (which were considered too dangerous for us to fire), firing normal single-shot rifles, erecting tents and breaking camp in as short a time as possible, protection against nuclear attack and first aid.

To further this education, during our summer vacation we spent two weeks in a real military camp on the upper reaches of the Volga River, sleeping in tents, exercising together with soldiers and eating food from their canteen. I remember that only the borsch was any good. Soldiers gave us daily lectures on various military subjects. The boys were keen to ask questions, but the girls did not appear particularly interested.

One day they called for brave volunteers to cross the Volga submerged in an amphibious tank, a distance of about 200 metres. Some of the boys volunteered and, to my horror, before the tank reached the middle it had submerged completely and all we could see was the radio antenna. I realised then that I was not cut out for a 'brave' life and perhaps the only heroic deed I might be capable of would be leading the retreat.

In fact, that camp exercise had the effect of putting me off all things military. In any case, I could never work out which eye I was supposed to close when firing a rifle and I still haven't learned how to follow compass directions, because I always confuse my left with my right.

Be that as it may, I was obliged as a member of my squad to do the best I could in order not to let the others down. We had borrowed the motto of the Three Musketeers, 'All for one and one for all', which was pretty much what we were weaned on as Communist babies. It must have been effective because, despite my shortcomings, our squad was awarded second prize in the town's squad competition.

It was the culmination of three years of competitive effort. First prize was a one-month visit to the All-Union Pioneer Camp 'Artek', located on the Crimean Peninsula on the Black Sea. Artek was a famous place in the Soviet Union and every Pioneer coveted the idea of getting there. We knew that to achieve it, we had to be either a 'hero' or simply the 'best of the best'. One of the boys in our squad was chosen to represent us and was sent to Artek, along with the winning squad. The rest of us were rewarded with a free 12-day boat trip to Uljanovsk on the Volga, the town where Lenin was born.

Matros Vaculenchuk was a three-upper-deck riverboat that carried about 300 Pioneers representing different towns. We stopped every day at towns and villages for excursions, lectures and museum visits, all connected to the Revolution, the life of Lenin and the establishment of the Communist Party.

In Uljanovsk we were able, with great excitement and reverence, to visit the actual house that was the birthplace of Lenin, as well as the school that he had attended at our age. Both of these venerated sites had been converted into museums. By the age of 14, our political education had been thorough and comprehensive.

In preparation for the 7 November anniversary of the Great October Revolution (a result of the Soviet government's altering the calendar by two weeks after the Revolution, which affected only Revolutionary anniversaries), four of us were nominated to stand guard of honour at the memorial to the Unknown Soldier, with its eternal flame. We wore our Pioneer uniforms and practised for several days marching with our drummer and Pioneer flag and standing to attention with the Pioneer salute for 15 minutes.

When the day came, it was cold and windy, with wet snow falling. Despite the jerseys we had on underneath our shirts, it must have been freezing. Our sense of pride and our Communist zeal was such that, at the time, I felt no discomfort. My only regret was that none of my family could see me or take a photograph of the proud occasion. They were at work.

I remember standing there, thinking how lucky I was to be such a happy girl, born in the best country in the world. The love and pride I felt for my motherland and the Soviet State filled my soul completely. I was consumed by thoughts of my future, of becoming a *Komsomol*, finishing school, living and working for the good of my great Soviet people and, ultimately, becoming a Communist like my parents.

I thought I would be prepared to give my life for our Communist ideals if necessary, like the heroes whose lives I had studied.

We remained members of the Pioneers until we turned 14, and then joined the *Komsomol* movement, which catered for ages 14 to 28 years.

8

Life's lessons

BEFORE I CONTINUE THE STORY OF MY POLITICAL EDUCATION, I would like to mention some events that occurred at this stage of my life. As with many young girls, I drove my parents crazy in my determination to be a ballet dancer. In the 14 square metre room occupied by our family of six, I would pirouette and take delicate steps round the confined space, disturbing my brothers who were trying to study.

Details of the first ballet I saw have long left my memory, but the event somehow made an indelible impression on me and provided me with a will to succeed at ballet that was totally disproportionate to my actual ability. My parents were at a loss to understand it, since nobody in their families had displayed any artistic leanings, let alone talent. When I was six, they finally capitulated and sent me to ballet school.

Lessons were held in the Palace of Culture building, which belonged to the chemical plant where my mother worked. Former professional ballet dancers gave free evening lessons, three times a week, to children of the workers. My mother made a special white dress for me and somehow produced a pair of ballet shoes, made by hand. It was great for me, but a member of the family had to take me there for every lesson and they soon tired of the chore.

Lessons were very formal and took place in a room properly equipped with bars, mirrors and a grand piano. We took part in many concerts and ballets that called for child participation. They were held in the theatre hall of the Palace of Culture, usually with large audiences present. I loved my lessons, and the teacher and other children soon became a second family to me.

When adults asked, as they do, 'What would you like to be when you grow up?' my answer was always the same, 'A ballet dancer.'

When I attended school I was keen to participate in all extramural activities such as sports, art classes and choir practice. This all went well until I was about 12, when educational inspectors arrived and decided I was one of three tone-deaf members of the choir. We were promptly asked to leave. I was shocked as I'd been in the choir since I was eight and nobody had even hinted that I might not be acceptable. What shocked me even more was the realisation that another consequence of this shortcoming would be the end of my dream dancing at the Bolshoi Theatre.

Only my pillow knew how many nights I cried myself to sleep, after lying awake for hours. My character would not allow me to share my tragedy with anyone else. I had to make the decision for myself: should I, or should I not, give up ballet?

For six years I had dreamt of the time we would be taught to dance on points, and it was about to begin. My parents had just bought me my first pair of real ballet shoes. How could I tell them? I was sure they would consider me capricious.

Finally, I chose to tell Father, thinking him likely to be the more understanding parent. He listened very seriously while I built an argument for my case to retire from ballet.

When I had finished he said, 'Are you sure you will not regret your decision, my girl?'

'No, Father,' I said.

'Are you sure you won't blame us in future?' he asked.

I gave a strong answer, 'No.'

I love ballet, but have never regretted the decision to give it up at age 12. That was my first real lesson in taking responsibility for my own actions and, to this day, I'm grateful to my father for always according me respect and giving me the time to discuss my problems in an adult way.

From nine to 14 years of age, I spent one month each summer school holiday at the Pioneer camp belonging to my mother's employers. It was in the same area as the kindergarten camp I had been to previously, and was typical of Soviet children's camps, with a rigid regime of daily activities.

Days began and ended with a parade, the raising and lowering of the flag, and the sounding of a bugle. In between, we moved in detachments, attending political lectures, movies, playing games, cleaning the camp and doing kitchen duty. I loved attending camps and those were probably the happiest days of my childhood.

During the time away from my parents, I enjoyed being independent and having responsibility for my own actions. It was a good opportunity to make new friends and learn about life. When the day was done and our tutors had checked us into bed, our secret nightly girlish conversations began in the darkness.

At nine years of age, we were very observant. We whispered about our tutors; who loved whom, who was dating whom and what adults 'did'. Crumbs of 'knowledge' provided an insight into activities yet to be discovered. Nowhere else was this kind of information available in what I now think of as a fairly puritanical society.

For instance, my aunt had given birth to a baby girl, but I had no idea of how that miracle of new life had come about. My mother ignored my questions on the subject, simply pretending that she hadn't heard me, and the only other information available was from the few 'knowledgeable' girls in our hut.

At camp, I learned about the process of girls becoming teenagers and how they became women and what to expect. As a result, I hid my bodily changes from my mother for many months and, when I'd already reached 14, she suddenly decided it was time for me to be enlightened. Her embarrassment was obvious and she seemed to stammer in her effort to explain. I felt quite sorry for her, so I took over and explained that I already knew everything. She was shocked at my knowledge about this delicate subject.

'What do you know and from whom?' she asked angrily.

My answer was, 'Everything, from the girls at camp.'

That was the end of my camping life. No matter how I begged, I was forbidden to attend another summer camp. It was another of life's lessons: to be careful revealing how much you know.

My childhood naivety was still in place, but I slowly began to question the motives of others. An example of this was connected with the famous Pioneer Camp, Artek.

When we were told that we had won second place in the Pioneer game *Zarnitsa*, our teacher instructed us to select among ourselves, by the following day, the best person to attend Artek for one month. There was great excitement, since we all wanted to be chosen for the honour. We set about choosing the one we considered best. There were five candidates, arrived at by their school marks, but there were other criteria too. The winner had to have leadership ability, be of good character and must have proved to be most competent at *Zarnitsa*.

It boiled down to three possibilities and we tried honestly, as we had been taught, to find the winner. We submitted our report to the teacher. None of us slept well that night and the following morning we couldn't wait to go to class.

Our teacher was a very beautiful young woman, who was fancied by all the boys and copied by the girls. During the period under her tutelage we had come to regard her as being perfect in every way. She arrived in the class that morning and announced the winner, a boy named Peter, who was to go to Artek.

Forty children exploded in unison. 'Why him?' we shouted. 'We didn't choose him.'

He was a mediocre student only, certainly not the best at *Zarnitsa*, not popular and very aloof. The teacher explained that we should show some sympathy for Peter. She said that he had not been well and would benefit from a month at the Black Sea. We were very indignant because he was one of the best physical specimens in our class and, as far as we knew, had not been off sick more than anyone else.

The teacher was stubborn and refused to entertain our objections. Peter was prompted by the class to stand up, say that he wasn't deserving of the honour and that others better represented our detachment. Ignoring our pleas, he sat in stoical silence. We were helpless to change the decision and eventually he went to Artek.

As the months passed, we tried to forget the bitterness caused by our teacher's dictate. Then, one day, one of the girls told us that she had overheard a conversation between mothers, and it became apparent that Peter had been selected by our teacher, regardless of our opinion, because his mother was our teacher's dressmaker. That meant that Peter had *blat*.

This is a Russian expression inferring bribery and corruption, nepotism, perhaps – an advantage because of 'a friend at court', or simply having something desired by others. It was the first time in our lives that we had experienced *blat*, which I learned to detest. It is one of the worst aspects of behaviour in a social society of supposed 'equals'. While *blat* probably exists to some extent in all societies, it found exceedingly fertile ground in the Soviet Union, in particular because of the supply structure and the lack of any transparency in decision making.

There were ongoing deficits, shortages of life's necessities, and a dictatorial, bureaucratic system. Backscratching was part of daily life, if standing in long queues for necessities, such as sugar, was to be avoided. And so *blat* prevailed, from hospitals to grocery stores.

In the same way, desirable items could usually be obtained through 'friends'. We had a saying, 'Don't have a hundred roubles, rather have a hundred friends.' I always found *blat* demeaning. Fawning over some mercenary butcher's assistant in order to get a reasonable cut of meat, instead of a bag of bones for the same money, was not something I could easily stoop to.

But I learned from this incident with Peter and our teacher that the system was not fail-safe, and that one can't always trust those who seem to be – and who should be – beyond reproach.

Thank goodness that not all of life's lessons are negative. When I was 14, I went swimming with friends in the Volga. The first public swimming pool had just been opened in our city of 700 000 people, but getting in and having swimming lessons was virtually impossible because of the crowds that flocked there daily. Of the 12 of us, only three could swim, but the rest of us were keen to learn. It was a warm sunny day with a water temperature of around 21 degrees Centigrade, tepid for the Volga. We were thoroughly enjoying themselves, laughing, running and jumping in, screaming and taking no particular notice of one another. I kept doggy-paddling into deep water, turning and heading back to the bank.

I don't know how it happened, but I suddenly found myself in trouble as I turned to go back towards the bank. In an instant I was under water. I watched the sun become dimmer as I sank deeper. The sunlight appeared to be like a tunnel that I was drawn towards, and the feeling was strangely comforting. In my mind's eye, I could see my life flashing by like a speeded-up movie.

To the left of the sunlit tunnel entrance there appeared to be something white. I don't know why, but I thought it was a woman, although it was small and did not even resemble a human in shape. Suddenly I felt as though somebody were questioning me. I didn't know who it was; maybe the white form near the tunnel entrance? Under the water there was no sound, so the voice must have been in my mind only. Someone said, 'Are you ready?' I knew I should answer, and said, 'I feel sorry for my mother, she will cry too much.'

Then my world went blank. Next thing, I was sitting on the bank, coughing up water. I couldn't breathe properly and my head was pounding. When I had recovered, one of the girls told me that she had seen me go under amid the noise and splashing. She had swum over, reached for me and pulled me out by my hair.

For years I pondered the incident, trying to find some answer regarding the tunnel, the white form, the voice I had heard in my mind and the light that had drawn me towards something unknown, but somehow strangely comforting. When I tried to discuss it with my friends and family, they paid no attention. They just laughed and said that nearly drowning must have affected my brain.

At that time, there was no literature available in Russia about religion, the afterlife, or any other subject considered contrary to Communist thinking or ideals. The drowning incident started me pondering on the possibility of there being a life after death, or even a God – concepts that had been absent from my upbringing and education. Only after *glasnost* was announced by Gorbachev in 1985, did any kind of publication on subjects such as mysticism and religion become available. When I finally managed to read books by people with similar experiences, I realised that a spiritual thread connected us all, pointing, perhaps, to a benign, all-encompassing God. But of course, at the time, in Soviet society, I was unable to discuss even this possibility.

9

High school

I N OUR EIGHTH CLASS WE BECAME MEMBERS OF THE YOUNG
Communist League of the Soviet Union *(Komsomol)*. It was
another step up in our political education, following our
membership of the *Octyabryonoks* and Pioneers. *Komsomols* were
regarded as the 'young brothers' of Communists and the first
assistants in the building of Communism.

One of the requirements for ultimate acceptance into the
Communist Party was prior membership of the *Komsomol*. The
structure of the *Komsomol* was a reflection of that used in the
Communist Party. It had its Central Committee situated in
Moscow under the direct control of the Central Committee of the
Communist Party.

As with the Communist Party, the *Komsomol* had central
committees in each of the 15 republics. Under them were
Komsomol provincial committees, then city and town committees
and finally countryside committees. Every four years there was an
All-Union Congress, similar to that of the Communist Party,
where they reviewed past achievements and formulated a new
'programme' for the future. The entire structure formed an
organisation that ran like clockwork in preparing the upcoming
generations for Communism.

Young people with criminal records of any kind, or whose ideas
did not conform to those of the Communists, such as churchgoers,
homosexuals or hippies, could not belong to the *Komsomol*. For
the rest of young society, it was 'voluntary'. But there was an
unwritten law: you either belonged or you were ostracised and
considered an outsider. For that reason, as 'normal' people, we were

all very keen to be *Komsomol* members.

Before acceptance into the *Komsomol* ranks, we studied their code, the congress programmes of both the *Komsomols* and Communists, the history of the Revolution and the Communist Party, and many other related political subjects. We were able to quote, from memory, special parts of the works of Karl Marx, Lenin and other Communist leaders.

Enrolment was no simple process. It required, in the first instance, a school interview, and, if the examiners were satisfied that your political education and viewpoint were correct, you were recommended to the next commission, the *Komsomol* district committee. That was made up of heroes of the Revolution and the Great Patriotic War, plus other distinguished Communists conscripted onto the *Komsomol* committee for the express purpose of ensuring our suitability to their cause.

Their main concern was ensuring the continuity of Communist ideology in the future. Questioning was rigorous and, if you were successful, you were later invited to a celebration at which you were decorated with a small red badge featuring Lenin's face, and given your membership book. It was the end of our Pioneer red ties. Our childhood was over.

From acceptance we were obliged to pay monthly membership fees, subscribe to *Komsomol Truth* (the newspaper of our central committee) and participate enthusiastically in *Komsomol* activities at school and, as dictates prescribed, nationwide.

A leader, who would be *komsorg (Komsomol* organiser), had to be elected from our school class each year, and I was surprised, proud and happy when I was chosen unanimously in my second year of membership. At 15, I was full of enthusiasm and wanted to work hard to show my patriotism. As *komsorg* I had to represent my class on the school *Komsomol* committee.

The chairman, who was a senior student, began by teaching us how to work with our classes, making recommendations that, in effect, were instructions for certain actions to be taken. His instructions emanated from the central *Komsomol* committee and were passed down the structure, ending with our classes.

Initially, I was given a plan to implement that was the same for every *komsorg* in the USSR. We were instructed in how to hold *Komsomol* meetings once a month and were given an agenda to follow. Attendance was compulsory for all members and no excuse was acceptable, other than serious illness. Each member had to bring along their *Komsomol* membership book so as to ensure that they were up to date in the payment of their monthly subscriptions. A responsible person would stamp the payees' books, indicating receipt of payment. Losing one's book had a severe consequence: loss of membership.

Since education was the main priority, part of the plan was to ensure that less bright students managed to keep up with the rest of the class. That called for the clever students to assist those who battled. Then, for the benefit of our general knowledge, someone in the class was detailed to provide information on political events of the past seven days occurring inside our country and worldwide. The lecture was called *Polit Informatsia.* Naturally, events were given a Communist bias.

Our active competitive duty continued in the collection of scrap metal and waste paper. Saturdays were *subbotnik* (voluntary, unpaid labour) spent, in spring and autumn, cleaning the city. At other times of the year, we did unskilled factory jobs and, instead of being paid, we were told that the money raised would go to the political development of less privileged countries trying to build the Socialist utopia.

During school holidays, we usually travelled to villages that had cemeteries of fallen Great Patriotic War soldiers, where survivors or heroes were sometimes invited to address us. Our *Komsomol* committee encouraged each class to select the name of a Communist as our honorary hero, and our good deeds were committed in honour of that person.

We chose Zoya Kosmodemyanskaya who was a heroine of the Soviet Union, a partisan who had given her life in the Great Patriotic War, and we applied to use her name. Such use was never taken for granted; we had to earn the right by being the best class by the year end.

Grandfather Ivan after the end of the Civil War, early 1922.

Grandfather Ivan and grandmother Katerina in Kalinin, 1935. I always hoped to inherit what I perceived to be strength in their faces. Although Ivan died tragically under Luftwaffe bombs, that strength served Katerina through many severe physical and mental tests, enabling her to live to the age of 95.

My father Daniel with his mother Elena, in 1939. At the time he was a student at
Kazan School of Justice, where he hoped to qualify as a detective.

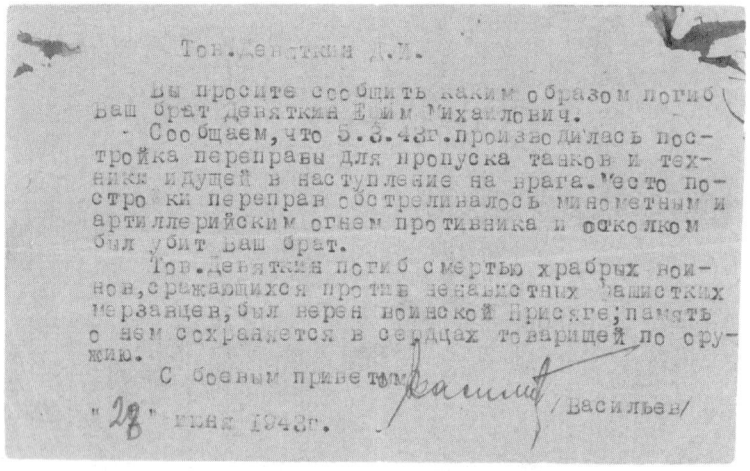

Note typed on the back of a piece of scrap paper, received from the army in response
to my father's enquiry regarding the fate of his brother Yephim during WWII.
Loosely translated it reads:

Comrade Devjatkin D.M.
You asked us to inform you of how your brother Devjatkin Yephim Mikhailovich
died. We advise that on 5.3.43 a river crossing was being constructed for tanks and
other equipment proceeding to attack the enemy. The site was attacked by mortar
and artillery fire and your brother killed by shrapnel.

Comrade Devjatkin died a brave soldier's death, fought against the hated Fascist
villains, was faithful to his oath, and his memory will remain in the hearts of his
comrades in arms.
With regards, Vasiljev.
28 June 1943.

Mother Antonina (back row, sixth from left) with her school class of 1939, two years before the beginning of WWII in Russia. Sadly, few of those pictured here survived to see Victory Day.

Antonina in Chelyabinsk, Urals, in 1942. She was 19, working voluntarily in a munitions factory, unaware that her mother and sisters were starving in Kalinin.

Daniel (second from left) in Kalinin, 1943, with comrades in arms.

Uncle Alex, a 17-year-old soldier, proudly displaying
the first of his many medals, end of 1943.

Antonina and Daniel with two-year-old Victor, their first child,
at Kalinin in 1947, just before moving to Orenburg.

The house where I was born in 1955 in a village in
Orenburg Province, near the Russian border with Kazakhstan.

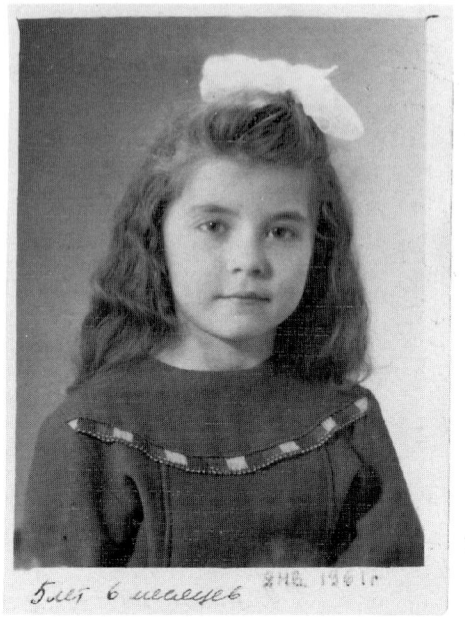

5 лет 6 месяцев

At the age of five, I asked my father what Communism was. 'Communism,' he said, 'will be the happy life that we are building now.'

Marching with Mother behind a picture of Karl Marx, on Labour Day, 1961. I was brought up like most children in the USSR to be patriotic.

Pioneer Camp, 1966.

With my red Pioneer tie
after taking the oath.

We were probably a typical Russian family, here in a portrait from 1967.
Victor (back right) had just finished university. Evgueni (back left)
was doing entrance examinations for the same university.

Subbotnik, 'voluntary' duty to clean the town twice a year, at the ends of autumn and winter. This photograph was taken after a snowstorm in 1960, when again the people 'voluntarily' cleaned up. It could happen five or six times during snowy winters. Mother is third from the right.

Memorial to The Unknown Soldier at The Kremlin Wall in Moscow. Unveiled with great fanfare on 8 May 1967, it may just as well have contained the remains of my grandfather Ivan. Who knew? Poor granny Katerina suffered such unnecessary indignity for 40 years.

These three certificates were typical of those issued to honour individuals in the USSR and could be awarded for a 'glorious job' well done (higher productivity than normal), attaining a high degree of knowledge of Communism, active participation in civic duties beneficial to Soviet society, etc.

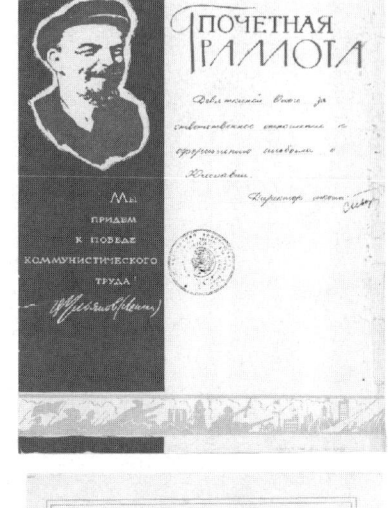

The first (right) was awarded to me in high school for a project I did on Yugoslavia. Under the picture of Lenin is a slogan, 'We will achieve a victory of Communist labour!' Lenin's signature is printed on it.

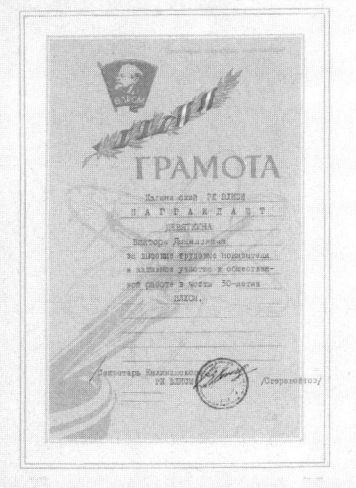

The second (above left) was awarded to me for being a socially active Pioneer. I earned it by collecting larger quantities of scrap metal and paper than my comrades and it was presented on the occasion of the Pioneer anniversary, 19 May 1966. Printed at the top is: 'Proletariats of the World Unite!' Under Lenin's picture is a slogan that reads, 'Under the flag of Marxism-Leninism and the Communist Party leadership – forward to Communism's victory!'

The third (above right) was awarded to my brother Victor, for his high productivity and active participation in Socialist life. The Regional *Komsomol* Committee, on the occasion of the 50th anniversary of the *Komsomol* organisation, presented it to him.

Mother with medals earned for her high degree of productivity on behalf of the Soviet nation and her participation in Victory in the Great Patriotic War, 1941–1945. The photograph was taken for display on the 'board of distinguished people' at the chemical factory at which she worked.
The occasion was the 20th anniversary of Victory Day, WWII, May 1965.

In March 1973, after the first semester at university, I was full of dreams to work, study and live for my beloved motherland. We had seven years left before our anticipated arrival in Khrushchev's promised Communist nirvana.

Our wedding in 1976. We were allowed use of this special room for 15 minutes. The mural in the background depicts our newly formed 'cell'.

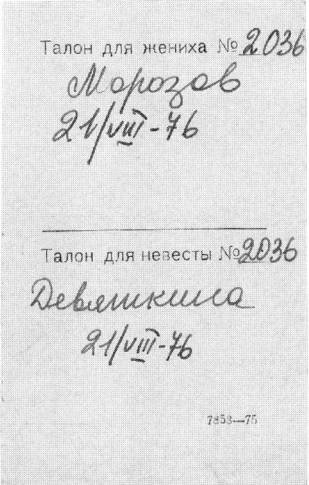

Wedding coupons issued to prospective brides and grooms to enable them to buy clothes, shoes and other necessary accoutrements for the big occasion. There was only one shop in our entire province able to supply wedding outfits.

By 1983 we were three years past the promised time for Communism in its final form, but, as a young member of the Party, I felt that I should be in the vanguard of our Socialist society.

My parent's *dacha* built in 1964. In compliance with the laws of the time,
it had no oven for heating, and no bathroom or inside toilet.
It was therefore impossible to live in as the weather cooled.

Our self-built *dacha*. Like most, it was never quite completed.

Military Prosecutor Colonel Grigory
Kroshner, now a retired General.
His determination to see justice
done helped those involved in
the hunting accident.

My visa to visit the
Republic of Bophuthatswana.

The two windows in the top left-hand corner are in the
two-roomed flat in which I grew up. My mother still lives there.

My beloved granny Katerina, a true
'survivor' and a wonderful human being.

The author outside the Kremlin with Roger Cartwright on a research and information-gathering trip to Moscow in October, 2003. The building in the background, behind the statue of horses, was the Kremlin stables.

A view of one of the city centre streets in Tver, 2003. These buildings were erected in the Stalin era and were superior to those built later, using pre-cast concrete panels. (The car in the foreground is a *Zhiguli*.)

The author, now living happily in Johannesburg.

Zoya had been 18, the same age my mother had been, when Germany invaded. She attended school in Moscow. From the age of 14, she had been a member of the *Komsomol* and, together with her younger brother, had volunteered to fight.

He had been sent to join the armoury, became a tank commander, was killed at the battle for Köningsburg and awarded the Hero of the Soviet Union Medal posthumously for his many acts of bravery.

Zoya was recommended to join a partisan detachment that, on 23 November 1941, passed through the attacking Nazi front line in order to obtain intelligence. She was sent alone to a village occupied by the Germans to glean information and had been captured there. Despite being severely tortured by her captors, she refused to reveal any information.

On 29 November, the Germans decided to make an example of her to discourage others from similar activities. They forced the entire population to turn out in the freezing cold to witness her execution.

She was led out in a torn undergarment, hands tied behind her back, a plaque on her thin chest bearing the words, 'I am a partisan', and forced to stand barefoot in the snow, while some Nazi officer made a long speech discouraging others from getting involved in partisan activities.

Exhausted from the terrible torture she had suffered, she was finally lifted onto a box, with a rope tied around her thin neck. But with the last strength she could muster, she managed to shout, 'Death to the fascists.' The box was kicked from under her and she hanged, dying slowly.

A German photographer took pictures of the whole procedure but the film later fell into Russian hands. To this day, I can still vividly recall those photographs. One in particular stands out. She had been cut down and left lying in the snow; her dishevelled hair was short like a boy's, her slip, which was all she wore, was torn, leaving a small breast protruding, and revealing ugly bruises up to her neck and over other visible parts of her pathetic body. Her heroism is well known among all citizens of the Soviet Union and she was honoured by having many towns, streets, ships and schools named after her.

Her mother was still alive in 1970 and living in Moscow. We wrote to her and to the *Komsomol* committee of Moscow School No. 201, which she had attended (and which was subsequently named after her and her brother), to tell them of our work in her honour. One day we received an invitation to attend a memorial day for Zoya and her brother, where we met her mother and listened to her tell of the lives and tragic deaths of her beloved children.

My year as *komsorg* was hard work, but at the end of it, we were awarded the right to name our detachment in Zoya's honour. For me, personally, it came as a reward for hard work and dedication. I was proud of what my detachment had achieved. But *komsorg* duty didn't bring me only satisfaction; there was also disappointment.

A year in that capacity taught me that there were also disadvantages to doing one's duty blindly and following instructions to the letter. For instance, I was told to hold a meeting to discuss '*Komsomol* conscience as a weapon against non-conformity'. I doubted that debating that particular subject would be a success, but I could not argue. It had come from the *Komsomol* committee and who was I to refuse?

As a disciplined *komsorg*, I began preparing for the debate. I was supposed to begin the discussion, then bring in the class to continue. It was a fiasco. I spoke for about 10 minutes, introducing the subject, then stepped back and waited for someone to grasp the nettle. There was a deathly silence. Nobody was prepared to utter a word.

There was something wrong with the subject; why, after all, should a *Komsomol* conscience be superior to any other? We knew from experience that Communists were opposed to 'non-conformists' who wanted to lead their own lives. But, secretly, we all hankered after a degree of nonconformism – the need to express our individuality. We secretly loved rock and roll music, avant-garde art, blue jeans and mini skirts, all of which were regarded as unacceptable. The words 'as a weapon' inferred fighting, which none of us really wanted. The subject was too personal and no-one was willing to divulge their thoughts; going along with the instruction would make us hypocrites.

As it was my responsibility to report on the outcome to the *Komsomol* committee, I had to attempt to save the situation. But, no matter how hard I tried to get people to stand up and speak, it was useless. In the end we all left for home in bad moods and I felt obliged to try to analyse what had happened.

It began to dawn on me that perhaps the system wasn't all it was cracked up to be. Maybe we were deliberately being told that we lived in a wonderful State when, in fact, it wasn't really 'nirvana'. Was it possible that all the parades, flag waving and speeches were intended to nurture a kind of *esprit de corps* that, in the end, just wouldn't take root? Were we being forced to play a political game? We had taken no part in formulating the rules dictated to us, so why should we be so enthusiastic about playing? They were even attempting to mould our consciences to conform to what was termed a '*Komsomol* conscience' or a 'Communist conscience'. I realised, with growing unease, that maybe someone was manipulating us.

I finished the compulsory eight classes of schooling in 1970. My parents and I decided that I would continue my education at another school for classes nine and ten, plus qualify for entrance to university. I had been with the same set of pupils for eight years, but now had to adjust to new surroundings, teachers and pupils.

I recall two political events from that time that gave me pause for thought. The first was my acquisition of an internal passport, which entitled me to vote. Not long after being issued with it, there was a national election for the Politburo chairman, Leonid Brezhnev. On our way to the polling booth, I asked my mother why we had to vote for him when he was the only candidate. Experience at school had shown me that voting was necessary when there was more than one candidate. So, to my mind, this election was farcical.

Mother maintained that it was a real election. If the whole country voted for him, then that is what they wanted. I asked what would happen if the people didn't want him.

She said, 'Don't worry, my girl, he will be elected anyway.'

In later years I took part in other elections, never allowing myself to question why there was only one candidate. It was simply acceptance of the status quo.

The second event occurred when I was in the tenth class. Our literature teacher, out of the blue, said that we had to write a composition on one of three themes. He favoured the first. It was a critique in which we were to analyse and censure the works of Solzhenitsyn. Since we'd never heard of him, we asked who he was and what he had written. The teacher appeared embarrassed and tried to explain that Solzhenitsyn was a contemporary writer whose work was critical of the Soviet State and leadership. Furthermore, he was against the Soviet people, which meant us. He had been declared an 'Enemy of the State' and his works banned.

Our teacher said he had had the opportunity to read only one of Solzhenitsyn's books before they were removed from sight, but he didn't enlarge on what he had read. He simply said we should believe what he told us, that Solzhenitsyn was bad, and that we should be able, in just one page, to criticise him. Despite listening attentively, we could not understand how we could be expected to write about something of which we had absolutely no direct knowledge, nor could we gain any, because his writings had already been banned and comprehensively obliterated.

We explained our sentiments and asked if it were possible to have another choice of subject for our compositions. He acquiesced, with a discernible sigh of relief. Obviously, being a reasonable man and a good teacher, he knew that it was unfair to ask us to do the impossible, but we still wondered why he had suggested this particular theme in the first place.

We chose other themes and set about writing our compositions. A few days later, the evening news announced that Solzhenitsyn had been deported in disgrace. It was emphasised that he was an 'Enemy of the State', and that even schoolchildren of the Soviet Union had written compositions decrying his work as anti-Soviet and anti the people. At that point it became clear that our teacher had been required to solicit such compositions in support of the State's campaign to discredit Solzhenitsyn.

At the time of *perestroika*, 18 years later, I understood more clearly how the Communist government had provoked a national campaign against Solzhenitsyn. They had infamously tried to crush a brave, dissenting voice, going to the extreme of using innocent and uninformed young scholars in their weaponry. I hope Solzhenitsyn was able to forgive the juveniles that criticised him in 1971. They were coerced and I can vouch for the fact.

Time in my ninth class passed quickly and I had still to decide what university course to choose. Having abandoned my ballet dancing aspirations at the age of 12, I now had a passion to become a fashion designer. The nearest university at which the subject could be studied was at the Moscow University of Light Industry.

To gain entry I would have to pass Mathematics, Chemistry and Physical Science and submit a composition on a subject yet to be announced. I would also have to be interviewed and submit my drawings. I worked hard at extra lessons and took a course at a drawing studio.

For some time I had been designing and making my own clothes, which were often admired by my friends and teachers. They were impressed with the way I sewed and said I had a talent for it. My father didn't take much interest and told me I should do whatever pleased me. Grandmother's attitude was that it was best to do in life what one enjoyed doing. But my mother was vehemently opposed to my choice of occupation.

Her main reason was that, as a fashion designer, I would have great difficulty in getting my own flat. According to her way of thinking, having one's own flat was just about the most important thing in life. In addition, she knew that if I went to Moscow, my parents would have to pay for my accommodation for the first two years, which they couldn't really afford. Student hostel facilities were available only for third-year students and upwards.

My mother suggested I choose one of four universities in our city, but I was stubborn and gave no thought to the problem of having a flat in my future life. I was on cloud nine, but Mother found a way to bring me back to earth.

One day, during the summer holidays between the ninth and tenth classes, she took me to Moscow to visit the university at a time when students were writing their entry examinations there. What we saw when we arrived shocked us: there were numerous ZILs and black Volgas (government-issued cars for high-level officials and Communist Party bigwigs) and taxis, prepaid and waiting for aspiring university entrants to finish their examinations. It was obvious to us, as ordinary folk, that getting in was going to be difficult at best and probably impossible if all of those high-level officials wanted their children to attend. This was confirmed by one of the examiners. He told us that Moscow residents were given preference; what's more, of more than 1 000 annual applicants, only 50 students were accepted.

My mother approached a well dressed woman who was also waiting, and asked how her daughter was progressing. She said she had no doubt that her daughter would pass as she had been given private lessons and coached in preparation for this particular university from age 10. She asked at what age my mother had begun preparing me for the entrance examination and reacted with disdain when my mother revealed that I had had only the normal school curriculum, with a few extra school lessons. My parents had never been in a position to pay for private lessons.

Another young girl, from the Ukraine, told us that she was being examined for the third year in succession, so desperate was she to gain admission. Her first question to us had been, 'Do you have *blat*?' As soon as she realised we were not from Moscow and didn't arrive in a government car, she looked at us with pity.

Again, the horrible word *blat* struck me. Of course we didn't have any *blat*; we could not be helpful to anyone on the examination commission, nor could we afford to use cash as a means to gain favour. I realised that I had to abandon all hope of gaining entry to that institution.

Of the four universities in Kalinin, I finally chose the Polytechnic, with the idea of studying civil engineering. Both my brothers had attended the same university. The eldest, Victor, had just qualified as a mechanical engineer. He had been posted to Tjumen in Siberia. The younger of my brothers, Evgueni, was in his final year at the Polytechnic and, on qualifying, expected a posting in the Urals. I was following what had become a family tradition.

My tenth class at school seemed to go even faster than the ninth. I was working hard in preparation for university and passed all of the final exams with good marks. After the school-leaving ball, I joined special courses at the Polytechnic to prepare for the entrance exams. The summer of 1972 was extremely hot and unusually dry – so hot and dry, in fact, that the peat swamps around our city caught fire and the entire area was shrouded in smoke. If we opened our windows to escape the heat, the flat filled with smoke and we battled to breathe or sleep.

I passed the exams and gained entrance to the Polytechnic. We were told to report at the university on 1 September, ready to go to work on a *kolkhoz* for one month. We were to wear working clothes and bring whatever else we needed in a rucksack.

As a reward for gaining admission to university, my mother announced that she was taking me to Orenburg province, to visit the village of my birth. It meant she would have to forego two weeks of work at our *dacha* at the most critical time of year, but it was a sacrifice she considered worthwhile in order to make this pilgrimage.

IO

Dachas

IF YOU LOOK UP THE WORD IN A RUSSIAN DICTIONARY, *'DACHA'* IS described as 'a country cottage', but Russian people use the word for other things too. For example, it is used to describe a place where children from a kindergarten would go for summer camps. So it not only describes a building, but also an area of recreation in the forest.

There is another kind of *dacha* that belongs to the State. These are houses, furnished, maintained and staffed by the State for use by high-ranking government officials. Stalin had numerous *dachas* in the most beautiful areas of the country, some of which he never even visited, although they were maintained in a state of readiness, just in case the whim took him.

Other officials, such as KGB bosses, members of the Politburo or Communist Party leaders, high-ranking military personnel, scientists, artists and writers considered deserving by the State, had *dachas* too. By Russian standards, they were luxurious, big houses with privacy, surrounded by spacious grounds, although the level of *dacha* varied according to rank or position. Creative people such as artists and writers sometimes lived and worked in their *dachas* all year, but most other privileged individuals used them only for recreation, without ever having to lift a finger to make improvements of any sort.

As a rule, State *dachas* could not be inherited and, in the event of a person losing his position for any reason, such as making a statement that offended the government, use of the *dacha* would be withdrawn, along with other privileges.

To the proletariat, a *dacha* meant something else altogether.

It was a piece of land of approximately 20 x 30 metres, cheek by jowl with many others, all belonging to gardening co-operative societies. The purpose of the proletariat *dachas* was to enable the 'owners' to grow vegetables and fruit in order to survive.

But the owners were employed elsewhere and able to work their lands only at weekends or after working hours in the long summer evenings. So a *dacha* for an ordinary Russian held very few pleasurable connotations. It meant hard work.

The system was introduced after WWII, when poverty and starvation became overwhelming problems and government was faced with the huge and potentially embarrassing challenge of how to feed the population. They came up with the cynical idea that it was the people's problem; and in a spirit of expediency, they decided to lend the land to the people, who would grow their own food.

The government lent land to big organisations, such as manufacturing plants, employing thousands of people. Those organisations were told to establish gardening co-operatives and encourage employees to join. But there were strings attached, the first rule being that only food was to be grown. Growing of flowers for commercial purposes was not permitted, and land issued but left fallow could be confiscated and given to other families. Selling any excess produce from one's land was frowned upon as being capitalistic and persons indulging in the practice were termed 'speculators', an epithet to be avoided at all cost in a Communist society.

Plots of the standard 20 x 30 metres were allotted to members who queued for the privilege and paid a small monthly subscription. The idea was popular, out of necessity, and more medium, and even small, organisations got involved.

In 1964, my parents managed to get their piece of land through the chemical plant. They had to enter into a lottery. Each plot was numbered and they drew lots, so there was no telling if their plot would be on better or worse ground than anyone else's.

The *dacha* they drew was in an area called Alexandrovka, situated some 30 kilometres from our city, on land that was virtually a swamp. It was one of about 10 000 adjoining plots, separated only by the gravel and dirt roads created for truck access. This didn't stop trucks from frequently getting stuck, though – the ground was simply too spongy to carry their weight. Had my parents held higher positions, either in the Party, Trade Union or administration, they would have been issued with better land, much closer to town.

There was a bus service every half hour, departing from a stop 30 minutes' tram ride from our flat, but the queues to board were kilometres long because it was the only way of getting there – none of the workers had cars. For thousands of families, mostly working the same hours, and each family wanting to take at least three members to work their *dacha*, you can imagine how difficult it was to get there.

On Saturdays we used to get up at six to ensure we were somewhere near the front of the bus queue. That was achievable, but coming home was a problem. Everyone wanted to work as late as possible, so they all wanted to leave Alexandrovka at more or less the same time. Often we didn't get home until 10 p.m. and the whole procedure had to be repeated the following day. Apart from having to take everything necessary to grow produce, first on the tram, then on the bus if we were lucky enough to get on, we also had to carry our baggage a further two kilometres from the bus stop.

There were no shops, so we also had to carry everything we needed to eat and drink, although, in a way, my parents had been lucky in the lottery; the plot most distant from the bus stop at Alexandrovka must have been a four-kilometre walk.

Big trees had been removed by a machine provided by the chemical plant; we had to dig out smaller trees and shrubs ourselves. Fortunately the spongy soil yielded them fairly easily – no wonder, as about 10 centimetres under the soil surface we discovered peat. This necessitated sand, topsoil and fertilisers, all of which had to be paid for out of inadequate salaries and brought in by truck. Having done that, it was still difficult to grow a good crop.

For 33 years my parents battled on the *dacha* and, in the end, the ground still gave way underfoot. One had the feeling that at any time it could give way altogether and one could fall into an abyss. No matter how much sand and topsoil they distributed, the peat perpetually swallowed it and returned to just below the surface.

However, after the first three years of clearing and ground preparation, they did manage to get a reasonable crop. An inadequate water supply had been installed together with electricity, but my parents, with assistance from one of their neighbours, dug a well to ensure a shared, continuous water supply for irrigation.

New regulations allowed a 6 x 6 metre house to be built as long as the height did not exceed seven metres and it did not feature a fireplace. The intention was to discourage people from living permanently in their *dachas*. Also permissible were a 1 x 1 metre toilet and a 2 x 3 metre shed, with a hothouse of the same proportions.

Although saunas are a part of Russian life, they were forbidden at *dachas* because the suspicious authorities thought they might encourage debauchery. Only at the front end of each *dacha* was a one-metre high fence permitted, which meant that all *dachas* were open on three sides. It seems the Soviet government's idea was that everyone should watch everyone else with a view to reporting any un-Soviet behaviour among neighbouring comrades.

After three years, my parents managed to buy second-hand materials and build a house. It had an entrance hall, where dirty boots and coats could be removed, a small bedroom with a single bed, a bigger room with another three beds and a veranda that doubled for a kitchen. It was no holiday chalet, and far too cold to sleep in during winter, which is most of the year.

Keeping the *dacha* buildings serviceable was an ongoing problem. No sooner did we manage to fix one thing than something else would need attention, which partly explains why there are so many derelict *dachas* in Russia today. Many people started building, then ran out of money, or became ill, or simply got too old to finish the project.

Robberies were commonplace, especially in winter when there were few people around and a complete lack of any kind of security. Reporting losses to the police was a waste of time; they didn't even open files. There was a token insurance premium paid to the State Insurance Company by all *dacha* house owners in respect of fire and flood cover only, but attempting to lodge a claim proved useless in most cases.

People were not lazy when it came to developing their ground and buildings, but often couldn't find the time over and above their other essential activities. Consider that a Russian parent was expected simultaneously to do his or her job, be a builder, a farmer and cope with a family and all its complexities and problems. Parents seldom had time for recreation.

My parents used what little spare time they had to study agricultural books in winter. Father took responsibility for the orchard and Mother for strawberries, potatoes and other vegetables. Over a period of 30 years they became proficient in growing those particular crops. In spring our flat became a nursery, with even window boxes used to grow seedlings. Seeds and seedlings were very expensive, so my mother learned how to prepare them from the previous season's crop.

Spring heralded a time of frenetic activity with regard to *dachas*. The population of Russia turned to discussing the weather and matters such as seed varieties. They would share past experiences and advice on how and when it was best to go about planting. Boxes of seedlings had to be carefully transported to *dachas* and, by the end of May, most people had finished planting.

Typically, they would have potatoes, onions, garlic, cabbages, carrots, beetroots, cucumbers, tomatoes, dill, parsley, strawberries; and in the orchard, apples, plums, cherries, black- white- and red-currants and gooseberries. After planting followed watering, weeding, spraying against pests and fertilising certain crops, such as cucumbers and tomatoes. Weather forecasts had to be taken note of because, even in the summer months, the central parts of Russia can be subjected to nights of icy dew that make it necessary to cover some plants with plastic sheeting.

Work at the *dachas* was ongoing in the summer months, which left no time for holidays away. By early June, we were able to enjoy spring onions, dill and parsley in our salad. That was always a welcome change; they would be the first fresh greens available since the previous summer's end. By that time, everyone, especially the children, would be badly in need of the vitamins they provided. In the middle of June we were able to get fresh strawberries; in July, cucumbers; later, tomatoes and, after that, new potatoes. In late August there was a rush to harvest everything before the rains began.

We realise now, of course, that the rest of Europe is usually enjoying holidays at the sea in summer, but we didn't know it then because of the information iron curtain. In Russia, there was always a need to take leave from work in the months of July and August, but it wasn't for going to the seaside – it was to gather the fruits and vegetables necessary for sustenance in the coming winter.

At the end of summer, everyone shared their opinions and recipes on the best ways of preserving what we collected in order to see us through the winter. Bags and buckets of fruits and vegetables had to be carried on busses and trams to our small flats, which became bottling plants. In our tiny kitchens, produce had to be washed and made ready for preserving. My mother would work through the night when necessary, until everything was done to her satisfaction. Big pots of fruits and berries had to be boiled with sugar, then bottled in sterile glass jars. Tomatoes and cucumbers were marinated or salted in large glass bowls, with nothing left to waste.

The last crops to be harvested were potatoes and cabbages. Potatoes were put into bags in the cellar; cabbages salted and kept in glass bowls and stored wherever space permitted. But the work was not over. Before the first winter snows, ground had to be turned over in preparation for the following spring.

It seems to me incredible now that we managed to grow all of those crops in such a short time, given that the weather can best be described as inconsistent. From the age of nine I spent two of my three summer months' holiday at the *dacha* each year, watering, weeding, picking fruits, vegetables and looking after my little cousins to keep them out of the way. All family members involved themselves in *dacha* activities and the only spare time came in mid-winter. I would spend the third month in summer at Pioneer camp — that was my real holiday.

Although there were thousands of *dachas* at Alexandrovka, which meant a multitude of people, there was nothing else there — no lake, river or anything to amuse children, other than a forest on one side that we were not allowed to enter unless accompanied by an adult. To add to the general discomfort, mosquitoes and horseflies infest much of Russia; as soon as the weather is calm and without rain, one is under constant attack by these pests.

From childhood, I hated the *dacha*, and swore that when I grew up I would do my utmost not to be subjected to that drudgery. (At the age of 25 and married, however, I was coerced by my husband into acquiring and maintaining one.) When I consider how hard my mother worked in summer, I realise that her normal job must have seemed like a holiday in comparison.

Despite the hard work, shortages of food forced more and more families to acquire *dachas*. Even the laziest, disabled, or sick grew a few potatoes. I don't think anyone ever calculated the actual cost of what they grew. It must have been thoroughly uneconomical but, given our circumstances, nobody cared. For us to have fresh greens in summer and preserves throughout the year was not considered a luxury, but a necessity.

When my parents acquired their *dacha*, Father was 50 and Mother 41. Over the 33 years that they worked on it, the *dacha* became an important part of our family life. There are many memories linked to that 600 square metre plot.

One, for example, occurred on the first day that we visited the site. I was nine years old and, walking through the grass, I came across a metre-long snake, the first I'd ever seen in the wild. There are only two kinds of snake found in that area, one is poisonous and the other harmless. It was just my luck to find the poisonous variety. I screamed like a banshee while running back to my father and swearing never to set foot on the *dacha* again. It was a type of adder and the whole family got involved in ridding our ground of the potential danger. We found a nest of adders and, to ensure the safety of the family, my father and elder brother set about killing and burning them.

I also recall that Mother had decided the first thing she would grow would be enough strawberries to feed the family. Previously, to spoil us, she would buy just a few in a paper cone. Now she set about her task with grim determination. In the second season she produced a wonderful crop, sufficient to fill forty 10-litre buckets. There were so many that we couldn't possibly eat them all, although Mother did her best to use the excess for jam and compote. There were still too many, prompting Granny Katerina to suggest that Mother sell what we couldn't use. But Mother wouldn't hear of it; she was a Communist and could not bear the thought of being labelled a 'speculator'. Her only solution was to reduce the size of next season's crop, when she grew potatoes in their stead. There were still so many strawberries that I can't face them even today.

For my family, the word *dacha* is directly associated with my grandmother, Katerina. She loved the place and considered it her duty to help my mother work it. Every autumn she would appear to decline in health, which I suppose is normal for ladies of 75 or more. She always said, 'I don't think I'll make another season.'

But every spring was a resurrection for her. She couldn't wait for my parents to take her out there to live, until the autumn cold set in. Later, we concluded that the *dacha* had actually kept her alive until the age of 95. Only in the last three years of her life was she unable to enjoy herself out there.

Most people had mixed feelings regarding their *dachas*. The system wasn't all bad and did provide benefits other than fresh produce. Working their land gave the people a chance to get out of the polluted cities, breathe fresh air and get some exercise. It also provided people with unaccustomed satisfaction, in the sense that what was produced there did not belong to the State, was not taxed and was solely for their personal benefit. For millions of Russian families who did not have the means to go away on holiday, the *dacha* provided some kind of escape and recreation, and kept them together. Children were brought up helping their parents and grandparents, gaining knowledge and a variety of basic skills that could be useful in later life.

There is no doubt that the tough years under Communism have left their mark on the Russian psyche. For most of the twentieth century, the Russian people faced serious shortages of basic foods: the famine during and after the war, the non-availability of bread in Khrushchev's time, empty shops under Brezhnev, and hunger resulting from unemployment that spread with the advent of *perestroika*. In addition, there were three currency devaluations in the 1990s, which resulted in the populace losing faith in the rouble and trust in the government.

For people subjected to such hardships, having fruit and vegetables available in their storerooms was more of a guarantee of survival than it was to have cash in the bank. My family was no exception and my parents gave top priority to growing crops on their *dacha*.

I can now appreciate the sacrifices my mother and family made when she took me to Orenburg. It was the only time she ever missed being at the *dacha* for the complete month of August.

II

Orenburg

AFTER THE STRESS OF EXAMS, IT WAS CERTAINLY A CHANGE OF scene, and of pace, to visit Orenburg, the place of my birth, and interesting to meet the many relatives and friends Mother was to introduce me to.

Mid-August is high holiday season for millions of Russian people – that is, for those not tied to *dachas*, or for family members not required for the relatively light work needed on the *dacha* by August. My mother's decision had been spontaneous, which meant that getting tickets for a train would be difficult. Our previous experience on a train had been 14 years earlier, in 1958, when we travelled from Orenburg to Kalinin in sleeping berths. This time, in her excitement, and because compartments and sleeping berths were unavailable, she bought tickets for seats in a 'common carriage'. The journey to Orenburg would take three days and two nights, but she thought we would cope. We took a train to Moscow and then changed to another for Orenburg.

Anyone who has ever travelled on the Moscow-Orenburg train, any southbound train out of Moscow, or any other train not made for foreign tourists, would understand something of our ordeal. It was extremely uncomfortable, the toilets were filthy and there was little service offered.

In compartments or sleeping berths, tickets are issued according to the number of beds, but in our common carriage, there appeared to be no limit to the number sold. Some people must have given cash directly to the conductor, who then allowed them onto the train. We could never have imagined what the conditions would be like. There were so many passengers that some were obliged to stand and those seated were squashed together like tinned sardines.

At the height of summer, without air conditioning, it was almost impossible to breathe. Passengers would not open windows on account of a commonly held belief that they might catch pneumonia. Mother and I took turns to visit the only toilet on our carriage because we didn't want to lose our seats or suitcases. As Russians, we took for granted that there would be no toilet paper, soap or towels, so we had come prepared. Still, the toilet, dirty to begin with, soon became unbearable.

There was absolutely no service of any kind. We had to bribe the conductor to get hot water to make a cup of tea. It wasn't long before the carriage completely ran out of water for both tea and toilets. The situation was desperate. Fortunately, there were *babushkas* (old women) selling food and drinks at stations, and we were able to get some sustenance, albeit at a price.

We had to try to sleep in torturous sitting positions for two nights, constantly assailed by the loud talking of standing passengers and noisy train wheels. I amused myself by attempting to imagine what the other passengers were like, what they did for a living and why they were travelling on the train. Some looked like criminals, others like hoboes and many seemed quite out of place, rather as I felt we were.

Somewhere in the middle of our journey, many more people got onto the train, and the carriage became even more packed. People had to stand for hours, hoping that seated passengers would get off. We deduced that, given the noise coming from above us, there were people on the roof of our carriage too. There was no relief; the journey was hellish and there was nothing we could do about it.

We finally arrived at Orenburg station, exhausted. It was a dirty place, full of unfamiliar faces. We bought tickets on a bus that transported us to the middle of nowhere, to a huge, flat, featureless area, part of the Great Russian steppe. It looked just the way I imagined it would, from lessons at school.

Orenburg was established in 1733, when Empress Anna (a niece of Peter the Great), Tsarina of all Russia, decided to expand her empire by sending Cossacks from the lower Don to settle vast areas of steppe lands in the southeast. Orenburg later became the capital of the Orenburg Cossack settlement.

Cossacks have their origin way back in Russian history. They were composed of assorted castes of the region and peasants who had fled serfdom in surrounding territories and lived in the northern hinterlands of the Black and Caspian seas. They had a proud tradition of independence. As free, self-governing military communities, they had secured a degree of liberty from Russian rulers in exchange for military obligations.

By 1916, there were an estimated 533 000 Cossacks living in the Orenburg area, of whom 27 000 participated in WWI. They were divided by the Revolution. In 1918, wealthy Cossacks joined the White Army under General Dutov and fought against the Bolsheviks. Poorer Cossacks joined the Red Army and established what they called 'the Ural Cossacks'.

The relative independence the Cossacks had enjoyed over several centuries gave birth to a unique character and culture that retains its romantic ring in folklore, with the music and unusual dancing of the frontiersmen well recognised. Their independence also resulted in their being able to accumulate wealth, as opposed to the average Russian military man who had little.

However, the Cossacks' fiercely independent spirit must have been a thorn in the side of the new regime, and was to lead to their demise. In 1920, they were designated part of the Red Army and the title 'Cossack' abolished. Stalin, in his time of great repression, further diluted the Cossack character by deliberately mixing them with other ethnic groups. The Great Patriotic War (WWII) served to accelerate their downfall, with many men of the area losing their lives in the struggle against fascism.

When the war was finally over, many people who had relocated to the southeast from western Russia, to escape the fighting, remained there because they had nothing to return to, having lost their dwellings to the destruction wrought by the Germans. Other families, including mine, had moved there to escape hunger in the west. Once settled there, my father invited his brother and family to join us, which is why, although my family subsequently left, we still have relatives living in the region.

From childhood, when people asked me where I was born and I told them in the Orenburg area, they would immediately ask, 'Are you an Orenburg Cossack girl?'

I would have liked to have been, but my roots are from a more prosaic Russian background.

When we alighted from the bus at its turn-around point, there was no other public transport to take us further, so we were left standing by the roadside on the vast steppe, waiting for any kind of traffic going our way. The temperature at the time must have been above 40 degrees Centigrade.

Fortunately, a truck picked us up and took us some distance. We crossed the Ural River, which is famous for the fighting that took place around it in 1918. Its banks were covered with lush green bush and it looked so tranquil that it was hard to imagine a battle ever having taken place there.

When the truck driver had to turn off the road, we hitched another ride. This time it was on a motorbike and sidecar. We put our cases in the sidecar and I sat on them while Mother rode on the pillion. I thought our journey would never end; the country was vast, with very few people spread out over a huge area. We were travelling on a sand road and, by the time we arrived at the village, were covered in dust.

I was so exhausted that I couldn't even take issue with my mother about her crazy idea of giving me such a 'holiday' as a reward for my efforts. I did ask her, though, why we had hitched rides when she had always forbidden me to do so in Kalinin. After all, we were two lone women with suitcases, surely sitting ducks for men of bad persuasion.

She said, 'We are very far from civilisation and people here are different. They are open, kind and helpful and, because there is no public transport, they help each other with lifts.'

I was to discover that she was correct. The lifestyle there was very different from that in the cities. People lived in small villages and *stanitsas* – large 'Cossack' villages that could almost be called towns. Over the course of the next two weeks, we visited friends and relatives, travelling many kilometres in the area. There were no hotels, so we lived as guests in their houses. We also spent two days in Burannoe, the village where I had been born 18 years before. There were about 100 houses there, constructed from a mixture of kaolin and *kizyak* (pressed cow dung), because, with the nearest forests being hundreds of miles away, there was little available timber. Local people collected cow dung throughout the year and dried it for later use. Since coal was expensive and hard to come by, *kizyak* was also used for fuel.

Each family had two houses, the larger to live and sleep in, the smaller used as a kitchen and social gathering place. The doors of the kitchen houses were always open, welcoming any passers-by during the long summer days. Doors and window shutters on the main houses were closed, intended to keep them cool for sleeping at night. Mosquitoes and other flying insects were kept to a minimum that way, but it was still unbearably hot inside at night.

Many people recognised my mother, even though she had left 15 years before. Most seemed to realise that I was her daughter and said she hadn't changed and that I looked like her. Everybody was glad to see us and Mother spent many happy hours recalling old times.

We stayed in my uncle Vasili's house at a *stanitsa* called Studernoe for a couple of nights. He was my father's elder brother who had come back an invalid from WWII and joined us in Orenburg. His two daughters were married and lived in their own houses with their families. Our relatives nearly tore us apart, all vying to show us hospitality in their homes. We moved from one house to the next, constantly being offered the best they had. There was delicious fresh fish from the local lakes, geese especially reared on wheat, lamb that tasted better than any I could recall, fruits, vegetables and home-made vodka in abundance. I thought we'd never stop eating, drinking and talking.

Of my two cousins, I became close to one named Nura. She was about 15 years my senior, had two sons and worked as a teacher in the local school. A strong, active woman, large, blonde and plump, she impressed me with her ambitious outlook. She appeared to know exactly where she was going in life and was not wasting time getting there. Her husband, an agricultural mechanisation expert, had been appointed to a career in the local Communist Party committee. When we parted, we promised to keep in touch and visit each other in the future. Over the next 20 years, Nura would sometimes come on excursions to Moscow with children from her school. She would invariably travel on to Kalinin to see us.

The last visit we made in Orenburg was to a friend of my mother's who lived in a village further south, near the Kazakhstan border. The area was like a desert, devoid of greenery, and the only bushes visible were those around houses.

Water had to be trucked into the area and was strictly rationed to each resident family. Even in the heat, there was insufficient to enable us to shower and we were given a bowl each to use for washing ourselves. I had never imagined that there were places on earth with so little water. I couldn't understand why anyone would choose to live in such circumstances.

We were shown a field of watermelons by our friends, which excited me because watermelons were rare in Kalinin and I considered them to be exotic fruit. We only ever saw them at the end of summer and, if we were lucky enough to get one, it was cause for celebration. Great green balls were lying on the yellow sand, waiting to be harvested below the highest blue sky I'd ever seen.

A farmer explained how, in spring, seeds were planted in a watered hole and, after they took root, there was no further need for watering because the roots went down deep enough to find sufficient moisture. It was amazing to me that any fruit could thrive in such arid conditions.

I was handed half a melon, broken on someone's knee and, without a plate or knife, couldn't wait to enjoy the treat. I was amazed at its sweetness, better than any I had ever tasted in Kalinin. Before long I was a complete mess; my face and clothes were covered in sweet juice to which the swirling dust stuck like glue. All I wanted to do was wash the gooey mess off, but there was no water available.

Quietly cursing my mother for bringing me to this waterless place, I overheard, to my amazement, my mother's friend telling her that she had been offered a teaching post in Orenburg, but had refused the transfer because she couldn't stand the thought of leaving this area that she loved so much. I had never before considered that people could adapt to the most uncomfortable places on Earth and could be happy living in such obviously adverse conditions.

The following day we departed for Orenburg. Mother's friend kindly arranged a car to take us to the bus stop a few hours away. We arrived by bus at the Orenburg railway station to take the train back to Moscow, where we would change to another for Kalinin.

For some reason, the trip back was easier; perhaps knowing we were going home made it so. I reflected on what I'd seen and concluded that it had been a pleasure for Mother, who had met her old friends and been able to return to the places where she had spent some of her best years, from age 25 to 35. My younger brother and I had both been born there, so the place held some nostalgia for her.

I recognised that we had been warmly welcomed; the people had shown us great hospitality and shared what they had, even down to their precious water. Our suitcases contained such a variety of presents for all family members, it was clear that the generosity of our Orenburg relatives was disproportionate to their standard of living. After all, we in the city enjoyed limitless water in flush toilets, theatres, cinemas and art galleries, all of which were a far cry from their rather basic living amenities. I concluded that, despite my having been born there and my relatives' kindness, my heart lay in Kalinin. I was thankful that my parents had moved back to the city when I was three and, if the choice were between water and watermelons, I would choose the former.

A rest was badly needed by the time we arrived home and, after recuperating for a day or two, we started making jokes about our trip in the 'common carriage'. We boasted that if we could survive that trip, we must be imbued with fortitude disproportionate to our appearances and, as tough Russian women, we could handle anything thrown at us.

I silently promised myself never to return to Orenburg. As it turned out, some 21 years later, it became necessary.

12

University

IT WASN'T LONG AFTER STARTING UNIVERSITY THAT IT BECAME MY complete and full-time preoccupation. Every day was interesting and different. For the first two years we studied subjects such as Mathematics, Physics and Chemistry, common to all student groups attending the institute. Only in the third year did we begin taking subjects necessary for our particular vocations; mine were Manufacturing of Building Materials and Construction.

There were two semesters per annum, the first from September to December, the second from February to May. At the end of each we were examined to assess our progress. After the winter examinations at the end of January, we had a short break of about 10 days and, after the May examinations, we were usually required to get practical experience or were sent to work on a *kolkhoz*. After that, we had less than a month of vacation time left.

I didn't find technical studies easy and was obliged to apply myself with some intensity. In order to qualify for a stipend I had to get good marks in all subjects, which I fortunately managed to accomplish. I also managed thereafter to qualify for stipends for the rest of my time at the institute, saving my parents 40 roubles every month. Forty roubles at that time was one-third of the average engineer's salary, or just enough to feed me.

After the first year, we were sent to the Crimean Peninsula for a month-and-a-half for geology practice. Fifty of us were billeted in tents in the mountains, studying rocks, caves, stalactites and stalagmites, earth formations and how to put different minerals to a variety of applications. It was one of the best practical studies we had; it was interesting, we were out in the fresh air, the sun shone warmly and the landscapes of sea and mountains were invigorating.

After my second year I went to work for a couple of months for the All-Union Student Building Detachment in Kalinin province. My brothers had both been members of the student building movement and its title evoked images of heroism, promoted through intense propaganda by government media: young students giving of their time to build a better country for the collective good of the nation. Even though it didn't live up to my expectations, I'm still proud of having been a member of the All-Union Student Building Detachment. It was on that assignment that I first met the man I would later marry.

At the end of my third year, I got a job working in the university test laboratory. It provided the opportunity to work as a scientist testing materials for strength and resistance in a clean laboratory, which was a welcome change from dirty building sites. The work was interesting and I gained valuable knowledge.

Another important practical test came at the end of year four. For two months we had to work in the industry, acting as foremen or forewomen. At the end of the period, I received a certificate of qualification for this task.

After four years at university, I had to have two months' practical experience in a ferroconcrete structures and parts production plant. It was one of the most modern and best equipped of four similar plants in Kalinin, and my department was housed in a huge building that resembled an aircraft hanger.

I was a forewoman in the steel-reinforcing department that prepared steel for encasing in concrete columns. We worked two shifts a day and I led one shift of 40 people. On receipt of drawings, I ordered the requisite steel and ensured that the skeleton was properly put together in its metal casing.

There were many different pieces of equipment for cutting and welding steel that I had not seen before. Reading drawings was easy because I had studied the subject at university, but I was lost as far as the equipment was concerned. I tried not to show my ignorance and learned about the workings of the machinery as fast as possible.

I liked the job from the start and didn't find being a leader inhibiting. Everything was going according to plan and life was great: I was 21, pretty, healthy, happy and had met a man whom I hoped to marry; I was fulfilling my promise to my motherland, about to qualify as a civil engineer, and would be able to take my place in Soviet society and make a worthwhile contribution. As a serious adult, I was full of enthusiasm for hard work and playing my part in improving our Communist State.

It appeared to me that my fellow workers were good, honest, down-to-earth people. Although most were years my senior, they treated me with respect, some calling me by the old-fashioned Olga Danilovna, others a more familiar, yet still respectful, 'little daughter' or 'pretty bride'. Everything was fine until the last Friday of the month when we received our monthly salaries.

On Monday morning there wasn't one worker in my department. The only person to arrive was a woman assistant whose job it was to calculate salaries for our shift. Where were my people? We had been given a job and I had nobody to do it. My experienced assistant calmed me down. She said it had always been a rule in big plants to pay salaries only on Fridays, so that the workers could drink over the weekend, plus Monday, and the more sober would return to work on Tuesday afternoon. She told me not to worry about it and that I would not be held responsible.

Head office knew from experience that it was the best policy, because, that way, the workers mostly missed just two working days. Had workers been paid on a Monday, the entire working week would probably be written off. I was shocked to learn that head office could do nothing about it. But my assistant advised me to accept it philosophically, as if it were a natural occurrence.

So, the entire plant was unproductively silent on Monday. I had nothing to do that day and sat around chatting to my assistant. What she told me came as a further shock: 85 per cent of my shift workers were ex-convicts. Some were sent to perform hard labour by the courts, as a punishment. The police were keeping a close watch on them. One man had served 20 years for murder, another 15 for rape. Some were burglars and many were habitual criminals. It appeared almost all had dubious backgrounds.

The most competent welder, an elderly man who called me 'little daughter', had been in prison for over 20 years for rape and murder. My colleague told me he was a chronic alcoholic and would be the last to return to work. Head office knew all about him, but kept him on because he was such a good welder and a hard worker when sober.

'Is there anyone without a criminal record on my shift?' I asked.

'Yes,' she said, 'but now that it's summer they are away on holiday.'

The workers returned exactly as she had predicted, the first arriving on Tuesday afternoon and the last, the welder, on Friday. By that time I had decided to change my appearance. Gone was my idea of looking young and trying to be attractive. I wore old, baggy clothes, and even a scarf over my head like a *babushka*.

Prior to hearing their background stories I had not taken their comments, jokes or hints seriously. That now changed, to the extent that I brought my fiancé along one day so that they would know that I wasn't entirely defenceless.

At that age, I still saw life in black and white, with no shades of grey. I could not accept the workers being irresponsible drunkards and going unpunished. I thought it my responsibility to tell them how I felt about their lack of self-discipline. University had created in us the idea that we, the young generation, were expected to lead our country to better things. I really believed that I was there to make the changes necessary for the attainment of the goals of a new Communist generation of builders.

On the first morning that all the workers were present, I called a meeting and told the staff that, when the time came for me to authorise their next salary payments, I would be honest and deduct payment for the days they had been absent. There was a terrible silence and 40 pairs of hostile eyes fixed on me.

My assistant led me out by the elbow and told me to stop trying to teach them morals or discipline if I wanted to stay alive. She reminded me that I would be there for only two months and that the best thing I could do was keep quiet, do my job and leave on the appointed date. She added that, before I had arrived, there had been a foreman who had tried to discipline the staff. He had been stabbed to death for his trouble.

She said, 'I will calm the workers down and tell them not to worry, they will get their full salaries at the month's end.'

It was another of life's lessons for me. At university and at home, I might have been seen as a future leader, but out in the harsh real world, I'd be lucky to have a future, unless I learned how to treat people. It was the ex-criminals who held sway in the plant; with no fear of losing their harsh and unpopular jobs, they had their own rules and traditions, not to be violated by someone like me or head office, the general director, or anyone else for that matter.

While this factory was one of the most modern plants of its kind, conditions were bad. There was dust everywhere, from stone crushing, metal cutting and cement mixing. It polluted the lungs, often making breathing difficult, so working with a facemask was essential. The noise level was deafening. Emerging after eight hours in the factory, I could hardly hear at all. When considering these factors, I began to realise why this had become a place of punishment for wrongdoers.

I was to discover later that the head office had 'traditions' of its own. One day, two shifts of the whole plant were told to stop work. We were instructed to clean and tidy the plant and surrounds because, the following morning, a high-level Communist commission was expected to check the plant.

Broken windows were urgently replaced and all were washed, letting in light that had not been seen before. Toilets and change rooms were hurriedly painted. Scrap metal that had for months been lying around uncollected by the people responsible was abruptly removed. Outside, paths were repaired and flowers planted. New uniforms were issued to all workers. For a few bigwigs, the entire plant had been stopped, in spite of the fact that I had been given to understand that I would be skinned alive if I didn't keep my department up to speed on the tasks given us.

The next day we were allowed to view the commission from a distance. I was angered and disappointed by the whole event. It was all so false. Our tasks had fallen behind schedule, which meant either doing a rushed job, at the possible expense of quality, or holding up a construction job. I believed that whatever problems existed in the plant should have been visible to the commission. Without that, how were they ever to know what was really going on in their sphere of responsibility?

Instead of discussing their problems with our visitors, our bosses from head office were hiding them to make themselves appear good. In my naivety, I had not yet realised that that behaviour was typical of our Socialist hierarchy, right up to the general secretary of the Politburo. 'Look good at all costs and don't bother me with your problems' was how it worked. I could not imagine then that, one day, all the problems swept under the carpet would accumulate to create enough tension among the people to bring about *perestroika* (restructuring).

One is reminded of the story of Prince Potemkin, who was one of Catherine the Great's many lovers. She sent him deep into the countryside, in the latter part of the eighteenth century, to see how her people were living. When they knew he was coming, the local landowners, who exploited their serfs in terrible conditions, built façades of villages, like a Hollywood film set, trained the serfs in how to answer questions and left the prince with entirely the wrong impression to be conveyed back to Catherine. The story spread among the people and, from that time, the saying 'Potemkin Village' has referred to the covering up of problems in order to give a false impression of good order. It became an everyday expression in Russia.

At about this time, I became very upset about my future occupation. I blamed my mother for encouraging me to qualify as an engineer, without warning me of the hazards involved. Would I have to work for the rest of my life in a filthy, polluted plant, among deafening machinery, and in the company of ex-criminals? But it was too late. Mother had the last word.

She said, 'My darling girl, nobody will force you to work in a plant like that. Just get good marks and you can choose where you want to work.' And she proved to be right.

I finished my two months' practical and came away with a letter of commendation as having done a good job, which qualified me as a production manager.

In February of my last year at university, all students were graded by their average marks achieved over the five-year course. We had started as 50 students, but only 42 finished. I was happy to be graded seventh in the class, so had seventh choice of the job opportunities on offer. By this stage, I knew better than to go for a job in a ferroconcrete production plant.

My choice was as a drafts engineer in an organisation called Kalininspetzstroy (Kalinin Specialist Construction), based in my home town. The job entailed designing and constructing huge sewerage purification plants, capable of servicing large towns. I chose it because I knew that I would be working in the city's centre, in a clean office environment, while contributing towards the wellbeing of my city.

13

Kolkhozes (Collective farms)

THE *KOLKHOZ* PLAYED AN IMPORTANT ROLE IN CITY DWELLERS' lives. It was supposed to supply us with our everyday food requirements, such as meat, eggs, milk and bread, and each of us had an 'obligatory duty' to work on one for at least a few weeks per year.

At the time of the Revolution, about 90 per cent of the population lived in rural areas. With collectivisation in the early 1930s came the destruction of the private agricultural system. As time went by, conditions in the rural areas deteriorated: pay and pensions were the lowest in the salary hierarchy; government restrictions limiting private ownership of livestock removed incentive for farmers to remain on their land; and all services were woefully inadequate in the rural areas. To make matters worse, many *Kolkhozniks* were killed in WWII, further depleting the labour force.

During Brezhnev's rule in the 1960s and 1970s, movement to the cities gathered momentum. Because the agricultural system had deteriorated to the point where it produced insufficient food, and because most farm workers had left the countryside to look for better prospects in the towns and cities, city dwellers were obliged to work on *kolkhozes*.

This 'obligatory duty' was, in Brezhnev's time, applicable to all citizens, including soldiers and students, regardless of rank or social station, and even included schoolchildren. The result was multitudes of people working on every *kolkhoz*. At certain times of year, work there was so intense that we didn't know what we were supposed to be – engineers, scientists, doctors or farm workers.

The Communist government proclaimed that only by collective farming could the nation be adequately fed. From the time of the establishment of *kolkhozes*, Russian people read glowing reports in the media of the production of tons of quality crops such as wheat, vegetables and fruits that would supposedly end up on their dining tables. However, reality was a far cry from that propaganda.

Exaggerated reports were obviously being produced for the benefit of the Soviet government and Communist Party congresses, and eagerly fed to the media for dissemination to the proletariat. When we listened to the reports of tons of quality produce being sent to State storage facilities, we joked among ourselves, asking who knew the storage facility address so that we could go there and find some food. In reality, agricultural production appeared seldom to function adequately, so that queues for food, empty shops and rationing of basic foodstuffs continued throughout the lives of many Russians.

I remember at the age of six, in Khrushchev's time, being woken at five in the morning to go, together with my family of six, to stand in a queue for white bread outside a shop that opened only at eight. Nearly asleep, but not allowed to leave the queue, even to relieve myself, was a form of torture that I remember well. One small loaf, about the weight of a typical French baguette, was given to each person, although the supply usually ran out before everyone got their ration. When we were fortunate enough to leave with bread, six small loaves had to last our family a week.

My first experience on a *kolkhoz*, albeit not as a worker, came at age five. I was taken by my grandmother, Katerina, to Rozhdestvenno, a relatively large and successful village where her sister, Sasha, lived. From then on, I accompanied her to Rozhdestvenno regularly during summer holidays, until my parents acquired a *dacha*, whereafter we spent all available time in the summers working our own land.

I recall my grandmother's elder sister Sasha quite clearly; she was old and completely blind. Her daughter, Varvara, who was deaf and dumb, lived with her. Varvara was then about 40, physically strong and capable of loading as much hay as any man. Unable to be educated, she had worked on the *kolkhoz* from age 15. It was her life; she worked with enthusiasm and dedication, putting all of her immense energy into what she could do, instead of the marriage and family that fate had denied her. She showed me great kindness, and would often gather wild berries or flowers for me from the forest.

Katerina tried to help them by cleaning and cooking in the house and working in their small vegetable garden. It was a happy time for me as a young child, and I ran around playing endlessly with other village children, unaware of any responsibility – as a child of that young age should be. Behind the village were huge fields of wheat and rye in which combine harvesters worked in unison. On the other side of the village were fields of vegetables and, for animal feed, they grew a type of green pea.

As children, we loved running in that field, collecting shirts full of fresh green peas and taking them home to eat with our friends. There were sheds at the end of the fields, used for storing fertiliser and other chemicals, and equipment not in use. Everything was tidy and an atmosphere of discipline and order prevailed.

Apart from the herds of cows, sheep and goats, there was a large coop of hens and geese, which contained an incubator for hatchlings. We loved that place because we could touch and play with the little birds.

The mother of one of my friends worked in the village bakery where fresh bread was produced daily. We were given brown bread hot from the oven, a delicacy unavailable in town. To this day, the smell of hot bread takes me straight back to that time and place. There was a cheese factory in the village too, which used wax to cover the cheeses. We went there to beg for coloured wax that we used as modelling clay.

In addition to other production facilities, there was a ladies' brassiere factory that operated mainly in winter, when there was no fieldwork. Women unable to do heavier work would usually occupy themselves there during the whole year, so it continued production even in summer, albeit at a slower rate.

There was a cinema club in the recreation centre where we went to see movies, and on Sunday mornings they had a special children's show. The big hall held plenty of children, but late-comers had to stand along the walls if they wanted to see the show. Then there were three food shops, a bookshop and a clothing store that sold straw hats, made in winter by the local villagers. Every time we arrived in Rozhdestvenno I was allowed to choose a pretty straw hat that, by the time we left, was so destroyed, it might have looked more appropriate on a donkey.

To me, Rozhdestvenno was a happy place. There were usually weddings in summer, and young couples built new homes and had babies. One young couple built a house adjacent to Sasha's, and each year I would discover that they had produced another baby. They kept bees in order to raise extra cash, so their garden was full of hives. It appeared that the honey business paid off, because they were the only couple in the village to own a motorcycle, albeit second-hand.

In the 1960s, villagers probably enjoyed a better life than most city dwellers, because on the occasions that my parents were departing for Rozhdestvenno they would call in advance and enquire as to what they could bring from town that could not be obtained on the farm. The usual answer was, 'Just herring, thanks.' – not because it was not available in *kolkhoz* shops, but because there was not as great a variety as could be bought in town.

My working experience on *kolkhozes* began at age seven, when it was purely voluntary, although my commitment finished only when I was 33. One day in Rozhdestvenno, volunteers were called for from children age 10 and upwards. All adults were occupied with higher priorities and weeders had to be found for the vegetable fields that were fast being overgrown. Because most of the other children volunteered, my grandmother was unable to persuade me that, at seven, I was too young to join in.

Very early in the morning, horse-drawn carts transported us to big fields some way from the village. Furrows were allocated to each child and we were all shown what to dig out and what we should leave. To me, the furrow had no end; it went on forever. Before very long I was tired of bending and, with the sun getting increasingly hot as the day wore on, I found myself some distance behind the other children who had begun at the same time as me. Looking across the furrows, it was evident that the village children of the same age as me were stronger than their city counterparts. I did not like to be found wanting, so I continued for another three days.

At pay time, I recall some children receiving as much as seven roubles. I got one rouble, twenty kopeks. Brimming with self-satisfaction I took my first pay home and pondered long and hard as to how best to spend it. Finally, I was persuaded by my parents to buy a book. I chose one from the village bookshop featuring historical stories for children.

On attaining the grand age of nine, my entire school class worked on a *kolkhoz* during the month of September, instead of taking the usual school lessons. However, we were shown some sympathy by the authorities, who sent us to work only until the weather turned inclement.

We gathered beetroots and carrots and left them in piles for collection. Older children might be given the more difficult task of digging up potatoes. Cabbages were the last crop to be harvested and the senior classes at school were usually sent to collect those in October.

By then the weather was cold, rain had normally set in, morning frosts might cover the ground, and there were occasions when it snowed. No matter how warmly we dressed, working in a windy open field was, to say the least, uncomfortable and children often became ill.

The school year began officially on 1 September, but, as a rule, after a few days, we abandoned lessons in favour of *kolkhoz* duty, until about 1 October. Teachers had to provide extra classes thereafter to enable us to keep up with the curriculum.

Nobody appeared to take our work at the *kolkhoz* too seriously. We were not paid, had to use our own clothing, take our own equipment, such as buckets and knives, and bring our own food and drinks. There were no ablution facilities, so we had to relieve ourselves in the nearest bushes, regardless of weather conditions.

Schoolteachers were supposedly in charge, but, as most children do, we played as soon as their backs were turned. That had a welcome warming effect in the otherwise bleak conditions.

One advantage was that we were permitted to eat as many carrots or cabbages as we liked, but were forbidden to take any vegetables home. Teachers told us that to do so would be stealing and that we could be punished, even jailed. They said the produce belonged to the State and we should buy food through the shops, because all people were equal in our society. We had difficulty accepting this, particularly as quite often we returned to the same place some weeks later, only to see our piles of produce rotting because nobody had collected them for distribution to the shops.

From childhood, we accepted that we would have to work on the *kolkhoz*, as did everyone else – with the exception of most Muscovites. Living in that city was a privilege, because it was always well supplied by the rest of the country. Even Moscow university students were exempted from this particular duty. But as university students in Kalinin, we certainly were not exempted. Consequently, our university academic year began on 15 October because, from 1 September, we were obliged to report for work on a *kolkhoz*.

In my first year at university we were sent to a *kolkhoz* 400 kilometres away, at a place called Lesnoy, which means 'forest area', in such a remote place that they didn't even have electricity. We called it 'Bears' Corner', expecting to see one behind every bush.

We were billeted in workers' houses in two villages and I was sent to an antiquated house with five other girls. There was a poor old couple living there and they had not been expecting six 'guests'. It was just as well that we had taken our own bed rolls and could fit in wherever space was found, sleeping on straw mattresses on the floor, on the big Russian oven or in the storeroom. Only one among us was lucky enough to get a proper bed.

The 'toilet' was in the animal shed attached to one side of the house. They did have a sauna though and once a week we were permitted that luxury; otherwise, we were reduced to washing just our faces in icy cold water from a small metal tank above an outside handbasin. The water in the tank was often frozen on very cold mornings.

Our diet consisted of porridge, macaroni, bread and tea, bought with our own money from the village store. The *kolkhoz* supplied us with meat and milk, and the old lady in whose house we lived did all the cooking.

The couple was happy with the arrangement because they ate with us, saving their money for the one-and-a-half months of our stay. The old lady once tried to get us to go to the chairman of the *kolkhoz* and tell him our meat was finished, but we knew that we hadn't eaten it all. It transpired that she had taken some and salted it for the coming winter, to save having to buy their own.

Apart from that, they were very kind and treated us like their daughters. Their children had gone off to towns to seek better lives, leaving them behind. They kept photographs on the walls of them and of their grandchildren, and told us that, in summer, it was usual for them to receive visits from their family.

Evenings were boring as there was no electricity, radio or other amusement. The shop and village cinema were a few kilometres away, too far to walk after a tiring day in the fields. All of the permanent residents in our little village were elderly and retired, so there were no local boys to take us to movies or dancing.

Our job entailed standing three abreast on the potato harvester, picking rubbish and stones off the conveyer belt and throwing them back onto the field. We did that from eight to five daily, except Sundays. There were unscheduled breaks, occasioned by the driver being too drunk to work, the machine breaking down, or very heavy rains.

Standing high up on the machine in the drizzle and, later, even snow, cold winds cut through us to the very bone. After eight hours on that noisy, vibrating contraption, continually watching the conveyor, it was difficult to walk on terra firma and to avoid the sight of moving potatoes when trying to get to sleep.

When we had harvested our first field, which took about a week, the *kolkhoz* chairman paid us a complimentary visit to congratulate us on a job well done. He said it was a tradition that they have a party whenever the harvesting of a field was completed and asked what we would prefer to drink, homemade vodka *(samogon)* or red wine from the village store. As 17- or 18-year-old girls, we had not previously been exposed to drinking alcohol. We declined his offer.

He scratched his head in bemusement, not wanting to break with *kolkhoz* tradition, then decided to offer us chocolate bonbons instead, to which we all eagerly agreed. He knew that there was a limited stock of 'Krasny Mak' (Red Poppy) chocolates in the village store and promised that he would have them reserved for us. That set a precedent and, every time we finished a field, we received a very large box of those chocolates. Although we welcomed the treat initially, by the time our six-week duty period finished, we never wanted to see a Red Poppy chocolate again.

The chairman had not been joking about having a party. After they finished each field, the permanent *kolkhoz* workers had a huge celebration, together with all the villagers, drinking their *samogon* and cheap red wine, which made them horribly drunk. It took them a couple of days to recover and get back into the fields. We couldn't work out if these parties were a reward for work done, or rather the stimulus for workers to finish the next field as quickly as possible.

One day, in our 'comatose' village, the atmosphere changed dramatically. People arrived from the surrounding areas, made fires on which they placed huge iron pots and began brewing some kind of beer. The aroma permeated the village and, finally, when the brew was ready, they set up tables with simple village food.

An accordion began playing while the people sat and drank. It was a most festive atmosphere and all the locals were happy, drinking, eating and singing. As time wore on, some of them collapsed in a stupor, but their places were soon taken by others arriving from elsewhere.

We were invited to join in, and they insisted that we taste their beer. It was as dark as chocolate, as thick as honey, had a completely foreign aroma and a bittersweet, pleasant flavour. After one glass we felt fine, with clear heads, and were perfectly capable of conversing.

Then one girl stood up and her legs battled to carry her. That was enough; we quit.

In what appeared to be a well-established tradition, the locals continued to party for the whole week, then moved their huge brew pots to another village and started over again. There is a common Russian expression, 'One's job is not a wolf, it will not run away to the forest', which seemed to be at the heart of these celebrations – no-one appeared to care in the slightest about going back to work. They probably thought it unnecessary because there were enough students on the job. So, instead of studying, we continued to work on that horribly uncomfortable, noisy machine, getting cold and sick, but returning to work each day because it was 'our duty'. It was obvious to us that a good part of the crop would never have been lifted without student help. It would simply have rotted in the ground.

We finally received our salaries of 120 roubles each. It was supposed to be a basic of 80 roubles per month, but we discovered that we had been paid for doing a 'skilled job'. That was lucky because, the following year, when we spent the same time doing back-breaking labour, lifting potatoes by hand, we received only a paltry 40 roubles per month for our six weeks of effort. It was far harder being bent double all day, but the job was graded as 'unskilled' because no machines were involved.

Office cleaners in town started on 60 roubles per month. All salaries were prescribed by government edict and had nothing to do with supply or demand, or even performance, with agricultural salaries the lowest of all.

My 120 roubles went quite a long way. I bought two quilts for my parents' beds that cost roughly 20 roubles each; 40 roubles went towards a warm dress for myself for university; and the other 40, I gave to the younger of my brothers, to buy a gold band for his forthcoming marriage.

That happened in 1972, and, as time went by, increasing numbers of poorly paid *kolkhoz* workers left the countryside to seek employment in the towns. As a consequence, progressively more townsfolk were needed to work the *kolkhozes*, so Communist leaders coined the term 'kolkhoz patronage', allocating farms to various individual manufacturing plants in the cities and eventually making them responsible for supplying the necessary farm labour, all year round.

Factory bosses had to create roster systems to supply labour to their allocated kolkhoz, at the expense of factory production. It meant that even educated factory foremen had to milk cows, and skilled machine minders had to plant and weed.

Truth was that the kolkhoz system was breaking down, but the Communist leaders refused to admit it. They tried to make the problem disappear by passing the responsibility to factory bosses. Pressure and responsibility were therefore spread in areas other than farming. Bosses in town were then obliged to submit false annual production reports if they were to keep their jobs. On the surface, everything looked good, but underneath was a different story.

On finishing university, I started work at Kalininspetzstroy. My job was categorised as 'white collar', but that didn't save me from kolkhoz duty; quite the opposite, in fact. Kalininspetzstroy patronised a kolkhoz, just like every other company, and therefore had to provide people to work on the lands. Unless there was an emergency concerning the lifting of crops, construction workers were seldom sent, as they had construction site deadlines to meet. It was easier to spare engineers, and those who went were expected to catch up on work after returning from a week or two on the kolkhoz. Workers in our office were sick and tired of this duty. They made every excuse to avoid being sent and, when three new faces (and potential kolkhoz candidates) appeared, they were delighted.

My two colleagues and I, fresh out of university, without the responsibilities of parenthood, young, fit and strong, were prime candidates for the task. In addition, we three were tied by law to the organisation for three years to refund the cost of our education.

When my boss tried to send me for two weeks to some 'Bear Corner', a serious problem arose at home. I had been married for just a year and my husband, Eugene, on hearing about my proposed kolkhoz duty, said that, if I went for two weeks, I might just as well pack my suitcases and not come back. I could understand his attitude because *kolkhozes* had a bad reputation as far as married people were concerned; in many instances marriages were irreparably harmed by a husband or wife's attitude changing after duties there.

Distressed, I cried pitifully in front of my boss, begging him not to send me for even one night. I was prepared to do my duty as long as I could get home every night. My weeping in front of the boss became a regular occurrence over the three-year period I was tied to Kalininspetzstroy. He was able to allocate me different duties, which smoothed the way for me somewhat, and placated my husband.

My husband had to go on *kolkhoz* duty too, but he was more fortunate than I. Also a qualified civil engineer, he worked as leader of a Student Building Detachment, which responded directly to our provincial Communist Party committee. Members of that committee had the responsibility of organising the requisite numbers for *kolkhoz* duty, a very important task, leaving them little or no time to do duty themselves. That annoyed us tremendously, but there was little we could do about it.

The first secretary of our provincial committee, comrade Ivanov, attempted for a couple of days each year to prove his equality. He announced to the media that he and his colleagues would be cutting hay the following day before sunrise. They would all turn out, at about five on a warm July morning, surrounded by obsequious reporters and photographers with cameras flashing, to work until about eight-thirty. By nine they were usually back in their offices, doing their 'important work'. The local paper would carry a front-page photograph with headlines proclaiming, 'Comrade Ivanov and his staff participate in *kolkhoz* duty'. Somehow they never got around to lifting potatoes or cutting cabbages. Perhaps the poor fellows had not been able to master the necessary skills?

Eugene always hated participation in that farce; he thought the committee members were simply making fools of themselves. They clearly had no idea of how to use an old-fashioned scythe. He contended that they could, collectively, be outperformed by one piece of machinery. He had to bite his tongue though, as his job was more important than his opinion.

So many townsfolk were mobilised for work on *kolkhozes* every autumn, that it looked as if a farming revolution had started. Hordes were visible everywhere, wearing battered looking clothes, old rubber boots and carrying buckets. If viewed from above, it may have resembled a colony of busy worker bees.

In the mornings, people left home sober, but, because of the amount of vodka consumed, by the time they returned, many could hardly get off the bus. Food was not provided at *kolkhozes*; everyone had to take their own supplies, so buckets usually contained thermos flasks of tea, sausages, boiled potatoes, or anything else available. To drink, people brought vodka, either homemade or store bought, together with cheap wine.

At lunchtime, all food and drink was laid out collectively, creating a common table from which everyone helped themselves. It was unthinkable for any individual to separate from the crowd in order to eat his own food. We had all grown up 'socially', so this 'collective lifestyle' was normal.

Vodka or wine was shared among all present, but the men were never upset if a woman declined her share. It was most unusual for a man to decline a drink because he would be thought of as either antisocial or sick. When the booze ran out, someone would always volunteer to walk to the nearest village store to buy more.

Vodka was relatively inexpensive then, at less than three roubles a bottle. After lunch, work was often left to the women and a few men, with the majority determined to enjoy their *kolkhoz* duties. There was little supervision, and they were being paid their normal office salaries anyhow. Out in the fresh air, at one with nature, was the ideal place to enjoy themselves.

It wasn't long before the authorities became aware of this particular folly. They forbade the sale of alcohol by all *kolkhoz* village stores during the cropping season, but traditions tended to die hard. People simply bought more in town and took it with them.

In the spring of 1979, I was sent to work at a potato storage facility on a particular *kolkhoz*. Normally, at that time of year, the vegetable shops were empty or were selling rotten items. Because we had previously participated in the harvesting and seen the huge piles of vegetables collected, we often wondered what really happened to them and where they were sent. It appeared that, after the glowing reports of record crops had been submitted by *kolkhoz* management to the central committee, nobody cared about what then happened to the glorious harvests. *Kolkhoz* management received the accolade; they had done their job. Central committee was satisfied by the good production figures they could report to the nation. What happened thereafter didn't appear to concern either of them.

In the old days, before the Revolution, generations of Russian farmers had known precisely how to preserve a potato harvest for up to two years, in case of a future crop failure. They would dig shallow holes in dry ground, line them with straw, fill the holes with dry potatoes and cover them with sods of earth. The principle seemed to be to maintain the potatoes at an even temperature, while keeping them dry and allowing them to breathe. In addition, they had many different holes for storage, never keeping all the potatoes in one place. It was their way of ensuring that, even if some went rotten, they could save at least part of the crop.

We were now living in booming, modern Soviet circumstances, or so we were told. Potato crops were being stored in vast concrete and steel buildings instead of in holes in the ground. Outwardly, the buildings resembled aeroplane hangers, and were fitted with the most modern equipment, supposedly showpieces of storage ingenuity. It was at one of those facilities that I was sent to work.

One day in March, when snow still blanketed the ground, six of us went to one of those buildings to sort and grade potatoes. On our arrival at the potato storage facility, we were met by the sight of a completely full building. There were potatoes from floor to ceiling and wall-to-wall. But what hit us was the stench of rotting vegetable matter. The potatoes could not be recognised outwardly as rotten, but when handled, those that had gone bad were jelly-like inside. We covered our noses and mouths with scarves, sat on our buckets outside the door and sorted the potatoes by feel into what we thought might be edible or otherwise piles. We were shocked when we realised the terrible waste that had taken place there.

When the *kolkhoz* foreman finally appeared, he informed us that the building was brand new, having been completed just before the crop had been brought in. Inside were heating, ventilation and air-conditioning systems intended to keep vegetables dry and at a constant temperature. Potatoes should have been stacked in separate piles, he explained, not more than a metre in height, with a clear path between piles, wide enough for the passage of small vehicles. However, last autumn the *kolkhoz* had been late bringing in the crop. As harvested crop reports had to be submitted to the provincial Communist Party committee by a certain deadline, the chairman of the *kolkhoz* had ordered that the potato crop be stored in the quickest manner, facilitating his timely report.

Reports were of vital importance to the Party, regardless of the fact that incorrect storage prevented the heating and ventilation systems from functioning, causing the crop to rot. What we were looking at was the result of a botched exercise, brought about by a serious lack of planning and management.

After eight hours of work in that foul place, the smell permeated our skin, hair and clothing, right down to our underwear. On the journey back, between our office and home, I couldn't have cared less about my looks; the stench was my main concern. I chose not to use the tram and walked all the way home to spare my fellow citizens the dreadful smell and myself the embarrassment.

At home I ripped off my clothes, hung them out on the balcony to air and took a long hot shower, but I had to dress in the same clothes the following day and return for another session of potato sorting.

After three days of the same routine, we all began complaining of headaches due to the ammonium gas given off by the rotting potatoes. We were then issued with respirators. By the time we completed that tour of duty, one week later, we found that we had broken out in skin rashes.

Experiences while on *kolkhoz* duty prompted me to think about what was happening in the USSR. Why, for example, should we have to grow our own vegetables at *dachas*, work on *kolkhoz* fields, do our normal jobs, and still be subjected to food shortages? To whose advantage was all of this? Certainly not ours. There were always more questions than answers.

On a rainy day in 1985, I drove through the village of Rozhdestvenno. I had not been in the area for 20 years, during which time it had changed beyond recognition. I remembered it as an active place where many people lived and worked, children played in fields, and weddings and other social gatherings took place. Now it appeared almost uninhabited, with just a few old people waiting out their remaining days, surrounded by abandoned houses. When I saw the ruins of what I'd known as shops, schools and the clinic, I was overcome by sadness.

We found a dilapidated store that stocked just five different food items, all of which had been produced in the city. Agricultural production had been allowed to stagnate to the point where there was insufficient to feed even just the few elderly locals. The brassiere and cheese factories had gone, along with the bakery. Sheds on the outskirts of the village, previously used to store fertilisers, were empty, except for what was being washed out by rain, forming rivulets of yellow slime running into the road.

I was moved to tears for what had been lost. The villagers had moved out and gone to live in the town just 40 kilometres away, and I couldn't help wondering how many other farming villages in Russia that had been taken over and collectivised had also been abandoned.

I thought of relatives I had visited as a child. Mother had told me how hard Varvara had worked as the *kolkhoz* crumbled – for which she had finally been rewarded with a pension of just 12 roubles per month.

The minimum pension for townsfolk at that time was 45 roubles. The government considered it unnecessary to pay higher pensions to farm workers, and expected them to feed themselves from their own gardens. It seemed that many sick or disabled old people, who had given their lives to hard labour on the land, were still living in the abandoned villages in the country, and were condemned to die in pitiful conditions.

Why had the authorities created circumstances so grim and uncompromising for people who had come from generations of successful farmers? Why had they been so determined to deprive them of a sense of responsibility and pride in ownership? It was no wonder the younger generation was unwilling to remain on the land.

At the turn of the millennium, with a progressive government in place in Russia, there is still no law allowing ownership of land by farmers, with all land remaining in the hands of the State. We were taught as children that the 'State' meant 'us', which supposedly means that the land belongs to all of the people. But, without individual title, who, as a farmer, would be prepared to invest money and hard labour to improve something that could be lost to a whim of the State?

14

Student Building Detachments

STUDENT BUILDING DETACHMENTS (SBDs) WERE ANOTHER remarkable part of Russian university students' lives prior to *perestroika*. First organised by the Communist Party in the 1930s (although not known as SBDs at this time), millions of young people from the cities were called upon to work in building huge production plants, power stations and river-linking channels. Unlike *kolkhoz* duty, participation was entirely voluntary, although workers were paid for their efforts.

Construction projects were part of the many Five-Year Plans put forward by the government, who marketed the idea by puting a patriotic slant on the call for volunteers to work in uninhabited areas. Young men and women (not necessarily university students at that time) were encouraged to leave their homes to travel to unknown areas, where many settled, creating new towns around the huge projects. They were told that they would be glorious pioneers, recognised for their ability to live and work in tough conditions for the benefit of the motherland. Their lives were far from comfortable or heroic; they had to live and work in extreme conditions for the same kind of salaries they could have earned back home. As the old saying has it, 'Pioneers can be recognised by the arrows in their backs.'

Completion of projects often took many years. Volunteers would marry, raise families and settle permanently in the area, often growing old there too, without receiving any special compensation for their pioneering exploits. Not even the promises of glory accrued to them; accolades invariably went to people higher up the ladder.

At the end of hostilities in the Great Patriotic War, more volunteers were called for to open up virgin lands in the south and southwestern areas of Russia. Thousands of young people again ventured into unknown, sparsely populated areas, where they settled in tents.

But perhaps, by the 1960s, enthusiasm for acts of patriotism was beginning to wane, with the number of people prepared to sacrifice what little they had on the Soviet altar definitely declining. And so, in Kalinin in 1965, the SBD programme was officially launched. School-leaving students (18- to 22-year-olds), would be mustered for despatch to construction sites and new farmlands. Since their education had been free of charge, why should they not repay the favour by working for the State for a couple of months?

The *Komsomol* that reported to the central Communist Party committee was delegated responsibility for organising the movement. The idea subsequently appealed to other countries in the Russian sphere of influence, and many adopted the same practice. Governments grasped it as another opportunity to further the 'political education' of the young.

Because participation was voluntary, the government had to come up with some incentive, and so they put a romantic slant on recruitment. Young people were going to be given the chance to make new friends, test their mettle and make a meaningful contribution to society. It worked, because young people seized on the idea and volunteered in droves. They were, after all, the cream of Communist youth, eager to show their ability for their nation's benefit.

The picture painted was that, when the day was done, workers would sit around campfires swapping stories and singing songs composed by some of the more talented among them. Some of these songs were glorified by the authorities and broadcast on radio, often becoming instant hits. Before long, the entire country was singing SBD songs of fortitude and courage, friendship and love.

In Kalinin province, the first SBD was established in 1965. One hundred and ten students were seconded to work together with others from a famous Moscow scientific university. They went to the Celinograd area in Kazakhstan for a couple of months, to help build houses and wheat storage silos.

By 1967, the movement had gained in strength and staff offices were built to oversee the organisation. There were, by then, 1 600 students allocated work in Kalinin province alone. They helped construct buildings required in agricultural areas.

Most rural construction workers took their annual leave in summer, and those that didn't were inclined to slow down to enjoy some respite from the drudgery of working through the long cold winters. Because students were enthusiastic about proving their ability, more progress was usually made on the sites in the three months of their summer stay than during the rest of the year. In this way, students succeeded in creating more work for themselves. Authorities were not slow to notice the positive difference made by student workers and construction sites constantly called for their help.

My elder brother, Victor, at the time studying mechanical engineering, was the first in our family to take part in the SBD. He was one of 110 student volunteers that went to Kazakhstan in 1965, returning after two-and-a-half months, having put on a lot of muscle. He had also gained both a suntan and new confidence in himself. From photographs he brought back, we were introduced to his new friends and given an insight into what he had seen and done.

His enthusiasm for what he had experienced rubbed off on those around him. His description of tough living conditions and long working hours did not diminish the attraction we felt for the idea of sitting around a campfire, singing romantic, patriotic songs and getting a tan during the day. He had also brought home the first money he had earned in his life and given it to our parents. It was more substantial than we expected, and the only items he wanted for himself were a guitar and a 'teach yourself to play' book. We took great pride in his efforts and treated him as if he were a conquering hero, returned home from battle.

The younger of my brothers was next to participate. Evgueni was also a mechanical engineering student and, in 1970, went with a detachment to work in a rural area of our province, returning with, what was for us, another substantial sum of money. It was very difficult for students to earn any money at that time; nobody wanted to employ unqualified young people for such short periods. The only opportunity of earning good money was with the SBD.

The SBDs had been organised along Soviet military lines and green uniforms with epaulettes bearing rank insignia were worn. There were detachment commanders, political commissars and other ranks, down to private. Strict discipline had become the structural base, so detachments were ready to do whatever the commander ordered. I was so proud of my brothers and swore to myself that, if I ever had the opportunity, I would definitely volunteer for that distinguished duty.

As it happened, I did attend university and, after the second year, my childhood friend, Raya, and I volunteered to serve. On learning of this, my brothers did their best to dissuade me from going. They said it was far too hard for girls, who really had no place in the movement, but I was too stubborn to be talked out of it.

To our surprise, getting accepted was more difficult than we had anticipated. When we went along to SBD headquarters, we were told that girls were not needed; they wanted boys for the hard work. We begged them to accept us and, finally, four of us were taken on as cooks only. And so we paid half of our 40 rouble monthly university stipend for our green SBD uniforms.

The idea of being a cook was not intimidating. I had cooked often enough for six people and never had any complaints, so I assumed that cooking in bigger quantities would be 'a piece of cake'. I also thought the experience would be a test of character that I was determined to pass with honour, making my contribution to the State and, at the same time, earning money for my parents. I suppose my brothers' descriptions of romantic campfire evenings had not entirely escaped my notice. All things considered, it was going to be the experience of a lifetime.

At the end of June 1974, 70 of us, mostly boys, went off to the Bezhetsk region of Kalinin province to build a school, a clinic and a few houses. On the outskirts of one of the rural villages we set up the tented camp that was to be our not very cosy home for the next two-and-a-half months.

The area was particularly featureless and flat, without hills, lakes or rivers. There was an incomplete building at the site that had a roof and little else, which our commander decided would serve adequately as the detachment's dining room. We were given two gas stoves with gas cylinders and informed that water would be carted in daily.

The following morning the boys left for work at a site not visible from our location. More kitchen equipment, crockery, pots, pans, tables and chairs arrived periodically during the day, but it was still inadequate for our purposes.

We four girls had a tent to ourselves and decided we would work in two shifts. However, when we tried out our plan, we found it impossible to cater adequately, because there was just too much for two people to do. In fact, it was too much work for four people.

We had to get up at four in the morning to prepare breakfast for seven a.m. The stoves were domestic sized, but the pots were industrial, holding about 50 litres each. It meant that each stove could take only one pot, which took forever to boil because the hotplates were too small. Cold porridge had to be served because we couldn't keep it warm while making boiled eggs on one stove and tea on the other.

When the boys left for work we had to wash up after waiting at least an hour for water on the stove to heat up sufficiently. Lunch was at one p.m. and consisted, for example, of borsch, a meat course such as stew, followed by coffee, cocoa or tea. After lunch there were even more dishes to wash, which had to be done quickly if dinner was to be served on time at 8 p.m. It took until midnight to wash the dinner dishes, which left just four hours a night for sleep.

After a few days of that routine, we were so tired that we couldn't even walk straight. When we had agreed to take on the job, we could never have imagined what we were letting ourselves in for. Cooking for 70, with such inadequate facilities, was very different from cooking for six at home. We had no idea of the quantities required to feed 70 people, so the amount of porridge or spaghetti put in the pot was a hit-and-miss affair, resulting in either feast or famine.

The pots were so heavy that we struggled to lift them. I weighed only 51 kilograms and I'm sure the pots sometimes exceeded my weight. We soon realised that catering for so many called for professional expertise way beyond our entirely amateur efforts. The SBD had turned into a nightmare for us.

The boys worked extremely hard all day, returning tired and hungry, often not in the best frame of mind. What was presented to them was often either under- or overcooked, which gave rise to loud objections, with our lives the only things not threatened, although I felt this might change at any time. If lunch were half an hour late, or there wasn't enough for dinner, a riot threatened to erupt.

After the first week of stress and overwhelming fatigue, I realised that I would be incapable of seeing out the two-and-a-half months. My dreams of romantic heroism were shattered completely. All we wanted to do was collapse in undisturbed sleep. I couldn't even look a boy in the face because we had become their enemies.

After 10 days, a commission arrived from headquarters to review progress on site. Their inspection was far ranging and included not only the construction sites, but also such diverse concerns as health of the students, general discipline, nutrition and sanitary facilities.

When they had completed their inspection, they asked the students if they had any comments or complaints. Nobody complained about having to sleep in cold tents, or the lack of water for adequate personal ablutions, or that there was only one long drop toilet for 70 people, and that it was located some way from camp, or that they were transported just once per week to a common sauna in the nearest little town, or that we had only two hours there to do our ablutions and whatever else was necessary in the way of finding personal requisites before being rushed back to camp. They expected such hardships on SBD camps. But when it came to the food and the cooks, there was a deluge of complaints. We had a lot to say too, pointing out that the construction work side had been well planned, but that little thought had been given to what would be needed in terms of the basic necessities of life.

As happened so often in Russia, the authorities had paid most attention to what they needed from a production viewpoint, with scant regard for the comfort of the people doing the job. The SBD had been in existence long enough for them to understand that, for large numbers of people, specialist cooks were needed. At the very least, we should have been given some basic training before being thrown in at the deep end. We also pointed out that, on Sundays, the boys took the day off to relax and play football, but their food requirements remained, which meant no time off for the cooks.

Members of the commission listened to our tales of woe. I doubt they had been addressed in such direct terms before, though only time would reveal if we had made any impression on them. That evening, we continued our criticism with the commander of the Bezhetsk regional detachment, one Eugene Morozov. We even asked if we could be bricklayers' assistants rather than cooks.

After a couple of days, two younger girls arrived at camp. They had attended a professional cooking school and volunteered to work at the camp to gain experience before going on to take up positions in industrial catering facilities elsewhere. They set about the task efficiently, ordering what they knew to be essential utensils and equipment. In addition, they asked the camp commander to second two boys to them each day to assist in the heavier work, such as lifting full, 50-kilogram pots.

Of course, the boys ended up doing a lot more than just lifting pots. Our new girls made sure that they peeled potatoes, washed dishes and helped with most other tedious chores. The quality of food produced improved dramatically. Complaints became a thing of the past and the new girls even found time to relax and get a suntan.

We, the original four cooks, were reassigned to assist bricklayers, as we had requested. However, before we began, I was offered an alternative. I was told that I could work as a secretary in the Bezhetsk HQ. I jumped at the opportunity. I was sick of being in camp without normal ablution facilities and the other basic necessities of a reasonably comfortable life.

My job at the office was easy. There were two other secretaries and the bosses were out checking on people at work sites most of the time. I had my own bedroom at a school that was in summer recess; we cooked for ourselves, went to movies at every opportunity – and I didn't miss camp life at all.

The two months I spent there passed in a flash. The detachment commander, Eugene Morozov, was paying me an inordinate amount of attention, which didn't upset me; in fact, I thought he was rather nice. He was four years my senior and had finished the same university course I was doing. Now he was busy creating a career for himself. He appeared strong willed, resolute, intelligent and active, and I enjoyed being in his company. When my SBD duty time was over, I returned home to begin my third year at university. Eugene and I continued to meet.

By 1974, students were being allocated activities other than just building and more in line with their future careers. Medical students, for example, went along to act as 'doctors' for their peers involved in construction. Those studying railway engineering worked as conductors on trains. Future art and music teachers went to rural areas to teach disadvantaged children and bring cultural performances to the adults. All of those activities were under the auspices of the SBD, whose reputation for doing glorious work grew to the point where it became an honour for individuals to participate.

From 1976 onwards, an SBD exchange programme was formulated. Kalinin students were sent to far-off places such as Astrakhan, Krasnodar, and later Uzbekistan, Azerbaijan and Ukraine.

At the end of every summer, progress reports for the working period were submitted upwards from one HQ to the next and, finally, to Moscow, where decisions were made about which detachments had performed best. Winners were invited to attend an SBD congress in the capital, where medals and honour certificates were bestowed on them for the wonderful work done in 'Building the Country for Communism'. When aggregated, what students achieved was quite extraordinary and the entire country applauded their efforts as news of their good works was broadcast.

Eugene Morozov enjoyed working in the SBD. He regarded it an honour, liked the responsibility and was very conscientious. As a lowly detachment commander, he had been acknowledged as having the best detachment in our province and, later, as commander of a regional HQ, again won the accolade for the best region in the Province. After promotion to provincial HQ commander, he worked exceptionally hard. His enthusiasm and diligence brought more students into the fold, productivity boomed and they were able to complete a variety of jobs in the province for the benefit of the rural population.

Despite his relative youth, he became well known to *kolkhoz* chairmen and the directors of a number of manufacturing organisations. His reputation did not go unnoticed by *Komsomol* and Communist provincial leaders, and his visits to Moscow, to both the SBD HQ and the central *Komsomol* committee, brought him into contact with even higher officials, whose respect he also earned, and whose support helped bolster his fast-moving career.

Working with thousands of students had its problems, though. Many saw the university summer recess as 'party time'. They may well have worked hard during the day, but at night and over weekends they were inclined to have fun. Spats frequently broke out between local boys and students, invariably involving girls, and there were a few occasions when fights turned very nasty, resulting in stabbings and even some deaths.

Carelessness on the job also made for traumas. People fell off scaffolding, bricks fell on heads and students got sunstroke. There were drownings, usually because students were inebriated, car accidents and all manner of other reckless behaviour.

Not a season passed without one tragedy or another. Eugene would invariably be faced with parents wanting to know why such disorder had been allowed. Tragedy was easier for relatives to accept if they could blame someone other than their children.

These mishaps affected Eugene badly. As a result, he began to impose ever stricter discipline in the detachments, often travelling hundreds of kilometres in the dead of night to visit camps unannounced, in an effort to ensure that discipline was being maintained.

If he found dereliction of duty in any shape or form, he was merciless. Those responsible bore his wrath and were fired immediately, regardless of whether they were workers or commanders. His subordinates began to fear him, but respected his intentions. In this way, he managed gradually to reduce incidents of injury and death.

I watched Eugene's activities with interest, took pride in his achievements and respected what he was doing. He was clever, hard working, of strong and honest character, and could be both kind and cruel, depending on what the situation demanded. I knew no other men of his ability and, after two years of courtship, had decided that I wanted to be his wife. We married in 1976.

For 10 years Eugene had been involved in the SBD, starting as a part-time student bricklayer, then joining full time, ending at the top of the provincial hierarchy as curator, positioned in the provincial *Komsomol* committee. He had 10 000 students under him at that time, participating in the Kalinin province SBD.

Their productivity was remarkable. Over the three-month period of summer university recess, they did the equivalent of the rest of the year's work of the full-time provincial building organisation, which resulted in Kalinin province SBD being recognised as the best in Russia. Moscow honoured Eugene with a 'Friendship of the People' medal, for his 'Contribution to Communism'.

The medal was pinned on his chest at a special Communist celebratory gathering, by Comrade Ivanov, the first secretary of Kalinin province Communist Party committee.

The SBD had played an important part in our lives. At the age of 30, Eugene was promoted to the provincial Communist Party committee. He was the youngest appointee and the only one with a medal from the central *Komsomol* committee. It was a great springboard for his future career.

15

The wedding

I n 1976, Eugene and I had been going out for two years. We had seen each other practically every day during that time, and had often travelled to other destinations with friends for weekends, holidays and hunting trips. However, the expression of love had been significantly absent from what was otherwise a close relationship. Nor had the topic of marriage been raised, other than in a rather oblique reference to it by Eugene after a quarrel; but it was somehow understood as being on the cards.

I had always thought that there should not be marriage without love. I had heard of marriages in which love developed over a period of time and thought that possibly this would happen in our case. And I wondered what I should do to advance the situation.

In March that year, Eugene went on a tour to West Germany and returned with many presents for me. It was flattering to realise that he had thought about me while he was away, so I decided to raise the subject of marriage, which had been hanging in the air since our quarrel a few months previously.

August was the most popular month for weddings because fresh fruit and vegetables were available at reasonable prices and the weather was at its best. But to marry in August necessitated a reservation four or five months in advance. I mentioned to Eugene that, if he wanted to get married in August, he would have to go to the registry office and apply immediately, or it would probably be too late. In our city of 700 000 people, there was only one registry office for marriages. Church marriages were not recognised then and, in any case, would never have entered our minds. We were frightened of even entering any place of worship, because we knew that if we were seen we would probably experience trouble with our careers.

The next day we went together to the registry office. It was a bleak place; the room was dirty and application forms lay in disarray on some tables. A few broken chairs opposite the counter were the only other furnishings in the office, which didn't feature the luxuries of carpets or curtains.

A large, cheerless woman took our passports and studied our application form for a long time. She finally announced that our time for registration would be 13 August, at 11 a.m. It immediately flashed through my mind that the thirteenth was not a lucky day.

Without any prompting from me, Eugene asked for any day other than the thirteenth. She had not been friendly up till then, but now she turned nasty.

In a loud voice she said, 'You are *Komsomol* members and he works in the provincial *Komsomol* committee. Shame on you for being stupidly superstitious.'

Eugene said, '*Komsomol* may be *Komsomol*, but I'm not getting married on the thirteenth.'

The official finally capitulated and gave us another appointment on 21 August. 'Don't forget to collect your vouchers 10 days in advance,' she said before shouting, 'Next.' These vouchers were for the shop selling wedding clothes for brides and grooms.

A month before our wedding day, I began looking for a bridal outfit. It was difficult to find something suitable because there was a shortage of just about everything in our shops. Appropriate white fabrics were virtually out of stock and the right sort of white shoes and a veil were unobtainable. I spent days running around local shops and finally decided I would have to go to Moscow to find these items. Even in that city it was not possible to find all the things I needed, not because I was that demanding; it was simply a problem for all brides and grooms throughout Russia.

Our Communist administration had made a feeble attempt to resolve the problem by opening one shop in each province. It was typical of decisions made by our Soviet government. Kalinin had one small shop catering for a provincial population of some one-and-a-half million people.

People were allowed to browse, but had to have the necessary vouchers issued by the registry office, enabling them to make purchases only in the last 10 days before the stipulated wedding date. Sales in the wedding shop were strictly controlled; just one of each item could be purchased. Once chosen, the item was marked on a list, precluding anyone from coming back to get an extra suit or pair of shoes.

Just as in other countries, weddings are inclined to be expensive affairs and, in Communist countries, young people with low personal incomes, even with the help of parents, had limited resources to finance them. When we had made purchases up to our financial limit, we allowed relatives and friends to buy desperately needed items still unmarked on our list, which were unavailable in the usual shops. The wedding shop had imported goods, the best Russian-made clothes and accessories, and was the only shop of its kind in the province. It later became the only source of essential clothing items such as raincoats and winter boots. For these reasons, people were obliged to become 'creative'.

Unmarried couples would go to the registry office, fill in all the forms required to arrange a marriage, and get the valuable vouchers. After buying what they and their friends needed, they would simply call off the wedding – pulling the same trick later, but with a different proposed marriage partner. Survival made such conduct extremely popular, and it was quite normal for people to ask around to find someone with vouchers to obtain what they needed.

I had bought white fabric and a veil in Moscow, and shoes and four down pillows for my trousseau from the Kalinin wedding shop. A dressmaker made my gown inexpensively and, together, our families agreed to split the cost of the reception. Eugene had a relatively well-paid job and had been able to put aside enough for his family's share, but my parents had to borrow money that took two years to repay.

Eugene accepted responsibility for organising the reception for 70 guests, who would be made up largely of family members. My brothers, Victor and Evgueni, had long since left Kalinin, were married, had families and were living in Tyumen and Sverdlovsk respectively. Thankfully, they all managed somehow to make it to the wedding.

My father's only surviving brother from Orenburg arrived with his wife. Their daughters had also been invited, but declined on account of having nobody to look after their young families. Nura, with whom I had become close on my trip to Orenburg with Mother four years previously, sent me a special present together with warm congratulations. And Eugene and I invited a few close friends.

Weddings in the European part of Russia are little different from those in other Western countries, but they have certain traditions that are, perhaps, unique. For example, brides can be 'kidnapped' and ransomed for vodka. Guests could break a cheap ceramic pot on the floor and give a broom to the bride to tidy up while poking fun at her with remarks such as, 'Look at her, she's slow and must be a lazy wife'.

Coins are sometimes collected from guests and dropped on the floor for the bride and groom to pick up. The faster either one of them works, the more ribbing they get for having a lust for money or for being greedy. Guests also pretend to want to know who the leader in the new family is likely to be. One of the tests is to give a flat round bread loaf to the bride and groom who are asked to take a bite each. The partner with the bigger bite is then labelled the future leader. Of course, it's all good fun and done only in jest. I was too shy for those games, though, and had asked my friends not to initiate any. As usual, escape proved impossible.

On the morning of our wedding I was dressed and waiting to be picked up by the cars taking us to the registry office. It is an old custom in Russia for the groom to collect his bride from her home and take her to the church or, in Soviet times, the registry office. It was also customary for neighbours, or the bride's family, to refuse to surrender her unless a ransom was paid.

In my case, I looked out of the second-floor window of our flat to discover, to my horror, that the neighbouring old ladies had run ribbons across the building entrance and were obviously intent on demanding ransom. I don't know how they found out about my wedding day as I had tried to keep it a secret.

In my anxiety, I suddenly thought that perhaps Eugene, who was not the most patient of men, might turn on his heel and leave. At that moment, six Volga sedans, borrowed from Eugene's colleagues at the provincial *Komsomol* committee, rounded the corner with hooters blaring.

When he arrived at the 'blocked' entrance, Eugene was 'detained', subject to payment of the customary ransom. Fortunately, one of his friends had anticipated such hurdles and had brought along a case of brandy. Once the old girls had a couple of bottles in hand, honour had been satisfied and Eugene was allowed in.

I sighed with relief and waited for his knock on the door. Having seen what happened, my brothers grabbed hold of me and pushed me into the room furthest from the front door, making it clear that I would not be surrendered easily. Again, I feared that Eugene would leave without me. I kicked and screamed, and eventually was released.

On the way out, the old ladies blocked the exit again, laughing and demanding more ransom. They were finally given another bottle because 'the bride is so beautiful' and the 'problem' miraculously resolved itself.

Driving in a cavalcade of hooting cars, we eventually arrived at the registry office. There was a queue of young couples waiting 'on the conveyor belt' to marry. By the time our turn came, the registrar was visibly tired of the repetitive ceremonies. Inside the registry room, the rings were hurriedly placed on a small silver plate, resting on a green baize-covered table, while the registrar hunted quickly through a pile of documents to find our file.

Her speech was short, read from a prepared text and delivered mechanically; it constituted a brief lecture relating to our future responsibilities. The most important point she made was that we were jointly becoming a new cell of our glorious Communist society. Eugene and I, together with our witnesses, were then prompted to sign. Rings were slipped onto fingers, we were told to 'seal our vows with a kiss' and, as she barked 'Next', we left the room. The whole ceremony had taken just 15 minutes.

Another 15 minutes were allowed us in a room used for photographs. Bottles of Soviet sparkling wine were opened. We were photographed in front of a painted backdrop of a couple touching hands, representing a 'cell'; then we hurriedly downed our wine and left so that the next couple, already waiting in the doorway, could repeat the performance.

It was a modern Soviet custom in Kalinin to drive across the seven main bridges in town, hooting all the way. A stop would then be made at the war memorials where brides would lay flowers as a tribute to the fallen who, through their selflessness, had given us peace. It was a very emotional moment for me and I silently gave thanks to the heroes for their sacrifice, allowing me to live happily, study, marry and be free of occupation by fascist invaders.

Our final stop was in front of a restaurant. My newly acquired mother-in-law met us, carrying a special cloth on which rested bread and salt, the most ancient form of Russian welcome. We broke the bread, dipped it in salt and ate, as the customary acceptance of hospitality offered.

On entering the restaurant we were shown to a room where everything was ready for the festivities. Eugene had used *blat* to secure the use of a restaurant that was prepared to cook food brought in by him. The wife of one of his friends was a director of the establishment and had been persuaded to make exceptions to the general rules. Normally restaurants added big margins to raw material prices, making it prohibitively expensive to host a party of 70.

The day before, Eugene had delivered cases of good quality wine and vodka, not normally available at those places. He had also managed, through his extensive connections, to acquire caviar and other delicacies that most guests had seldom had the good fortune to taste. It had been his intention that our guests enjoy the party fully. However, he put so much effort into the arrangements that he looked more like a *maître d'hôtel* than a groom at his own wedding reception.

There were so many matters to oversee, and a good few that went wrong. Waitresses, after being instructed to the contrary, brought open bottles of wine and vodka to tables. We took that as a sign that they had purloined some and diluted the rest. They had been told to open the tins of caviar and place them on the tables to allow guests to eat the delicacy in their own, preferred way, but they served made-up, open caviar sandwiches, which made it impossible to check how much had disappeared.

Eugene ground his teeth while trying to remonstrate unobtrusively with the manager because the pre-agreed arrangements were not being adhered to. The *pièce de résistance* came when the baby chickens arrived, one on each guest's plate – and every chicken had a leg missing. The waitresses must have thought that the guests were sufficiently inebriated not to notice one-legged chickens, but Eugene was beside himself with anger.

At that time, clients were defenceless when it came to dealing with restaurants, butchers or other food purveyors, who all operated on the *blat* system. Party officials or other people of influence were always prepared to defend them, regardless of what was right or wrong. The unions always defended them too, purportedly in the cause of 'workers rights'. We recognised that, as engineers, we had less access to *blat*. After all, what did we have to offer? Besides, the restaurant had broken the rules for our benefit, so there was little we could do to be compensated for what the staff had stolen. Trying to sue would be a waste of time; the evidence had disappeared down the staff's throats.

The serving of one-legged chickens was the last straw as far as Eugene was concerned. He was not the kind of man to withhold his opinions. Nervously, I watched his face take on a reddish hue. With a look of murderous intent, he leapt to his feet and hurried for the kitchen. After a few minutes he returned to our table and appeared to have calmed down a little. He told me he had given the staff hell; but perhaps doing that had not been the wisest option.

Revenge on their part was swift. There was a shortage of good coffee in Russia, and Eugene had spent time and money to get the best for our reception. When it was served, it came in cheap tumblers, not coffee cups as would be expected in a restaurant of that class. Specially iced cakes that Eugene had ordered in Moscow were deliberately cut into squares and piled pyramid-style on plates so that the icing messages were obscured. There was no telling how much coffee or cake had disappeared, but our guests enjoyed themselves and didn't appear to have noticed being 'short changed'. The restaurant staff probably enjoyed our reception more than we did.

It is customary at Russian weddings for the groom to make a speech at the end of proceedings, thanking the bride's parents for giving her to him and the guests for attending. I tried to prompt Eugene, but to no avail. To my dismay he simply refused to stand up and speak.

In order to bring our two families closer together, I felt it was necessary for someone to speak. I thought the wedding would be incomplete without it. My anxiety prompted me to act spontaneously. I stood up, went to the microphone and began an impromptu speech of my own.

'My dear relatives and friends,' I began. 'Today is a very happy day for everyone, especially me. Today is the end of adolescence and the start of a new adult life for me. I am grateful to all my family for everything they have done for me. My special thanks to Grandmother Katerina for teaching me to read and write, cook soup and clean house; to my brothers for loving and caring about me. I'm glad they were able to come with their families from so far off, all the way from Siberia and the Urals. They were always so kind to me; Mother even remembers their putting a live squirrel in my bed when we lived in Orenburg. Thanks to my parents for giving me life and education. It didn't matter how difficult finances were for them, they always tried to give me everything I wanted. Thanks, Mother, for your love, for raising me strictly and with a sense of responsibility. Thanks, Father, for teaching me the importance of kindness and honesty ...'

I glanced at my father and he was crying. Immediately something caught in my throat. I couldn't utter a word. I turned to the guests and realised that many sat tearfully silent. I had to force myself to continue speaking.

'And now I am entering a new family. I love my husband, promise to be a good wife, support him in life and keep our home fires burning. I want to be a good daughter to my new mother-and father-in-law.'

There was thunderous applause that prevented me from thanking the guests for coming. I was so overwhelmed with emotion and trying not to cry that I returned to my seat with my head bowed.

Our day finished in the small hours of the following morning. I was exhausted. When I went to my new home, which, in fact, was that of my new parents-in-law, I fell into bed. Eugene and my mother-in-law sat in the kitchen sipping brandy and talking until sunrise. I was relieved that nobody saw me crying. I wasn't even certain why I was crying. Was it because of what had now finished in my life or what was beginning?

At 11 a.m. the following day, our guests regathered at the same restaurant for a second celebration, this time for lunch. There was another team of waitresses serving, but they obviously knew about what had happened the previous day and went about helping themselves with a little more discretion. The atmosphere was relaxed and the guests danced, joked and enjoyed themselves.

Then I learned about a problem that had occurred the previous day. My two brothers had three young children between them and their wives would not leave them with anyone outside of our family. Everybody wanted to attend the wedding and it was decided that only two candidates were suitable as babysitters. One was my 14-year-old cousin, Lena, and the other, my grandmother, Katerina.

Because my grandmother was 76 years old, would tire quickly at the wedding and was more experienced with children, they considered her the best for the job. She had dug in her heels and stated quite firmly that she had every intention of being at the wedding. No-one had taken her too seriously, because she had always been ready to do whatever had been asked of her.

She was living with my aunt at the time, which meant that, although my attachment to her was as strong as ever, I didn't get to see her that often. When the family awoke on the morning of the wedding, she had disappeared. Nobody knew when she had left or where she had gone. That's how a tearful 14-year-old cousin Lena came to be left at home with the children. Nobody saw Grandmother Katerina until she arrived at the wedding at three in the afternoon.

It transpired that she had dressed and left home at five a.m. to avoid any pleas from the rest of the family for her to babysit and miss the wedding. I had made a special invitation for her, so she knew exactly where and when the reception would be held.

From five in the morning, she had moved from one bench to another to prevent anyone in the family from finding her. She had left home without a kopek, so had been unable to eat a thing before arriving at the reception. I saw her among the guests, but had no idea of the circuitous route she had taken to be there.

When I found out, I was furious with my family because I could not imagine my wedding without her. She was my guardian angel, who had given me so much in my life. I asked her how she could have been so brave as to withstand the pressure and, for the first time in her life, go against the wishes of the rest of the family?

'How could I miss your wedding? I raised you from a baby and you gave me a special invitation,' she replied. 'I have never attended a proper wedding and this could be my last chance. I've spent my life, from the age of 11, bringing up children, first my elder sister's, then four of my own and, after that, six grandchildren. It's enough now, let someone else look after the great-grandchildren. The only way I could get here was to run away early in the morning and that's what I did. I simply had to be at your wedding.'

My dear old granny had walked the town for 10 hours just to be with me on that important day. I will never forget her remarkable effort.

There is something else that I remember particularly about our wedding party. At the time, there were exchange students from the SBD in Krasnodar working in Kalinin province. When they heard about Eugene's wedding they volunteered to send their musical group, free of charge, to play at the reception. Five of them arrived with their instruments and set themselves up.

They turned out to be much better than we had anticipated. They could play any request the guests made, their versatility was impressive, and their repertoire was unusual in our region. They began playing old Russian romantic songs with which we were not familiar.

They were beautiful but sad songs about officers of the White Army, men who defended the Tsar and their motherland in the 1917 Revolution. Having lost their desperate struggle against the Bolsheviks, they were forced to leave the country or die. About to board the ship that was to take them away to an unknown land as refugees, one bitter officer asked his friend, 'Poruchik Galitzin, will we ever come back? Why do we need another country?' The guests were enthralled and moved as they listened to the words.

It was the first time that I had heard good words spoken of White Army officers. I'd never considered that they were pure Russians who loved their country just as we did, and that they had defended what they believed in. And that among them were heroes too. The only heroes I'd learned about were Red Army heroes. We had been taught that those in the White Army were our enemies and devoid of all human emotion. Supposedly, only those in the Red Army were capable of loving their motherland and sacrificing themselves for it. These songs came as a revelation to me and I remember breaking out in goosebumps.

Eugene leaned over and whispered to me that the lyrics were banned, but no-one attempted to stop the singer. I studied the guests who were spellbound by the performance and it was obvious that it was the first time they'd heard these songs too. The performance by the student singer was so heartfelt that our guests clapped rapturously and requested an encore.

Afterwards, we wondered if we might be reported and punished for allowing these songs to be performed. Thankfully, the government's attitude had softened a little by then and nothing came of it.

We could not have imagined then that, within 10 years, we would be able to speak our minds, and read books and sing songs of our own choosing.

16

Travel

FROM EARLY CHILDHOOD WE WERE TAUGHT THAT WE, THE SOVIET people, had many foreign enemies, especially in the capitalist world. As children, we were led to believe that there was a threat to our very existence on the periphery of our country, and that it did not come only from a few individuals, but rather from whole countries. They wanted to destroy our society because we were busy building the dream of the world's proletariat, Communism. That had been proven, they said, by our war against the capitalistic, fascist Germans.

We were told that the KGB and other government agencies eager to ensure our patriotism were watching us. To deviate in any way meant bringing attention to oneself that might result in one's name being on their 'blacklist'.

All media broadcasting information to the Russian populace were given material checked and approved by our government censors, which, in turn, responded to the KGB and Communist Party. Growing up, we were taught that this was for our own safety, and that listening on transistor radios to propaganda broadcasts by the BBC or Voice of America was forbidden. Western music and literature, considered 'decadent' by the censors, was also banned.

Contact with foreigners was strictly controlled and, if a penfriend were established, all letters or parcels were opened and checked by the authorities, with no guarantee that they would ever reach the addressee. Holding of any foreign currency was forbidden. Until I was 19, I had not seen a US dollar banknote.

My family was typical of law-abiding Russians, and I had been raised to respect authority. Life was simple as far as I was concerned;

if something was banned, that was alright, I could live without it. Millions of Russians lived their lives thinking that way; after all, what was the point of putting oneself in jeopardy with the authorities?

The rest of the world was selectively displayed to us on TV. There were news programmes, political reviews and travel items that gave us the impression that certain natural or historical wonders were great; but that foreign societies deserved our sympathy because they were divided into just two categories: rich and poor.

Our society was made up of 'equals' and this was the reason why other countries didn't like us and wanted to see our destruction. The thought that there could be a better life than ours seldom entered our minds. At every opportunity, the media in Russia inspired us with the idea that ours was the best and most just way of life on the planet. We were living a delusion.

My first introduction to 'foreigners', who were in fact also from the Socialist camp, came during my time as a Pioneer. All Pioneers were obliged to subscribe to *Pioneer Pravda*, a special newspaper for members of the organisation. In one edition, I found addresses of Pioneers in other Socialist countries who wanted to correspond with us.

There was a simple explanation for this: after WWII, in countries that had become Socialist, the Russian language was included in their school curriculum. The advertisements in *Pioneer Pravda* were intended to get Russian children to assist in teaching the language to their foreign counterparts.

I established connections with girls and boys in Poland, Czechoslovakia, East Germany and even Yugoslavia. In our letters we always enclosed some simple token gift, such as postage stamps, postcards, photographs of ourselves or stickers. On one occasion, I received a parcel containing lollipops from a girl in Czechoslovakia. They were beautifully made with flowers on the suckers and they tasted better than our simple Russian equivalents. I showed them to my mother and commented that we didn't have such nice sweets in our shops. But she said I should not worry because the time would come when ours would be even better.

As the years passed, more information about other countries slowly began filtering into Russia. Not even an iron curtain could keep some things out. Attitudes in the media evolved over the years too. Criticism of capitalist countries slowly became less vitriolic and, on celebratory holidays, the entire country could see concerts by groups like Abba, although they were screened late at night. The best concerts for young people were reserved for Easter Saturday night, when screening lasted all night. I'm sure it was intended to keep the youth from attending the parades around our churches that are so much a part of Russian Orthodox tradition.

We were surprised and delighted when we found imported clothing items making brief appearances in our shops. I say 'brief' because they didn't last on store shelves for very long. The quality was far better than we had been accustomed to, and the designs were more attractive. Patriotism flew out of the window when it came to dressing up and looking good.

Overseas tours became available, but the prices, as far as our salaries went, were bordering on prohibitive. Those who managed to travel returned with tales that led us to believe that life on the outside was not nearly as bad as we had been led to believe. No-one in my family had travelled outside of Russia, but my curiosity made me hanker after it.

In 1974, in my second year at university, a sign appeared on our notice board inviting staff and students to apply to tour East Germany and Czechoslovakia for 10 days at a cost of 400 roubles. The tour was scheduled to depart six months later, during our winter break.

At the time, my parents' salaries totalled 250 roubles per month, which made it very difficult for me to expect them to fund such a trip. I mulled over the question for a few days and finally plucked up the courage to ask my father if I had any chance of going. He pondered for a long time and eventually said, 'Okay, go and fill in the application form and we will try to save the money for you.'

I was elated, and pestered a university friend, Marina, to go along with me. She finally agreed; money was not a problem for her as she came from a relatively wealthy military family.

I loved that trip. It opened up new horizons for me and exploded some myths. Having at last witnessed conditions first-hand, I now realised that people in other Socialist countries, in this case East Germany and Czechoslovakia, lived a *better* life than we did in Russia. They were better paid and their lifestyles more modern. At the time, I consoled myself that it was like the Czech lollipops; as my mother had said, our standard of living would eventually overtake theirs. I was filled with patriotic optimism, but, in retrospect, I think I was 'the sucker'. My high ideals would set me up for a shock towards the end of the tour.

Overseas tours had to be prepaid in roubles, and the government laid down rules that dictated how many roubles could be taken out as a daily spending allowance. The allowance would be exchanged for the currency of the countries being visited. For countries in the Socialist camp, we could use more roubles, but illegally carrying other monies in excess of the amount permitted, or changing foreign currency without authorisation, was categorically forbidden. Anyone caught would feature in the KGB files and would be unlikely to be allowed out of Russia again. Our spending allowances limited us to buying small souvenirs only.

There was a constant shortage of goods at home, and what was cheap for foreigners in their countries was either unavailable to us or would cost too much on the black market. Because of that situation, Russian travellers would seek out and buy cheap goods that were hard to come by at home. We viewed the opportunity as compensation for the cost of a tour.

Once abroad, an extra coffee or beer was an unnecessary luxury to us, because we knew that, on getting home, the same jeans available cheaply here would cost two months' salary there. Platform shoes or elasticised boots, as worn by foreigners, were not available at all in Russia.

We found the variety of goods on offer in foreign shops mind-blowing. Tour members would find fashion items reduced on a sale and the news would spread like wildfire. In the limited time available, we would rush to the store to find bargains, diving into sale bins with little restraint. We understood that we appeared to be lacking in dignity, but were inclined to blame it on our government, which displayed little concern for the needs and desires of its people.

It was customary for us to behave in ways that proved we were beyond suspicion; so, on getting back to our hotel, we would lay out our purchases for all to see. Any individual not doing so might be suspected of having had extra money to buy luxury items beyond our common allowance. We all knew that, on returning home, the tour leader and perhaps two or three other 'fellow travellers' would submit written reports about our behaviour to the KGB. Those 'spies' also looked for unusual behaviour such as conversing or even walking with 'strangers', so we didn't dare go out shopping alone.

Seven days in East Germany provided us with the time to make interesting excursions to different towns. I was happy with the items I had purchased for my parents and myself because, priced at home in Russian roubles, the cost would have exceeded the price of the whole tour.

Our next stop was in Czechoslovakia. We spent three days seeing the cities of Karlovy Vary and Prague. I found the cities beautiful and their history fascinating. We were due to travel home by train from Prague and, on that last day, were given a final opportunity to shop for two hours.

The Czech allowance was 130 Czech crowns and, with so little, I could find nothing to buy. Marina and I, together with a few others, rushed from one shop to another, determined not to have to repatriate our allowances.

Suddenly I came across some magnificent underwear in a shop window. There were sexy bras and panties in pastel colours, trimmed with lace and beautifully cut. I had never seen anything like them before and was positively giddy with excitement. The prices in the window read –5.50, –6.00 and –7.00.

In my fervour, I ran into the shop and stood in a short queue at the cash desk. The Czech system was the same as that in Russia: customers paid for the goods, were given a receipt and then collected their purchases from the salesperson. Standing in the queue, I was transfixed by the display of underwear. How many would I buy and in which colours?

Marina appeared and asked me what I was doing. She said, 'Don't stand here – go upstairs, there are so many beautiful dresses there.'

In my hypnotised state I replied, 'No, I want to buy that underwear.'

The woman in front of me opened her purse and took out money that was quite unfamiliar to me. It wasn't roubles, it wasn't crowns, nor was it marks. I was thunderstruck. At that moment, I realised the prices were in US dollars. The pictures in my mind of myself in that refined and elegant underwear evaporated instantly. The money in my hand would not have been enough to buy the clasp on one of the bras.

The realisation hit me like an express train. There I was, a hardworking, disciplined Soviet citizen, not permitted to carry US dollars, limited by my government in my capacity to spend my own money. Why should I be forced to buy rubbish in our shops? Why could I not be a normal person, like the woman in front of me, who could buy with dollars? The answer came to me in a flash. It was because I came from the USSR where everything desirable was 'RESTRICTED'.

I concluded that, through no fault of my own, I was a second-class citizen of the world, subject to inescapable indignities and injustices thrust upon me by my own government. The shock of arriving at that conclusion was too much for me. I suddenly found the atmosphere in the shop claustrophobic and oppressive. Dashing outside, I gulped for air.

Marina found me, took my arm and tried to shepherd me back to see the dresses on the upper floor.

'What is the point, Marina? They're not for us,' I said dejectedly, as I wriggled free and turned in the direction of our hotel.

I was terribly disappointed and embittered by the experience. It had ruined what had otherwise seemed a good tour. For perhaps the first time, I was disillusioned with our Soviet life, but kept the fact to myself for fear of being listed in a KGB file.

On returning home, I found everything to be grey: the streets, the buildings and the people appeared lacklustre. But life slowly returned to normal and I was able to fit back into my old routine. One of the advantages of youth is that bad memories are not kept for long, so the unfortunate Prague underwear experience faded.

Some four years later I was able to travel again. In 1978, I went on tour to West Germany. By that time, many changes had taken place, both in my life and in Russia. I was 23, married and employed as a civil engineer.

Arrangements had been made by the Russian government to adopt 'twin cities' in Socialist countries, with the aim of generating reciprocal tourism. Cities were adopted in capitalist countries too, but they were called 'partner cities'. Osnabruck, West Germany had been designated Kalinin's 'partner city' and a variety of 'exchanges' were taking place. Tour groups, trade delegations and administrative officials visited each other often.

Tour groups to Kalinin could stop at motels specially built for them outside the town, where the KGB would watch them constantly. There was a *Beriuzka* shop at the motel, which sold goods for foreign currency only. Russians wishing to shop there had to provide proof of their right to hold foreign money. It was obviously the same type of shop in which I had seen the underwear in Prague in 1974. By that time I had learned to accept that there were shops for 'them' and others for 'us'.

In 1976, Eugene had been to Osnabruck as a tourist. Later, after we married, he suggested I go on the same tour because it was interesting and reasonably priced.

The group I joined was made up of young *Komsomol* members and the leader was the second secretary of the provincial *Komsomol* committee. In order to qualify for the tour, we had to undergo numerous interviews that were far more investigative than those I had undergone in order to travel four years earlier.

We had to submit character references from our places of employment, confirming our trustworthiness and reliability. Three signatures were required on the document asserting that we had been politically educated to the highest ideals of Communism, one from our office director, another from the secretary of the Communist organisations within our offices, and a third from the chairman of the Office Workers' Union. Then there were multiple KGB forms to be completed, attesting to such things as our not having convicted criminals in our families or anyone who had been in an enemy prisoner-of-war camp. If we had any friends or relatives in foreign countries, we had to list them too.

With our sheaves of forms, we were interviewed by a special commission in the city Communist Party committee, which comprised WWII veterans, long-serving members of the Communist Party and other dignitaries. They asked us to relate our biographies, questioned us on our political opinions, both inside and outside Russia, and tested our general knowledge of Communism, in order to be assured of our patriotism. I spent hours before that interview reading up on everything I thought might be of assistance.

Our next interview was with another special commission, this time of the all-powerful provincial Communist Party committee. That was even more frightening and required a lot more reading of subjects likely to arise.

From all the applicants, 30 of the most 'politically suitable' were selected. I was lucky enough to be one of them. The tour included a free night in Moscow, to ensure that we received a compulsory lecture on appropriate Communist behaviour in an 'enemy country'. Instructions were delivered in very serious vein and related to situations in which we might unexpectedly find ourselves. Examples were given of previous experiences and what we should be wary of, such as certain types of provocation, which were to be avoided at all costs.

We were told how to answer provocative questions such as 'Why are there no millionaires in your country?'

The correct reply was, 'We have millionaires, *kolkhoz*-millionaires and plant-millionaires.'

If the question, 'Why are you not allowed your own businesses?' were asked, the answer had to be, 'Yes, we are allowed to have our own businesses. Private people (anyone not employed by government) sell flowers at our flea markets.'

We had to be accompanied by other tour members at all times and being alone for even a short time was not permitted. The group leader was the responsible person and had to be obeyed without question. Then we were told outright that the group leader and three other tour party members had been delegated the responsibility of submitting written reports on our behaviour as soon as we returned.

In retrospect, it is clear that the authorities had employed all means at their disposal to intimidate us to conform, but at that time I thought the instructions were for our own protection, which was the spin they put on the process.

Having listened to the lectures, I was really scared to travel. My 10 days in West Germany were spent continually looking over my shoulder, expecting to be abducted for forced conversion to a 'false capitalistic faith' and then 'used' against my own country. The fact was that nobody interfered or even went out of their way to speak with us, but we were not nervous without reason.

We knew that if a suspicious report were submitted about our behaviour, it could have a detrimental effect not only on our lives, but also on those of our relatives and friends, who might also find themselves included on the KGB's blacklist. If we tried to stay in West Germany, claiming political refugee status, they would most definitely be on the blacklist.

There were other people likely to be punished too: the signatories to the documents attesting to our suitability for the tour. Tour group leaders would be in serious trouble and at risk of losing their jobs. Although they didn't pay for their tour and had a bigger foreign currency allowance, nobody really wanted the job of tour leader; it was too risky.

Some moments of the tour were particularly interesting or amusing. One day we gathered in the foyer of our hotel and were told that, according to our itinerary and in the spirit of 'partner cities', we were scheduled to meet young West Germans for discussions, set to last an hour. A party of unknowns eventually arrived and, with an interpreter on each side, we sat looking at each other, wondering what to say.

One of them suggested we discuss the origin of the human race. We didn't understand the point of that discussion because, to us, it was common knowledge that the human race had evolved from apes. Darwin had made the case for evolution and there were no possible doubts about it.

They asked why Darwin should be believed and said there were many other theories on how man had originated. They suggested that the origin of man may, in fact, lie somewhere else entirely; for example, we may well have come to Earth from another planet.

That came as a complete surprise to us and we sat gaping at them in incomprehension. I realised later that Darwin's theory had been particularly suitable for Communist ideology, suggesting that man had evolved from the ape through work. Man had evolved precisely because the ape had been required to get up off all fours to reach higher for food. According to Communist theory, work had created man and only ongoing work would continue that process of evolution.

With that, discussions collapsed. We were not prepared to ask their opinion on other subjects as our tour leader or his anonymous 'fellow travellers' might see it as expressing too much interest in capitalist views and ideas.

Eugene had been on the same tour two years earlier and his tour leader had been quite liberal. A number of people had decided to see an erotic movie that, of course, was forbidden in the Soviet Union. Before I left, he had suggested that, if the opportunity arose, I should go along because it could be the only chance I'd ever get. Naturally, when something is banned or forbidden, interest in it is heightened. In any case, I was curious to be able to keep up with my husband.

I plucked up the courage to ask our tour leader if it might be possible to go to such a movie, because I thought he would probably go anyway with a few selected members of our group, without making it known to the rest of the tour. In any case, I knew the man reasonably well because he was a colleague of Eugene's and, as families, we had met on social occasions.

He took the question badly, not because this was a generally taboo activity, but rather because he thought I was testing his resolve as a Communist.

His response was unexpectedly harsh: 'Why do you want to see erotic movies and why are you pushing me to agree?' he asked.

I was stunned by the severe way in which he spoke and stammered, 'Eugene advised me to go, to broaden my general knowledge.'

'Isn't your general knowledge as a Soviet woman broad enough?' he shot back.

'Yes it is, but I've been told that the capitalists are degenerate and I want to see how they are bringing about their own demise,' I said pathetically, as if I was being questioned by the KGB.

He ended the discussion: 'None of us will see an erotic movie and I advise you not to try.'

I realised, with regret, that he had taken me as a provocateur and thought I might report him if he acquiesced. On reflection, I realised that he had been the wrong person to approach on such a subject. As a brainwashed young Communist, he was clearly terrified of making a mistake that could cost him future promotion.

His cowardice and lack of vision were to create further embarrassment for us all in Hamburg. Included in our itinerary was an excursion to the Rieperbahn. After dinner we were joined by a small group of West Germans who were to act as guides. We boarded our tour bus and, on arrival in the area, the driver parked in a vacant lot at the entrance to a pedestrian walkway.

The drive had taken us past windows that revealed to our tour leader what we were about to see at closer range. He suddenly announced that the walking tour was for men only and all women were to remain seated in the bus. The women went crazy. We had paid the same as the men for the complete tour, and the Rieperbahn excursion had been arranged with the knowledge of the authorities in Russia, so we had every right to go along with the men. He was adamant and nothing we said could persuade him to change his mind. As far as he was concerned, there was nothing for us to see there and, in any event, he thought the area 'dangerous for women'.

Pandemonium broke out on the bus. The Russian males offered to look after us and the German guides, who had girls with them, tried to convince our tour leader that the area was in fact safe and no harm would come to us.

I elbowed my way to the front of the bus and began shouting at him. 'Let us go. We are here for the first and maybe last time in our lives. Everything that we have seen in West Germany has been great, but we were told that capitalist life is so tough that women are forced to sell themselves on the streets to survive. Please, allow us to confirm that we are privileged to live in Russia and will never have to do that.'

He would not bend. 'Comrade Morozova, you and all women will stay on this bus and that's final,' he shouted.

'Okay comrade tour guide,' one of the women said, 'but you stay with us.'

His display of sanctimony had not fooled us for a second. It was obvious that he couldn't wait to see what the Rieperbahn had to offer, but he persisted with the line that he was going along only because it was his duty. The argument had taken almost an hour; it had got us nowhere, and resulted in 15 unhappy young women sitting in an open bus without security in an unlit parking area on the periphery of that popular tourist attraction.

We were exasperated by this injustice. We all, in turn, expressed dissatisfaction with our tour leader. We were not even concerned that someone might be recording our words. One of the girls suggested that we might go it alone, but the majority opinion was that we had been told to obey our tour leader and to deviate might not serve our long-term interests.

Having expressed my anger, I sat quietly trying to figure out what I could do to achieve a modicum of revenge. After another couple of hours, a few of our male tour members returned, saying they were concerned about us sitting on the bus without security of any kind. We asked them what they had seen and they said 'women' on the street and, scantily clothed, in windows – beautiful, but so expensive. Our foreign exchange allowance, they told us, was not even enough to raise a petticoat.

Everyone drifted back in batches, with the tour leader last. He found the women uncharacteristically silent. We wanted nothing further to do with him. His overcautious approach, engineered to protect his own rear end, had spoiled what for us would have been a fun, eye-opening evening.

The following day, when I had a chance to speak alone with him, I told the man, in a very firm tone, that he had been wrong the previous night.

'You are fully responsible for our security in West Germany,' I said. 'But you left 15 young women in an open bus, while you went off to satisfy your lecherous nature. Do you know that, last night, two strange men came to our bus on motorcycles? They were wearing leathers and had metal everywhere, maybe even guns. We were scared and thought they might do something bad with us. Had something happened while you were busy ogling prostitutes, at the very least I would have had to tell my husband, friends and acquaintances, because your behaviour as our leader was irresponsible.'

With great satisfaction I watched him blush and squirm with embarrassment. It was clear that he was thinking about what effect this could have on his future career. Personally, I was satisfied that I had been able to scare him a little in revenge for the night before. He would be unlikely to sleep well for a couple of nights, pondering his possible fate.

I had not lied about the motorcyclists. They were skinheads, not seen in the Soviet Union, but while we were really apprehensive about their intentions, they'd paid no attention to us, just parked their bikes and walked off.

On our last day in Germany, the tour leader told me he had bought two tee shirts that had turned out to be too small for him. He wanted to know if I'd like to buy them for Eugene, who was a size smaller. Since I had spent my allowance in German marks, I asked if he would accept payment at home in roubles. He agreed – but later refused to do the deal. I asked Eugene why. He explained that, to buy something overseas, bring it back to Russia and sell it to someone else, was classed as 'speculation'. It was specifically forbidden by the authorities and would be severely punished if perpetrated by a member of the Party. Of course, he was a 'very good member' of the Communist Party.

Something else on the tour had set me thinking about our situation in Russia. One of our West German guides had been a young, unmarried woman of 19 – a qualified secretary. She drove her own car to our hotel whenever she had to meet us. In conversation with her, I learned that she had her own flat, purchased with a mortgage granted by a bank, and her second-hand car had been bought on credit from a finance company. That made me think about our situation back in the Soviet Union.

At the time, I was in my third year of marriage, a qualified engineer, as was Eugene, with both of us, by Russian standards, in reasonably well paid jobs. Collectively, we earned 270 roubles per month, but it was insufficient to rent our own flat and buy a second-hand car. At that time, the cheapest used car cost around 3 000 roubles and a new Zhiguly or Mosckvich, 5 000 to 8 000 roubles. For us, that was huge money.

How was it that a 19-year-old, single girl could own her flat and drive her own car? How did the West German banks give her credit? We had better jobs than her, so why were we not able to enjoy equivalent luxuries? Why was it that, in Russia, the banks did not provide these facilities to private citizens? I was coming to the conclusion that our lives were not the best in the world, as constantly claimed by our government. I had seen the proof and would not be inclined to believe their propaganda in future. I had to force myself to be calm and put doubts away in the back of my mind.

The tour finished and everyone returned home without any attempted defections. I suppose, in that sense, it could have been classified as 'successful'. I had enjoyed it and it had left me with much to think about, although I never knew what the tour leader's report about me to the KGB contained, and there was no way that I could find out if I would be allowed out of the country again.

When friends asked me about the trip, I decided it best to answer that I hadn't found a great deal of difference architecturally between East and West Germany, but that many roads and buildings in the West were signposted 'PRIVATE'. When they heard that, they invariably shook their heads and said, 'That's bad, because everything should be common and belong to the people.'

A month after our tour I received, quite unexpectedly, a letter from an unknown woman in Osnabruck. It was quite cheerful and asked if I was interested in establishing a pen friendship. I searched my memory, trying to establish how she had my name and address. We had all been warned not to divulge such information to foreigners and I was sure that I hadn't done so. I was also convinced that the letter must have passed through KGB hands before reaching me, and the thought filled me with dread. It was probably the start of an effort to recruit me for some foreign cause, or a test of my loyalty by the KGB. If I answered it, they would definitely open a file on me, so I deemed it prudent to ignore the letter. We had been brainwashed into regarding with suspicion any contact made by foreigners, convinced that they would turn us to their evil ends, against our beloved motherland.

In 1978, had it been suggested that Communist Russia would change dramatically within the next seven or eight years, we would certainly not have given it any credence. But Gorbachev announced *perestroika* in 1985 and the rules of the old game collapsed.

Suddenly we could travel to any destination in the world, if we could afford it. Nobody need vouch for us; there were no signatures needed from Party officials, no reams of forms and no interviews necessary. The only prerequisites were visas and tickets, just as would be needed in any civilised country.

It prompted an about-face by countries that had previously been happy to consider providing succour to emigrants (also known as 'political refugees'). The numbers wishing to leave Russia in order to find a better life were then so great, that other countries closed their doors to all but a few.

17

Economic woes

A T THE TIME OF MY MARRIAGE TO EUGENE IN 1976, WE MOVED into the flat of my parents-in-law. My mother-in-law, Larissa, was then 47 years old, an imposing and attractive woman. She worked as head in the copy bureau of a building project institute in Kalinin, and had acquired their two-roomed flat after 20 years of loyal service.

My father-in-law, Yuri, was 45. A retired air force colonel, he had been a test pilot, grounded three years earlier because of a chronic heart condition. His pension was equal to two normal monthly salaries, and, at the time of my marriage, he did not work. He spent his days sitting at home doing crossword puzzles or talking with friends. The inactivity was bad for his heart and had resulted in his putting on weight, which made him appear much older than his actual age.

I had grown up in a naturally democratic family, in which Father was our president, Mother our vice-president and Granny Katerina our prime minister. We children were members of parliament with full rights to voice our opinions. As the youngest member, I had not felt discriminated against or had my dignity infringed upon. I was always given encouragement in my endeavours and felt secure, loved and respected.

My new family was a full dictatorship. Mother-in-law was the self-appointed dictator-for-life. Eugene was her shadow minister and dictator-in-waiting, while Father-in-law represented the voiceless population. For his intelligence, loyalty and bravery, the Russian defence force may have seen fit to bestow the rank of colonel on him, but in the home brigade he was lower than a private, without any hope of promotion.

One of my mother-in-law's characteristics was a peculiar ability to create an argument whenever or wherever she saw fit. Her colleagues at work, including the director of the institute, sprang to attention when she appeared, just as privates were expected to do on seeing their commanding officer. At home, she regularly issued standing orders to remind everyone exactly who was boss.

When I first arrived among them, Mother-in-law could not figure out exactly where I fitted into the pecking order; although I was definitely below her, of course. Whenever there was a family argument, I would stay out of it, and I tried never to give her cause to argue with me. I maintained a calm, impenetrable aura that protected me from criticism, but had the effect of infuriating her.

I got into the habit of calling her 'Mum', although it was difficult initially. Before moving in with them I had discussed the subject with my grandmother, and she told me to try to do that from the beginning, for the sake of good relations. She said I should close my eyes the first time and thereafter it would be easier. That's exactly what I had done.

About a year later, Mother-in-law started some facile argument in which she tried to involve me, but I kept my cool and didn't rise to the bait.

Finally she screamed, 'And don't call me "Mum". I'm not your mother.'

I was furious and said, 'It was difficult to call you "Mum" in the beginning, and now I'm not going to change just because you want me to.'

Her reaction was immediate and unexpected. She began to laugh. It became a favourite story of hers and was related to all her friends. For some reason she considered it a compliment that I refused to call her anything but 'Mum'.

After living in the flat with my parents-in-law for three years, we had a lucky break. My father-in-law had originally come from Moscow and, after a few years of waiting in line, he was issued a two-roomed flat in a large, modern 16-floor block at Ostankino, a suburb of Moscow that is also home to the main Russian television broadcasting station. This was in line with a custom whereby military people were allowed, on retirement, to return to the city or town from where they had originally come, and were given flats there.

Eugene and I took over their flat in Kalinin, together with items of 20-year-old furniture, and cutlery and crockery that my mother-in-law decided she didn't need in her new flat. We used the furniture for another 18 years, with the exception of a fold-out double bed that was replaced after 13 years. Inheriting all this furniture saved us a lot of money, for which we were extremely grateful.

My relationship with my mother-in-law, traditionally fraught, became easier once they had moved out and settled in Moscow. When food was scarce, as was often the case, we tried to help each other. There were times they sent us a case of meat or fish cans that were obtainable only in Moscow, and I would give them fresh vegetables and fruit from our *dacha*.

After marrying, I became a typical Russian wife. I worked eight hours a day, five days a week, as did my husband. When I left the office, I had to rush home and, on the way, scavenge around the shops to buy food. At home I had to cook, clean, wash and iron, which didn't leave much time for relaxation. Russian wives did not expect help at home from their husbands. Perhaps this was rooted in historical circumstances. So many men had died in wars or returned home as invalids, that women took it upon themselves to do all the work they could cope with.

Towards the end of Brezhnev's 'time of stagnation', we noticed the deterioration of food items in shops, from both a quality and a quantity point of view. The word 'deficit', frequently heard, meant that a particular everyday item had disappeared from store shelves and could probably only be obtained through the use of *blat*. That gave rise to new expressions, such as 'get' replacing the word 'buy'. Buying was easy, but getting was another story. 'Getting' meant standing in queues for hours on end or using *blat*, if you were in a position to offer it.

Normal foods like salami, coffee, chocolate, good cheese or

bacon gradually ran short and then disappeared altogether. Inferior quality items that we considered inedible replaced them. Nobody wanted to buy these items, but the food industry continued to produce them, regardless of consumers' preferences.

Around 1980, the authorities found a way to force us to buy these products, and a new meaning was given to the Russian word *nagruzka*, a slang expression adopted by the people. Under normal circumstances, the true meaning of the word is 'load' (as in that which is carried), but in this case it meant that we couldn't buy what we wanted without having to take some poor quality products as well. If we wanted to buy a tin of good quality instant coffee, we had to take a can of locally produced, unpalatable chicory along with it. They were packaged together and fully priced; what we did with the chicory was of no concern to the authorities. So foods were generally categorised by the people as either 'deficit' or *nagruzka*.

We got used to having to buy, for instance, two kilograms of fresh meat, which would consist of a kilogram of reasonable meat that was 'deficit' and a kilogram of bones that were *nagruzka*. A half-kilogram packet of Italian pasta could not be bought without two kilograms of local, tarmac-coloured macaroni that our dog would not even eat in his soup.

The idea worked so successfully, as far as the government was concerned, that it wasn't long before we could not buy things like clothes or bed linen without being forced to pay for some unwanted rubbish too. The quantity of available goods regressed to the point where store shelves were practically empty. The further one lived from Moscow, the worse the situation became until, to all intents and purposes, Moscow was the only place to buy anything. Muscovites were always better off because the government didn't want foreign tourists to be exposed to *nagruzka*.

By 1985, large numbers of people from all parts of European Russia were travelling to Moscow to obtain food. It was the only city in all of western Russia where a decent choice of food was available. In order to get there, people took leave or used public holidays and long weekends. Sometimes they had to sleep at

Moscow railway stations because they could not afford hotels. They stood for hours in one long queue after another to fill their shopping bags, or even suitcases. Transport there was expensive, and standing in long queues all day without sustenance or convenient toilet facilities was hardly a pleasure, but they didn't have any choice if their families were to survive.

Big production plants often had company buses, and staff, with the consent of their bosses, used them over weekends to travel to Moscow. The trains were always packed with travellers to and from the capital and often, on the return journey, I recall having to stand for three-and-a-half hours holding two shopping bags weighing about 25 kilograms. More often than not, it was impossible to find a place even to put my bags down. Conversation flourished on the crowded trains, from swearing and cursing the government to jokes about the public transport system out of Moscow. Every train or bus smelled of smoked sausage and bacon, just like a meat-processing factory.

What we couldn't understand was what was happening to the food products that had been produced in our own cities for decades? We had huge production and processing plants for meat, cheese, biscuits and sweets, but it was anyone's guess as to where the end products were sold. Perhaps the control and supply system had collapsed, or all of the production was being shipped to Moscow; nobody was able to tell us.

Muscovites began to hate the literally millions of outsiders descending daily on their city, and dubbed them 'baggers'. As shops opened in the mornings, locust-like hordes from out of town invaded, snapping up the stock, much to the chagrin of locals who considered it their privilege to have the run of the city.

Outsiders reciprocated the bad feelings and grew to hate the Muscovites too, because they felt just as entitled to shop in Moscow as were the locals. As far as we were concerned, we worked the same hours as they did for the good of our wonderful Soviet Union, and were entitled to buy food just the same as they were. What was more, for all we knew, the products may well have been produced by us in our very own city.

The Moscow administration tried to close the city to baggers, and shops stopped opening at weekends, but that didn't last for long because the mood of the people began to be felt. Civil disturbance and riots were on the cards and the government did not relish the idea of facing them, so they came up with a marvellous 'new' idea: ration cards for food and consumer goods.

Every citizen over the age of 16 had to have an internal passport that listed their domicile. Addresses within particular areas were allocated to house management offices that kept up-to-date lists of persons living at all addresses in their territory. Those offices were given the responsibility of issuing and controlling vouchers, without which little of any consequence could be purchased.

Each family member was entitled to the same set of vouchers, regardless of age, but because my family consisted of just two, we had the following combined monthly entitlement: two kilograms of sugar and flour or pasta or rice, two kilograms of porridge, one litre of vegetable oil, two bottles of vodka, two blocks of bath soap, two blocks of kitchen soap and two kilograms of washing powder. However, this could vary depending on what was or was not available.

At one stage, apparently to address a shortage, they decided to issue washing powder vouchers of two kilograms only, for three months. Vouchers were dated for use and a family representative had personally to take their internal passport to the office to sign a receipt for them.

On one occasion, I went to the office to collect vouchers for my three-months' supply of washing powder and was told that I had already had my ration. The clerk said someone from my family had already signed for and taken it. I knew that Eugene would certainly not have gone there to collect our washing powder, so I asked to see the signature. I didn't recognise the scribble at all. The mix-up was quite serious because we could not be without washing powder for three months.

Trying to persuade the clerk that somebody had purloined our washing powder was futile. I realised that I would get nowhere by getting excited, so asked if I could see the list of signatories for our block of flats.

On closer examination, I discovered that an old, half-blind neighbour had signed in the wrong place. The only course of action open to me was to pay her a visit, explain that she had made a mistake and get her to go back to the office to sign for her vouchers to hand over to me, which thankfully she duly did.

It is almost inconceivable how much I came to hate living in such degrading circumstances. We lived with the voucher system for about three years, until the government abruptly decided to cancel it. However, the situation did not improve.

The older generation may have understood the reason for food shortages. They had suffered wars and a Revolution, and had been told that suffering was necessary to build Socialism. But my generation was supposed to be living in an already completely Socialist society.

Khrushchev had promised that my age group would live in a Communist utopia by 1980 and Brezhnev continued the myth. What we could not understand was that, although we lived in relatively peaceful times with all manufacturing facilities operating normally, as far as we knew, our shops were empty and unable to cater for the people (of whom there were approximately 280 million in the USSR).

Everyone tried to find as much food as possible, even if it meant storing it for a year. There was no spare cash; it was kept aside in case the opportunity to buy food arose unexpectedly. People began working harder at their *dachas* and trying to find food such as mushrooms and berries in the forests, while membership of hunting and fishing clubs increased dramatically.

City dwellers began raising poultry on their balconies and those working *dachas* started, of necessity, to use them as small livestock farms, raising chickens, rabbits and even goats. The most sought-after domestic item was a deep-freeze cabinet. Rationing no longer existed, so anyone lucky enough to find a supply of butter, for example, would buy as much as they could afford or whatever their storage space permitted.

Nobody cared if essential items, like bags of sugar, had 'fallen off the back of a truck', or if the trader was unknown to them, claiming to have come from far off, but looking as if he'd just left prison. Everyone bought what they could without asking too many questions.

By that time, Eugene and I were earning relatively good salaries and our two-roomed flat became a storage warehouse. Even in the wardrobes we had 50 kilogram bags of porridge, flour and sugar, and boxes of pasta. Under the sofa were cases of vodka and brandy that were as good as cash, if not better. Our cupboards were full of tins of meat, fish, condensed milk, and bottled fruits and vegetables from our *dacha*.

We had installed more shelves in our bathroom and toilet to hold quantities of soaps, toothpaste, toilet paper and cleaning materials. It may seem crazy, but many of those products might only become available in stores once a year, at best, and everybody was determined not to run out. There were times when we swapped items with other people, but exchanging goods was not very popular because we were never sure when the goods we gave away in the swap would next become available in the shops.

Foreign visitors in Kalinin at that time would have noticed that store shelves were nearly empty, but had they been invited into a Russian home they would have found a variety of foods and vodka on the table. It is part of Russian custom to put whatever food there is in the home on the table for guests.

In spite of this, we became accustomed to being told, when visiting friends, 'Sorry folks, we have only boiled potatoes and sour cabbage today.' On another occasion, we might be offered steaks, vegetables and other delicacies – it all depended on what was available at the time.

Life continued, despite the shortages. Eugene and I were young, so were our friends and our main leisure activity revolved around socialising in each other's homes and enjoying whatever was available to eat and drink. But conversation invariably turned to our circumstances. Who was responsible for our miserable lifestyles? What did the future hold for us?

The economic crisis, unemployment, poverty and starvation

were impacting on the suffering populace, creating new occupations in Russia such as street trading, prostitution and even hired killing. As their only means of survival, thousands of people were becoming street traders, under the old rules condemned as 'speculators'. They travelled to Europe, Turkey, the Middle East and Thailand, buying cheap goods to sell on the streets of Moscow and other cities and towns. Reminding them of the old rules was likely to provoke a very bitter reaction.

The younger generation was badly affected, too, and the daughters of some of the proudest Soviet mothers, unable to find ways of earning a living, were forced to turn to prostitution. Others tried to find foreign husbands via the Internet as a means of survival.

Some young people considered their only hope of survival to lie in criminal pursuits and turned to racketeering and robbery. After two years of compulsory military service, often in lamentable conditions in places like Afghanistan or Chechnya, some returning soldiers appeared to know nothing other than how to kill, and sold that 'skill' to anyone prepared to pay.

18

My career

AFTER UNIVERSITY I BEGAN WORK AT KALININSPETZSTROY, A building project organisation that was responsible for drawing plans, quantity surveying and prefabrication required for the building of reservoirs and sewage purification plants for cities, towns and large production plants.

At the time, much emphasis was placed on creating a cleaner environment – an imperative that had been lacking in the past. I worked at the head office as a civil engineer and was happy to feel that, through my occupation, I was contributing to the improvement.

I used topographical maps and geological surveys of large areas to calculate the sequence of events necessary for the construction of upcoming projects. For example, if we had to construct a reservoir in some hilly area, I had to determine where the roads should go, where the storage facilities would best be located, calculate details of all machinery needed, how many cubic metres of earth would have to be removed and where it could be dumped, what type of retention wall was necessary and the reinforcing needed to achieve it. If surveys indicated the existence of underground water of any kind, I had to determine the technology necessary to overcome that particular problem.

It was an exciting occupation as far as I was concerned, because each project was different and presented a new challenge. The creativity was stimulating and the independence to make my own decisions very satisfying.

At 120 roubles, my starting salary was the lowest for engineers. But compared with other occupations it was quite good. Men from the age of 18, married or not, and women from the date of marriage, had to pay 'childless tax' until they produced a child. After paying that, plus normal tax, Trade Union and *Komsomol* dues, I took home the sum of 101 roubles. Our two-roomed 40 square metre flat cost 15 roubles per month (once my parents-in-law had moved out), which left 86 roubles to live on for the next 30 days. That meant 2.86 roubles per day, which was just sufficient for food, transport and a few necessary odds and ends, such as cleaning materials. This is what it would have cost a qualified engineer, earning the average salary of 120 roubles, to live alone in a typical two-roomed flat. Had I been single, or not sharing a flat with my husband and in-laws, there would have been no possibility of buying anything such as furniture, a refrigerator, or an essential winter coat.

Eugene's monthly salary was 150 roubles. After taxes and paying for his food, we were able to put away a little for our annual holiday. Compared to other young couples, we were well off, especially when his parents moved to Moscow, leaving us with a fully furnished, two-roomed flat.

My salary as an engineer had a ceiling of 180 roubles, but reaching that lofty height would take a minimum of 10 years and was not necessarily achievable, unless I was promoted to head of department in a big organisation.

Two years later I was given a 10-rouble increase. I was happy in the job and would have remained so were it not for one problem: *kolkhoz* duty. I accepted this duty as necessary, but it was a threat to my marriage if it meant spending many consecutive nights away from home. I was obliged to continue in my current job for a total of three years, in order to repay my university education. That deadline was fast approaching, and I hoped at that point to resign and look for another job that, above all, would allow me to escape *kolkhoz* duty.

I became obsessed about finding such a position, but all organisations in Kalinin were compelled to send staff on *kolkhoz* duty. There was no point in leaving Kalininspetzstroy for another organisation that would send me anyway.

I was close to abandoning hope when an answer to my problem came in the most unexpected way – while walking the dog that we had recently acquired. I had taken him on a leash to a popular dog-walking area, where I met and struck up a conversation with someone else walking their dog. The subject of *kolkhoz* duty arose and I complained bitterly about having to participate.

She said, 'Our staff never does *kolkhoz* duty.'

I could not believe what I had heard, and asked her where she worked and what she did. She was also a civil engineer, employed as a group manager in a military project detachment. Their office of 40 people fell under a huge military building organisation, with its head office in Moscow. But the provincial Communist Party committee, which organised *kolkhoz* duty in the province, was unaware of the existence of the detachment. The old wooden building they occupied, in the centre of town, did not have any signboards denoting their presence and the detachment was not registered in Kalinin.

She said I might be able to get a job there, but employees seldom left, so it wouldn't be easy. How jealous I was of those 40 people never having to report for loathsome *kolkhoz* duties! I undertook to do everything I could to get a job there.

A few weeks later, I decided to find the office and eventually arrived at the unpainted wooden building. I asked to see the boss and enquired about employment. He was a lieutenant colonel and reacted in a brusque, military manner.

He gave me the shortest possible answer, 'No.'

I left the building feeling deflated and depressed at the thought of having to stay at Kalininspetzstroy.

But I wasn't going to give up that easily and, three weeks later, returned to knock on their door again. This time I was greeted by a cheerful civilian and asked to see the lieutenant colonel. The civilian said that the lieutenant colonel had been transferred to the Far East. I took a chance and told him that the departed military man had promised me a job.

'Well,' said the man, 'If he promised, I suppose we'll have to find one for you.'

As soon as my three-year obligatory stay at Kalininspetzstroy was up, I went directly to my new office, without taking even a day's break. My new job involved building projects for the residents of military bases scattered around Russia. The woman I'd met while walking the dog turned out to be the manager of the group to which I was assigned. Delighted to be there, I was happy to continue working for the same salary.

My new job differed from the old in that I now specialised in central heating systems, ventilation and air conditioning. I tried to learn fast and was promoted after a couple of years to senior engineer. Without the stress of *kolkhoz* duty hanging over me, I became more relaxed, but the mere sight of people dressed for such duty brought back horrid memories of those days of drudgery. Of 700 000 people in our town, just 40 lucky individuals were exempt. Being one of them was a real triumph.

The seven years I was employed there were the happiest of my career. I enjoyed the job, liked my colleagues, especially our group manager, and the atmosphere was more akin to being part of a family than being in a working environment.

In 1982, while there, I became a member of the Communist Party. Working in a military, rather than a civil organisation, provided an easier opportunity to join, so it seemed like a good time to make the move.

However, after 10 years of being employed and 11 married, I began feeling that I had to achieve advancement in my field. My relationship with Eugene had matured and stabilised, and I was no longer that concerned about having to do *kolkhoz* duty which, now that I was 32, allowed me exemption from overnight stays and long periods of duty; although, of course, I would have preferred to remain exempt.

What was making me restless was the fact that I could not get further in the organisation until my group manager retired, and she still had many years to go. I had reached the top level as senior engineer, with a monthly salary of 165 roubles, and felt that I could handle something bigger or more challenging. Broadening my experience would not be possible if I remained in that position and

I was becoming frustrated through lack of opportunity. I resigned with a heavy heart.

Finding another job proved not to be a problem, and I soon started with a big agricultural building project organisation as a group manager in the central heating and ventilation department. My starting salary, at 180 roubles, was the maximum available to project engineers. Exactly as I'd calculated at the start of my career, it had taken me 10 years to rise to that level.

My new job involved designing heating and ventilation systems for specific buildings used in agricultural applications such as crop storage facilities, poultry and pig farms, cow sheds, garages for repairing implements and machinery; and houses, clinics, clubs, schools, shops and administration buildings for *kolkhozes*.

In the beginning I found the situation awkward, because I had been thrust in as a manager without having had experience in agricultural projects. Seven women, all civil engineers of different ages, worked under me, four of whom had young children who often kept them at home when they were sick. The organisational structure was such that those who were highest paid were given the most difficult projects and, because I was the highest earner, I was given them. In addition, I had the responsibility of overseeing the work of those under me.

Work was piled onto my department and, had I worked for eight hours a day, without standing up from my desk, I don't think it would have been possible to get through it all. We always had deadlines to meet and, when one of my people, for whatever reason, did not come to work, her job had to be taken on by the rest of us and completed by due date. It put enormous pressure on me and I began having to work much longer hours than I had anticipated. At weekends I found myself at home, trying to finish projects that I knew were fast approaching deadline.

I approached Mondays with a degree of trepidation, knowing that staff were often absent because of illness in the family. One of the more humane USSR laws allowed mothers with children who were proven to be sick to stay at home on full pay for as long as the doctor prescribed. I had no criticism of that law, but the repercussions were considerable for those at work. When two or three mothers were absent simultaneously, which occurred all too frequently, it caused a catastrophe for the rest of us. Unplanned consequences of this law were to stimulate the birth rate while placing increasing pressure on childless colleagues, who were obliged to do more work with no added incentive.

At 32 I felt that I was at the very pinnacle of life. I was bursting with energy, felt close to the top of my professional ability, and wanted very much to contribute through greater input, but my enthusiasm was backfiring on me. Weekends and evenings were spent working and, gradually, I became tired and disillusioned, wondering why I was obliged to work like that and how long it would continue.

I had been a member of the Communist Party for more than five years and wanted to believe that the Party would ultimately resolve the existing problems and everything would turn out fine. However, I was having nagging doubts about the likelihood of this happening.

Over the years of Soviet power, specific economic mechanisms had been put in place throughout Russia. For decades, factories had produced the same products and delivered them to the same distribution networks, regardless of whether there was a market for them or not, and with no cognisance of the opinions of consumers. The entire population seemed to work in robotic fashion and to collect their salaries without questioning the worth of their labours, or showing concern for the quality of the products they made.

Nobody ever appeared to question whether a product was really required, or to consider whether it would have been prudent to close certain factories and save the costs of worthless production. What was produced was expected to be bought by the populace, regardless of whether they liked it or not. The government's policy was to run a Socialist economy, which meant keeping everyone employed.

Production reports to the Communist Party congresses were based on, and given recognition for, quantities produced, not quality. There was a captive market that certainly wasn't free. There must have been some intelligent people who wanted to improve our lives, but the risks of being called an 'Enemy of the State' in Stalin's time, or later a 'dissident', were all too real.

Examples of the lack of concern for consumers could be found everywhere, and my Agricultural Building Project Institute was no exception. After WWII, some clever individuals had seen the need for such an institution to further the 'organised supply' of essential buildings for rural collective farming that had been devastated during the conflict. Included in the organisation were: the project institute, employing 400 people; a precast concrete plant producing items according to the details provided by the project engineers at the institute and employing 1 500 people; and a construction team of 1 000 to build the projects designed and overseen by the engineers. The three teams of people had worked satisfyingly well together, providing buildings for the collectives.

Project engineers also had to design houses and flats, but within strict parameters, in accordance with State standards that had been laid down decades before. That meant little or no latitude was available as far as architectural design was concerned. This restraint may well have served a purpose straight after the war, enabling construction to proceed at the necessary pace, but it resulted in a ubiquitous uniformity of uncomfortable, square-looking boxes with windows.

By 1988, nothing had changed. Project engineers had to make use of designs created as far back as the 1950s, with variations only for location and ground levels. The precast concrete plant was the same as had been created after the war, with metal moulds that had never varied in size; and the construction teams had been doing the same basic job for so many years that they could have built with their eyes closed.

The repetition resulted in high production levels, allowing the director to provide glorious reports of the quantity of square metres completed during the year, for which he and the institute were rewarded with medals, certificates and bonuses. Theoretically it looked great, but the majority of people in the rural community would not live in the houses or flats built for them.

Part of my responsibility included visiting the projects I'd designed to ensure that construction proceeded according to plan. The first village I visited had identical houses built at different stages by our institute – approximately 20 years before, 10 years before and brand new ones, which I had gone to inspect. The oldest houses were unoccupied, full of cracks and falling apart because of the weather. Ten-year-old cloned houses differed from the older ones only by the size of the weeds growing from cracks in the walls. I was shocked to think that my new houses would suffer the same fate.

On returning to the office, I sought out the project controller, who was a highly respected and very knowledgeable man, but not a member of the Communist Party. I asked him why the houses and flats we built were not being occupied. With a sad smile he explained that the authorities certainly knew about the unoccupied buildings, and that there were many reasons why the rural community did not like them. The first was that farmers had lived in houses at ground level for generations, with their gardens directly outside, so flats were unacceptable to them. Another reason was that the animal sheds of our freestanding houses (for reasons of health and sanitation) had been sited too far away from the houses to allow convenient access for feeding and milking in bad winter weather. Traditional farmhouses had been built with animal sheds leading conveniently off the main buildings, providing easy access without farmers having to venture outside.

New flats and houses that had initially been occupied would be vacated after the first winter, because electricity, plumbing, gas and heating were provided by centralised systems that often broke down without anyone able to service or repair them. It was widely recognised that maintenance services of that sort did not exist in rural areas. Just one experience of living in a cold concrete building, with outside temperatures sometimes reaching minus 30 degrees Centigrade, was enough to deter anyone.

So they returned to the traditional way of living in wooden houses, with big stoves for warmth, adjoining animal sheds, gardens close at hand and water drawn from their own wells. It was simple, functional and more comfortable, with less risk of breakdowns.

I asked the man why we didn't give the people what they wanted and he laughed at me.

'Olga Danilovna, you are a member of the Party,' he said sarcastically. 'Why don't you ask your Communist bosses?'

What I'd seen in the country disturbed me, and when I tried to calculate what the State was wasting throughout Russia, my head spun.

Attendance at monthly meetings of the Communist Party was compulsory for members. A few days later, I went to one and was subjected to a litany of favourable reports about our good work at the institute. Before the meeting closed, the chairman called for questions.

I nervously raised a hand. 'May I ask, comrade chairman, why we are building houses that we know are never going to be occupied by the people they are intended for, and why we continue to use 35-year-old plans? I'm sure we are capable of designing other houses, better suited to individual needs. Why is the State spending such a lot of money for nothing?'

It was as though someone had suddenly died. It felt like a minute's silence before the chief of the institute replied:

'Do you think, Comrade Morozova, that you're the cleverest person here? We all know about the situation. But, if you are so smart, why don't you work out what it would cost the State to organise that? To vary production to that degree is totally impractical; we would have to close our precast plant. Would you like to be responsible for thousands of unemployed workers? You're too young to teach us what to do. By the way, we are holding information that your group did not perform well. Go and fix your mistakes before you criticise the administration. Be careful, Comrade Morozova, perhaps we will ask you, as a young Communist, to report on your group productivity at the next meeting.'

When I looked around the hall, expecting some support, I thought the roof was about to fall in. Everyone was gazing upward with vacant expressions, as though my questions and the chief's answers were meaningless and all they wanted was to go home.

An empty feeling came over me. I realised that continuing my criticism would be worthless, if not detrimental, to my future progress. The chief's threats had been baseless because the performance of my group was no worse than the others.

What had shocked me was the scathing way in which I had been treated. His intimidation had obviously been intended to shut me up and, I suppose, I had allowed him to succeed. With very bitter feelings, I left the meeting and went home.

All things considered, I realised that, at 32, with 10 years of practical experience behind me, I was not being given the opportunity to make the contributions I had always hoped to do. My ambition and self-respect were suffering, especially when 'comrades' tried to manipulate me to recognise myself as a cog in a massive machine that I could see would trundle on in one direction regardless. Designing projects that would remain unused appeared futile to me and I determined not to continue.

More disappointing, though, was my membership of the Communist Party. I had been brought up believing that the Party and its members were the pride and vanguard of our society, without whom progress would not happen. But now, having been a member myself for more than five years, I had to accept that membership meant being an accomplice to hard-headed stupidity. As a member, I was an accessory to incompetence that, left unrecognised, would ultimately implode. It was the first time, as a Communist, that I felt shame, and I knew that I had to dissociate myself from the Party.

That evening I related everything to Eugene. He said I should calm down because I couldn't change the system. I knew he was right and concluded that, if the system could not be changed, my life certainly could. Nobody could stop me from doing that.

19

Hunting accident

MY HUSBAND WAS A HUNTER, AS WERE MANY OTHER RUSSIAN men. He took it very seriously and had all the necessary equipment: special camouflage clothes, high rubber boots for wading, rucksacks, knives, rifles, shotguns and cartridge belts. Our dog was from a hunting breed, a German wire-haired pointer.

Eugene was a member of our Provincial Society of Hunters and Fishermen and, in order to qualify, had to pass a number of tests, both medical and psychiatric. He had to have knowledge of the rules of hunting and to submit character references from responsible, experienced hunters. Licences had to be bought for each hunting activity, with strict controls on the number of birds or wild animals taken during the restricted hunting seasons, which Eugene and his friends respected.

The chairman of the society was a retired military man who had hunted since his youth. His son, Andrey, had grown up hunting with his father, and was also a member. They were wonderful people and Eugene became a close friend of theirs and the other members; they formed a close-knit group.

In our area, spring and autumn were open seasons for hunting duck, geese and teal. Although permitted in spring, the society was reluctant to shoot migratory birds then; they knew that the newly arrived birds had come to nest and felt they should be given a chance to settle in. Autumn hunting was far more popular; by then the chicks had grown and the birds were fat and gathering for the migration south. There were vast numbers of them at that time of year.

Our dog had been acquired for the express purpose of hunting birds. It was interesting to see how hunting had been bred into the animal and how he shivered with excitement at the prospect of a hunt. Running about 50 metres ahead of Eugene, he would traverse the ground, always staying in sight of his master. When he picked up a scent he would freeze, with his tail ramrod stiff, not moving until given the signal. Jumping forward, he would put up the bird and give a clear shot to his master.

So keen was he that, even in late autumn, when the swamp water had already started to freeze over, he would leap onto it, cracking the ice with his chest in order to get the bird for Eugene. Plants in the swamps sometimes had sharp edges that would have cut a normal dog, but because of his wire hair he managed, to our amazement, to retrieve birds without injury.

Hunting in our area for wood and black grouse took place at the end of winter and into early spring, without the participation of dogs. Clearings in the forests were found where birds normally performed their courtship rituals. Although it was legal to shoot these beautiful birds, they were not shot, but rather observed for their wonderful courtship performances.

I occasionally took part as an observer in duck hunting. At sundown we would sit in a boat in the reeds or in a hide and, as we waited for flights of duck to arrive, get eaten alive by swarms of ravenous mosquitoes. As a rule, ducks would arrive after dark had set in, and Eugene would blaze away, missing more often than not. Sometimes we would go home completely empty handed, but in a good frame of mind because it was the excitement and atmosphere of the hunt that we enjoyed most, not the result.

When he was successful, I was the one who plucked and cleaned the birds for the pot. Thankfully, we didn't have to depend on hunting for our food, although the birds were a treasure for us since they were never available in shops. I had a variety of recipes for preparing game birds, and we usually invited our friends to enjoy the meal with us, with Eugene relating the story of the hunt.

In winter there was a period for hunting moose and wild boar. If Eugene was lucky, we would have an abundance of meat at a time when none was available in the shops.

Sometimes he arrived home with sackfulls that I had to prepare for storage. There was far too much for immediate consumption, so it had to be preserved in one way or another. Some was salted and dried; other meat I cooked in a pressure cooker and put into sterilised glass jars that had to be sealed airtight for keeping over a period of time. Then there were sausages to be made, meat in aspic, meatballs, soups and *pelmeni* (Siberian meat dumplings). Our parents also benefited from those times of plenty and we were able to entertain more than usual.

In January 1983, an accident happened that had a profound effect on Eugene and his hunting partners. Eugene had left on a hunting trip on a Friday night. I did not expect him back until late Sunday night. To my surprise, he arrived home on Saturday night and told me he would be leaving again at five the next morning to hunt in another area.

Saturday had been unlucky; they had not found any game. To add to that, on the way back they had had an accident in the forest. A party of 12, they were travelling in two heavy four-by-four vehicles. The lead vehicle had skidded sideways on an icy road and the second had narrowly missed ramming into its side.

One had slid into deep snow and, to retrieve it, they had tried to tow it out using the other vehicle and a steel cable. But tension on the cable had caused it to snap, nearly killing one of them. Fortunately for this man, he was heavily clothed and suffered only a glancing blow. I listened to the story of the close shave and details of other problems that had befallen them. Eugene had supper and then dozed on the couch.

Alarm began to well up within me. I felt strongly that Eugene should not go on the hunt in the morning, but I knew that trying to dissuade him would be impossible. I tried broaching the subject carefully, but he was adamant that he was going and asked me not to talk about it any further. So I set the alarm for four a.m., in time for the hunting trip.

On that particular Sunday, I had arranged to go skiing in the forest with a friend. The day was clear with bright sunshine, the temperature minus 20 degrees Centigrade, a typically good winter's day. The forest, covered in snow, was like something from a fairytale. Skiing lifted our spirits; we breathed in the pure fresh air and found the atmosphere exhilarating.

After a while light snow began to fall. Suddenly a very uncomfortable sensation broke my mood. I looked at my watch; it was 12.30 p.m. Nothing had visibly changed and I could not understand why I had this ominous feeling. Despite my friend's protestations, I insisted on going home immediately.

When I got there, I felt a little easier and settled down to wait for Eugene. At four the following morning the phone rang. It was Eugene. He explained that a tragic accident had happened on the hunt. Andrey had been killed around lunchtime on the previous day and they were all in the custody of the local police.

I recalled then that, a couple of years earlier, we had spent a weekend in the countryside in autumn. There were five of us, including Andrey.

After a good lunch, I was busy washing dishes in the kitchen. The men were talking at the table, discussing death and what kind of death they would each choose for themselves, which made me anxious and uncomfortable. I vividly remember Andrey saying thoughtfully, 'I don't want to die sick in bed. I would prefer a quick death, like a bullet in the forehead.'

I had been brought up from childhood without religion or any form of spiritual enquiry, told that there was no God and that any kind of mysticism was a lot of nonsense. In the wake of recent happenings and the premotions I had experienced, I began to question those dictates; there simply had to be some power that imparted such feelings.

The following day I met Eugene and his friend after their intensive questioning by the police. None of us could have predicted the extent of the nightmare that would be thrust upon us by that terrible accident.

At the time, Eugene was employed as an instructor in the provincial Communist Party head office and his boss was Comrade Ivanov, first secretary of the provincial Communist Party. Under the first secretary fell the police, civil prosecutors and the complete administrative machinery of the province. When Comrade Ivanov heard of the accident, he opined that all those present on the hunt should be sent to jail.

As soon as Eugene arrived at his office the next morning, an urgent meeting was called by the boss and all Party head office staff were expected to attend. The only item on the agenda was the supposed bad behavior of Eugene and the others involved in the hunt. At that time, the only people aware of what had really happened were those who had been on the hunt and, to some extent, the police, who had not yet completed their report or submitted it to the Communist Party authorities.

It is possible that certain people working in that office were eager to advance their careers by any means, including condemning those on the hunt. They might have thought that vociferous vocal support of the boss would enhance their prospects for advancement. As a result, there was considerable, clearly premature, criticism of those involved in the hunting party.

Eugene was dismissed from his job, without being given any opportunity to explain what had happened. His friends on the hunt, half of whom were military people, were also fired from their jobs and, almost every day, for weeks, were summoned to meetings for questioning by one Communist Party commission or another.

Kalinin was a small town and the accident had been well publicised, so nearly everyone knew about it. We had grown up there and knew many people, if not by name then definitely by sight. In the street, people who recognised us looked the other way. Our friends no longer called us.

Eugene tried to get other employment but, under the circumstances, found it impossible; no employer wanted to be in opposition to the provincial Communist Party boss.

Two years earlier, the first secretary of the provincial Communist Party, the very same Comrade Ivanov, had publicly awarded Eugene the medal of 'Friendship of the People,' in recognition of his work organising students into a detachment to build public facilities. In his speech, he had lauded Eugene as being one of the up-and-coming young people in whom we could take pride, and who would take over when the old Communists retired. Now the same man had called for him to be jailed, along with his hunting friends.

We were ignorant of the laws governing such circumstances, but, as it transpired, if just one military officer was involved, the investigation had to be held by military authorities. Fortunately, the regional military prosecutor reported directly to the chief military prosecutor in Moscow, and was not obliged to respond to the first provincial secretary.

A new military prosecutor, Colonel Grigory Kroshner, had arrived to take up his post just two weeks prior to the accident and was unknown to us, so we had no idea of what to expect of him. He might choose to back the first secretary or, on the other hand, maintain his independence from the politicians. The uncertainty gave us sleepless nights.

A completely new military inquiry was then instigated and the true facts of the matter began to emerge. On that Sunday, 12 fully licensed hunters had set off to hunt moose, together with a couple of professional hunters from the region. Witnesses vouched for the fact that they were all sober when they left.

In the forest, the 12 men had spread out in a line, waiting for moose to be driven towards them by the two professional hunters who were acting as beaters. Andrey was on the left flank with a military man next to him, then nine others to his right, and Eugene on the extreme right flank.

A moose was chased from right to left in front of Andrey, who fired a shot, wounding the animal. It veered away from Andrey and made for cover in high bush directly ahead of the military man to Andrey's right. Andrey knew perfectly well not to leave his position before the signal was given to all by the professionals, who traditionally lead the hunt.

However, quite out of character, given his experience, Andrey had followed the wounded moose without giving notice to the other members of the party. We can only presume it was anxiety at not having taken the animal down cleanly with his first shot. When the man to his right saw the moose directly in front of him he fired twice, killing the animal.

The professionals then signalled the end of the hunt and the hunters gathered around the dead moose. Andrey was missing, so they shouted for him. There was no response and they spread out to look for him. He was soon discovered on the other side of the high bush, beyond and directly in line with both the moose and the military man who had been to his right.

There was a bullet hole in Andrey's forehead. As it dawned on the men that Andrey was dead and that nothing could be done about it, they decided they had better inform the police. Neither the body nor the moose were moved until the police took Andrey to the mortuary. The dead moose was left to the professional hunters. News of the tragedy spread quickly around the province.

Fate had fortunately provided a new military prosecutor of strong character. Despite pressure from the likes of the Party secretary, he stood firm in his resolve to handle the matter his way and was fully prepared to take responsibility for his decisions. He called all involved parties back to the site on two occasions and made them demonstrate exactly how everything had happened, ensuring that the highest-ranking officer from the military prosecution establishment in Moscow was present on both occasions. The report of the Commission of Inquiry took half a year to be made available. To our great relief, the tragedy was deemed an accident for which no-one could be held responsible.

From that time, we became close friends with the military prosecutor and his family. His resolve to make the truth known, despite the Party secretary openly demanding jail sentences, set him apart as a man of courage and character.

The episode left Eugene sadly disillusioned about his political ideals and career as a Communist.

20

Communism

COMMUNISM MEANT MANY THINGS TO MANY PEOPLE, AND THE system has been both revered and reviled. While its impact on ordinary people's lives was characterised by a certain grimness, its designers and enforcers maintained a relentlessly upbeat and starry-eyed approach, as shown in the following exerpts from the Programme of the Communist Party of the Soviet Union:

Communism is a classless society with one national ownership of all means of production, complete social equality of all members of society, where people are comprehensively educated and their productive forces developed on a constantly improving scientific basis.

All sources of national wealth will pour like a torrent in recognition of the Great Principle, each person contributing according to his capability, for the needs of everyone. Communism is a highly organised society of free and conscientious workers with self-Government, where labour for the improvement of society will be a vital necessity for all.

I was relatively lucky growing up as I did in the period of Russian history known as 'the thaw', after the death of Stalin, whom Khrushchev blamed for the loss of lives of innocent people. The atmosphere in the USSR had improved somewhat: the war was over, Stalin had passed on, people were happy at having survived, and they displayed great enthusiasm for life and rebuilding their motherland.

At a Communist Party congress, Khrushchev had announced that, by 1980, our society would be 'living Communism'. Nearly everyone supported the idea. At a very early age I became curious about 'Communism', a word so often heard in adult conversation. It prompted me to ask my father what Communism was.

He said, 'Communism, my girl, will be the happy life that we are building now.'

'What will be good, Dad?' I asked.

'Public transport will be free.'

'Great,' I said, 'I can go on the tram as often as I like.'

'Food will be free,' he added.

'Good!' I exclaimed, 'I can eat as many sweets as I like.'

He laughed and said, 'You've only got a tiny stomach.'

'Clothes will be free,' he told me.

I liked that too, remarking that I could have many different dresses.

'Oh no,' he said. 'You will have the same as other girls.'

'Why must I have the same dresses as other girls if I don't want them?' I questioned disappointedly.

'You should be the same as everyone else,' he explained.

I didn't like his answer because, at age five, Mother had made me pretty dresses from old clothes she had found and our neighbours had admired them. Even at that age I enjoyed flattery.

I remembered once having seen a group of little girls on the street, all dressed identically, and my grandmother had told me that they were from an orphanage, had no parents and were looked after by the State. That, she said, was why they were all dressed the same. I had understood that people viewed them with pity and I definitely didn't want to be in their situation.

'But why will everything be the same?' I asked.

'Because, my girl, in our Communist society, everyone will be equal and money will not exist,' my father explained. 'But you will have to work for society if you want everything free,' he continued.

'What will I be?' I asked.

'It depends on your talent,' he told me. 'When you grow up, we will see what you can do.'

'What should I do, Dad, if I don't have talent.'

'Those with no talent will have to do dirty jobs, like cleaning streets.'

My concern was for the word 'talent'. I didn't know what it was and I didn't understand how I would get it.

'I don't want to be a street cleaner. What if I have the same talent as everyone else?' I asked. 'Will we all do the same thing?'

'No,' he said, 'That's impossible. People's abilities differ.'

He chuckled and said, 'In a Communist society everybody will have to work and all the people will have jobs. Nobody will ask you what you want to do.'

I didn't like that answer; I'd already understood that a street cleaner was not a high position in the scheme of things.

He looked at me in a kindly way and said, 'Don't worry, my girl, if you are good at school you will get a better job. Each person will contribute to the needs of everyone according to their capability.'

I couldn't have been less impressed with his explanation of Communism.

'How old will I be when Communism comes?' I asked.

'In 1980 you will be 25,' he told me.

I sighed with relief, realising it would not be soon.

My parents had made it clear that I had to behave well at school and learn diligently to attain a position in society in which to make a meaningful contribution. Schools inculcated ideas of a perfect 'Communist State' in our young minds. Socialism, according to our teachers and lecturers, had been established before WWII.

'Now,' they told us, 'we are in a state of "developed Socialism" and firmly on the road to creating the perfect society, Communism.'

During class debates about the great principle of Communism, I struggled to come to grips with how it would work in real life, but thought I might be too young and would understand later. However, the moral code applicable to Communists had appeal and was easily understood, even at a young age.

Years later, after being able to read the Bible, I discovered a distinct similarity between the moral code and the Ten Commandments. Plagiarism perhaps? Anyway, I was proud that my generation was building equality, not only among our own proletariat, but helping other peoples of the world too.

A university education meant being subjected to more of the same. Of the five years I was at university, I estimate that approximately two-and-a-half were spent studying all aspects of Communism. Examining our grasp of Communist ideology was more important to the authorities than our levels of professional competence. Leading industries down the ideological path was of greater importance than designing and building appropriate, high quality projects.

In retrospect, I see myself as having been an ideal, mouldable individual for furthering the interests of the Communist Party, so it's not surprising that I ultimately decided to join the Party. To do so, one had, in the first instance, to gain entrance to the Communist organisation within the institution one attended, or the company in which one worked.

My first approach was to the University Communist Committee where I requested membership, but was told that they had a long waiting list and I had no chance of becoming a member. The fact that so many people were waiting to join only served to elevate my opinion of the organisation.

My second attempt came at Kalininspetzstroy, where I started my first job, but it turned out that there was a queue there, too, and I could not get membership. I asked why and they explained the in-company Party make-up in relation to the national Party constitution. The majority of members had to come from the proletariat workers, collective farmers and soldiers. White-collar workers were allowed to fill a smaller percentage, but the proportions had to remain as laid down nationally. It meant that there was no limit to the number of blue-collar workers who could join, but until there were sufficient, no additional white-collar members were accepted.

It appeared that the proletariat workers were not that eager to join, which was putting a restraint on the number of eligible higher-grade workers that could be accepted. Sixty-five years after enthusiastically participating in the Revolution and succeeding in their objective of achieving 'equality', the proletariat's interest in the party had perhaps waned somewhat.

My understanding of the situation was that uneducated workers might not be enthusiastic about joining because doing so would not necessarily advance their careers. It may, in fact, put considerable personal strain on them. Apart from having to attend meetings and vocational education courses, accept responsibility for workplace discipline and results, plus pay party dues, they were unlikely to gain any material benefit.

White-collar workers, on the other hand, might more easily get promotion, which meant a higher salary, in addition to which it was an unwritten rule that certain higher positions were not open to non-members of the Party. In any event, I was told at Kalininspetzstroy that, if I insisted on being in the queue, it would still take many years before I could become a member.

On joining a military organisation in my second job, the situation changed. Young soldiers were inclined, through their training, to be patriotic and joined the Party with enthusiasm, creating scope for the small number of white-collar workers attached to the military to become members if they so wished. The opportunity to realise my ambition had presented itself and I applied immediately.

The procedures involved in joining the party were both protracted and serious. I had to get a character reference written by the secretary of our Communist Party department, signed by our director and the chairman of our branch of the Trade Union, together with three letters of recommendation from long-serving members of the Communist Party. Then I was interviewed and grilled by the Communist Party members within my department.

Thereafter I had to travel to Moscow to be interviewed by the Communist Party members at our head office, before which I studied hard to ensure that I would be able to come up with the right answers. The last interview was with the Communist Party committee to which our head office responded. I was finally congratulated and given candidate membership, on probation for one year. When the year was up, I was issued with a Party card and granted full membership status.

Despite Khrushchev's earlier announcement that Russia would be a fully-fledged Communist society by 1980, there was little sign that the promised Utopia would, in fact, dawn. My school and university years fell during his successor Brezhnev's time, which was later known as the 'period of stagnation'. During this time, the bureaucratic apparatus stifled initiative and encouraged waste, until his death in office in 1982.

It was possibly to divert the attention of the people from internal problems that, in 1979, the Soviet army embarked on an invasion of Afghanistan, and that the Moscow Olympics were staged in 1980.

The verbosity of government pronouncements, so prevalent in past years, were gradually being toned down. It appeared that the promise of an ideal Communist society, which I had grown up in anticipation of inhabiting, had been no more than a glorious myth created by Marx and Lenin. The 'torrent of national wealth' had not materialised; in fact, our quality of life was deteriorating while our government failed to give recognition to the fact.

I recall that, in my youth, Father had quoted a phrase about the 'Great Principle of Communism' that I was later to encounter as part of my studies at school and university: 'Each person will contribute according to his capability, for the needs of everyone.'

That phrase played on my mind. How could 'needs' be measured for everyone in common, when people and their individual needs were so different, and some people's needs apparently having no limit? It was obvious that some people's capabilities, and therefore their contributions, were going to be greater than others whose 'needs' may well be in excess of their particular capabilities and contributions.

I decided that, although the philosophy sounded great, the question of individual 'needs' had not been resolved. A few years later, something happened that finally convinced me that I had been right.

The occasion was a New Year's Eve party at which I caught a glimpse of how great some people's needs could be.

In 1985, Eugene and I had taken a holiday at Sochi on the Black Sea. There we had met a Moscow couple of our age and their two children. After returning home, we maintained contact and made occasional visits to each other.

Late in 1986, they invited us to a guest house for a party to celebrate New Year's Eve. We were told that everything would be provided. That was unusual because we were accustomed to 'chipping in'. Our friend told us on the way there that his father worked at the central committee of the Communist Party, held a very responsible position and, prior to that, had been one of Brezhnev's personal assistants. His father was a regular guest at the establishment but, on that occasion, had gone elsewhere and offered the opportunity to his son. Security was tight and we passed a number of checkpoints at which we presented our pre-issued passes before finally arriving at the venue.

We had plenty of time and decided to explore the estate. I thought we'd arrived in paradise. The interior of the huge 'entertainment centre' was impressively decorated, with no apparent expense spared. Lighted Christmas trees and beautiful decorations had been tastefully distributed throughout the building. Our friend explained that the upstairs suites were allocated to high-ranking staff of the central committee, for free use as long as they remained in their jobs

In the building was a large covered swimming pool, a tennis court, a gymnasium, saunas, massage rooms, medical consulting rooms, a cinema, a library and an impressive-looking restaurant and bar, rendering self-catering unnecessary. All that, together with sleigh riding in winter and horse riding in summer, made it an impressive health and recuperation centre. A week in such a place would clearly have cost a lot of money.

Our friend told us that his father enjoyed the guest house and always felt rejuvenated after staying there for a few days. We hadn't met the father, but imagined him to be a man of worth, hard working, highly paid and able to afford the services on offer at the obviously very pricey establishment.

After our tour of the facilities and a brief look at our friend's father's suite, we returned to the main hall where a band was playing festive music. In every corner there were tables of snacks and drinks that we were invited to enjoy. Clowns, a Father Christmas, an Ice Queen and sundry other entertainers roamed the building, providing amusement for the guests.

We decided to take a walk in the floodlit grounds to pass a couple of hours before midnight. The weather was perfect, with clear, crisp air and a fresh layer of snow blanketing the ground. Surrounding an ice-skating arena were hills for children to slide down on toboggans, available free from a nearby kiosk, together with skates. Little children took pony rides and adults rode on horse-drawn sleighs through the fairytale park, filled with snow-laden pines and twinkling lights. Kiosks around the ice arena served hot blinis, *pirozhki* (Russian pies) and other snacks, plus whatever anyone wanted to drink.

Having had a lot of fun, we returned to the restaurant for the main party. A table had been allocated to us; we could help ourselves at a huge buffet or order from a very extensive *à la carte menu*, and drinks of every kind were available from the bar. We decided to take a look at the buffet, and what we saw laid out before us was just incredible.

There were great mounds of caviar, dressed crabs, whole sturgeons and salmon, cold meats and a variety of other delicacies, some of which I didn't even recognise. So many exotic dishes were on display that I couldn't take it all in. I could never have pictured the quality of the food or its presentation, all of which was a far cry from what we had been obliged to accept on the other side of the high walls.

The bar was a sight to behold. They had an array of bottles we'd never seen before and, on request, a drink from nearly any part of the world could be served. Back in Kalinin, we had a very limited choice that consisted of vodka, brandy, wine, beer and the odd liqueur, all from Russia or from one of the surrounding Socialist countries.

Our host was obviously familiar with most things on offer and asked what we would like to eat and drink. The answer was not going to be easy. We were mesmerised by what we had seen, and making a simple choice became problematic.

Suddenly Eugene and I found ourselves looking at each other with the same silent question. 'How much do you think this evening is going to cost and do we have enough cash to pay for it?'

We had our December salaries, together with both of our bonuses. We knew the cost of a New Year's Eve party in a normal restaurant, but this was going to be far in excess of the norm. Prices were conspicuously absent from menus and there was not a wine list or bar prices to be seen anywhere.

Simultaneously, our expressions made it clear that we were going to enjoy the evening without concern for the cost, realising that it may well be the last time we'd have such an opportunity. We ate, drank, danced and enjoyed the party until sunrise, which is quite late in Russian winters.

I wondered how I was going to describe the night to my friends. I imagined that this was how the Tsars had celebrated. Was this, finally, Communism? Or perhaps this was what Communism would be?

When the time came to leave, we insisted that our friend allow us to contribute our share of the bill, to which he finally agreed, and produced the slip. We could not believe what we saw: it came to a total of three roubles. With some embarrassment, he explained that, while the evening would have been entirely free before, it now cost a little because the central committee staff were not yet familiar with the sentiments of the new President Gorbachev.

Three roubles, at that time, bought three kilograms of sugar. Our good humour vanished. We sat on the train back to Kalinin in silent reflection of the experience. The idealistic dream of a future state of 'equality for all', towards which I had devoted my energies, had been shattered in one night, and my belief in the system appeared embarrassingly naive.

Official interpretation of 'for the needs of everyone' had become startlingly clear. In reality, it was nothing like what Marx and Lenin had theorised. The truth was that our high-ranking members of government had no limit to their individual 'needs', whereas the people's 'needs' were limited to what the government considered necessary for survival.

For government members, the closer to Moscow they lived, and the higher their positions, the better their 'needs' were catered for.

They became easily recognisable in autumn and spring by the specially designed government hats and coats they wore, in winter by special young reindeer fur *shapkas* (Russian fur hats) and throughout the year by the black, government-issue Volgas they drove at no cost.

Those in government were conspicuously absent from food queues, so conscientiously attended by the rest of the proletariat. I wondered how they intended improving our lives while remaining completely out of touch with the majority – and behind very high walls.

They claimed to be 'servants of the people', owning little of personal value. We all knew that their salaries were far in excess of ours; the best flats were reserved for them without waiting lists; telephones, for which the rest of us might wait 10 years, were immediately installed for them; *dachas* issued to them were on the best sites available, never on a swamp such as my parents had been issued; free luxury holiday houses and special shops catered exclusively for their every food and clothing 'need'.

They even had their own private hospitals, with the most up-to-date equipment and the best qualified staff in Russia.

We, the ordinary citizens, were rapidly becoming aware of what was happening at the top. The notion that the system wasn't going to last began to spread among the people. Indeed, the people were right: 70 years of idealism and hypocrisy were about to be consigned to the trash heap of failed ideologies. The endlessly repeated canon about 'building a society of equals' faded, and, in 1991, Yeltsin abolished the Communist Party (although it was later re-established).

It was the ignominious end of the theories of Marx and Lenin in the USSR, and many Russians, including Eugene and I, began returning to God, believing it wiser to abide by the Ten Commandments.

21

Caviar

RUSSIA HAS BEEN BLESSED WITH TWO OF THE WORLD'S MOST sought-after foods – red and black caviar.

Red caviar is obtained from salmon that are abundant in the rivers of the Russian Far East, the area east of Lake Baikal and north of the Chinese border. While red is delicious, Russian opinion holds that black caviar is superior in terms of its therapeutic properties and flavour. It is less easily available and more expensive.

The sturgeon provides black caviar and is found, among other places, in the Volga River, which flows into the Caspian Sea. The length of the river, from source to mouth, is 3 650 kilometres.

The Great Russian River Volga, known fondly as 'Mother Volga', has for centuries provided fish in huge quantities and great variety, feeding millions of people. It is a vast highway along which goods and people move great distances, by boat in summer and by sled in winter.

Flood plains are found along much of its lower reaches; farmers use them as grazing areas for their animals in summer. At times in history, the river has flooded so badly in early spring that it has destroyed many housing settlements. Nevertheless, people always return because of the plentiful supply of food provided by the 'Mother'.

In the province of Kalinin there is a small spring from a swamp around Lake Seliger in the Valdai Hills. That spring is the source of the mighty Volga. Many people visit the site to marvel at the tiny spring that becomes such a huge and life-giving river. Only 200 kilometres away, at the city of Kalinin, the river has already widened to 400 metres. By the time it flows out of Kalinin province, it is two kilometres wide.

It divides the city into two parts and lends some beauty to an otherwise ordinary place. People take pride in living in close proximity to Mother Volga.

After the October 1917 Revolution, many dams were built. Lenin, as leader of the Soviet government, declared the aim of electrifying all Russia – an aim that was achieved.

Hydroelectric power stations were constructed, one after the other, but their huge sluice gates cut the body of the Mother Volga into sections. Vast reservoirs flooded the countryside and, in some cases, small towns. My great-grandparents' farm, which had been handed down through generations before collectivisation, was inundated, along with the apple orchard, which was regarded as exceptional at the time. Later, their graves, too, were lost to the rising waters, with other cemeteries and low-lying churches disappearing progressively. Should you decide to take a boat trip on the Volga, don't be surprised to see church spires and bell towers protruding above the water, which stand today as symbols of the people's faith. The Soviet government was aggressively opposed to religion and displayed a total lack of concern for the loss of so many beautiful places of worship.

In the Soviet era, huge factories were constructed on the banks of the Volga, and the river used for evacuation of the effluent they created. Scientists attempting to protect the environment were labelled 'Enemies of the State' and ran the risk of severe penalties, particularly in Stalin's time. Environmental warnings were ignored, even post-Stalin, and the resultant damage became evident.

Prior to the Revolution, sturgeon were able to swim up the Volga far inland. In fact, my ancestors were able to catch the fish as far up the river as Kalinin province – and in past centuries, even higher up – and enjoy the delicious meat and wonderful black roe.

Because of the many hydroelectric power stations, sturgeons' natural spawning habits have been affected. They are able to swim upstream only as far as Volgograd, which has a giant chemical factory that damages the ecology and, at times, kills fish downstream.

In Old Russian engravings, the sturgeon was revered as 'Tsar among fish'. They can grow to be enormous, reaching a length in excess of seven metres and weighing more than 1 000 kilograms, but they are normally caught as tiddlers at around 20 kilograms. Tough scales and skin cover the fish and make it difficult to fillet, but the flesh, when sliced, resembles the grain of a beautiful hard wood, with shades of pink running into yellow, and makes delicious eating.

There are various ways to prepare sturgeon, including a famous Russian soup, which can be found in the most expensive restaurants. Other ways of preparing it are by smoking and salting. It can also be prepared in aspic.

A bucket or more of black caviar can be taken from a big sturgeon. My ancestors used to eat volumes of the delicacy, using wooden soup spoons. Sadly, the roe has become hard to find. It is recognised for its excellent therapeutic properties, especially after surgery and for cancer sufferers.

In 1978, a fish shop opened in Kalinin amid much fanfare, where I saw, for the only time in my life, caviar being sold by weight from big wooden barrels. Then, in 1995, it appeared again, but this time only in small glass jars or tins. Whatever we got was kept for very special occasions such as New Year's Eve, a birthday or an anniversary. It can be stored frozen for long periods and is usually eaten in Russia on a thickly buttered slice of good white bread, with nothing else to detract from the delicious flavour.

Occasionally we made a small Yorkshire-type pudding called *bulochka* and filled it with a teaspoon each of red and black caviar, together with a rose of butter. It looks mouth-wateringly good and the taste doesn't disappoint. It can also be served in half a boiled egg, with the yoke removed and replaced with caviar. The most important thing is to be able to roll the caviar slowly on one's tongue in order to get the full benefit of the delicious taste. It is savoured when broken against the roof of the mouth and, like good wine, is best taken slowly.

Once, on holiday with friends who had good government connections, we were presented at breakfast with a pile of blinis and a big bowl of black caviar, to be enjoyed without reserve. It was the most ancient of Russian ways to eat caviar – and confirmation of the fact that it's who you know that counts.

In 1987, my husband and I, together with two other families, decided to take a holiday down the Volga in the region of Astrakhan. A friend had been there a year earlier and told us tempting stories about the area, fishing for sturgeon and eating buckets of caviar. He said we would eat without limit and even be able to bring some home. But, he added, 'The area is a bit wild.'

We set off, in early August, in three cars carrying six adults and four children. Each car towed a trailer carrying cans of petrol to enable us to reach the Astrakhan area, a distance of around 1 500 kilometres. Petrol was in very short supply and there were no service stations en route.

We had been advised not to carry too much cash, but rather take as many bottles of vodka and cans of meat as possible. In that area, such produce was valued more than money. We also took three 50-kilogram bags of salt, tents, cooking pots, buckets, axes, fishing rods, rifles for security – in fact everything necessary for a 10-day stay on an uninhabited island with no easy access to civilisation. An emergency medical box and insect repellent were also packed. The food we took along had to be able to survive temperatures of up to 40 degrees Centigrade.

It took two days to get there and we spent the first night camping as far from any habitation as possible. Three cars with laden trailers of food and fuel would have been outstanding targets for criminals. The men took turns in keeping guard with rifles while the others slept.

Being a tourist in rural Russia has always been a problem. As one travels further from the capital, towns and villages become increasingly poor. Shops display fewer goods and, at times, even basic foods are scarce.

At midnight on the second day of the journey, we arrived in a big village on the banks of the Volga, about 150 kilometres south of Volgograd. From that point we travelled on a ferry, together with our cars and trailers, to an inhabited island. There we left our vehicles in the care of a local family, with promises of compensation by way of vodka and meat cans, should we find all in order on our return. We loaded our vast supplies of food and equipment onto a hired boat, which transported us out into the unknown. Finally we reached our uninhabited island of destination. Totally exhausted, we managed in windy darkness, with the aid of our inadequate torches, to erect three tents and collapse into sleeping bags.

When a still dawn broke, we awoke to a vast area covered with green grass, huge trees, bushes of all sizes and a variety of indigenous wild flowers. Birds were singing in the early morning sunshine and there was a pretty little sandy beach. I thought I'd woken in paradise. We had been told that the island measured 17 x 35 kilometres. Each year, the early spring floodwaters completely covered it, along with most of its neighbours.

Our 'paradise island' was situated at the top end of the vast Volga delta, which features hundreds of islands of varying sizes. No accurate map detailing them can be made because, in some years, depending on flood conditions, a number of the smaller islands disappear. Most islands cannot be permanently settled, but are used as lush grazing pastures by farmers of the region who transport cattle there on boats. However, there were no cows visible on our island.

We reconnoitred the territory and were delighted to find a small inland lake with fishing nets full of fish. Local customs had been explained to us on the boat ride to the island. Anyone could help themselves to netted fish, providing they replaced the nets. Fish were plentiful and the custom had come about because the netted fish would not last long in the heat. The lake was some distance from our camp, so at no stage did we meet the net owners. They must have arrived at regular intervals to collect the catch, because we never found rotten fish in the nets.

Afternoon temperatures in our tents reached as high as 42 degrees Centigrade. In such intense heat, the only relief to be found was on our little sandy beach in swimsuits, hats and sunglasses. When the heat became unbearable we jumped into the Volga. Emerging with wet swimsuits, we found we could breathe again.

It was stifling having to cook on an open fire. Boiling water to wash dishes was unthinkable, so they were washed in the river. This gave rise to the possibility of picking up diseases, and a couple of days into our stay we all got the 'trots'.

The medication for our malady quickly disappeared down eager throats, but one man in the party was not able to overcome his problem and had to be treated by an old Russian remedy. It involved a 250 ml glass of neat vodka, two heaped teaspoons of salt and a teaspoon of ground black pepper, mixed together and swallowed in one gulp. We surrounded the poor man shouting 'Drink, drink, swallow, swallow', until he managed to get it down. Fortunately, it appeared to have the desired effect.

Our hope of relief from the daytime heat did not materialise at night. As soon as the sun set, we were attacked by swarms of mosquitoes. The only respite we found was to sit in the smoke from our fire. We had the choice of either being eaten alive or dying of smoke inhalation.

We also discovered that we had neighbours, everywhere, in the form of snakes. They were even in the water. When my turn came around for washing dishes in the river, I would stand on the bank trying to pinpoint their location. Only when I was convinced that there were none in close proximity would I attempt to wash up.

None of us had ever seen a sturgeon 'in the flesh' before our arrival on 'paradise island'. Our friend who had originally recommended the wonderful area, had said we should not be tempted to buy sturgeon from anyone, unless it was still alive. Local people were not beyond taking dead fish from the river and selling them to unsuspecting visitors. This was possible because the huge chemical plant in Volgograd, upstream from our location, occasionally pumped effluent into the river, poisoning the fish. On such days, dozens of dead fish, with distended stomachs uppermost, could be seen floating down the Volga. We witnessed that heartbreaking sight on our third day on the island.

How would we get hold of a live sturgeon? Our men had no idea of how to fish for them, and, in any case, our equipment was for catching normal river fish, not the mighty sturgeon. They didn't need to catch normal fish because we had a plentiful supply from the nets in the lake.

On day one, they had brought many fish from the nets, including pike, perch and bream. Back home we were not spoiled by an unlimited supply of *fresh* fish and when we saw so many, some of them still flapping, it created great excitement. Decisions had to be made as to what to do with them. Some were salted to take home, others used to make soup or fried for immediate consumption.

The salting method had been detailed to us by our friend. The fish were gutted then rubbed with a great deal of salt, inside and out, until they were completely covered. They were then put into a thick, airtight plastic bag. The bag was then tied securely to ensure that no sand or air could enter. Then it was wrapped tightly around the fish. A hole about half a metre deep was dug and the bag buried in sand. Stones were piled on top to create more pressure on the fish.

After a couple of days, the bag was dug up, the fish taken out and strung up on a line to dry, completely covered with a muslin-type cloth that was impenetrable to flies. When completely dry, the fish was put into thick cotton bags. Like this, it would last indefinitely.

In Russia, this type of salted fish is called *vobla* and is extremely popular, particularly when taken with beer. What jerky is to an American, *bundefleis* to the Swiss, *biltong* to a South African, *vobla* is to a Russian. The mere mention of the word is likely to bring a grin to the face of most Russians.

One evening we were gathered around the campfire while the men cooked soup and fried fish, when a stranger quietly appeared out of the night. I was immobilised with fright. He must have been in his forties; a ragged, dirty, sick-looking apparition. His eyes were piercing and his gaze danced about in all directions. However, he greeted us quite affably, enquiring if we were newly arrived tourists.

Quite unexpectedly, he asked for a cup of tea. One of the men in our party seemed more confident in handling the situation than the others. He asked the stranger what strength tea he would like. The answer was, one whole packet, not just a sachet, should be used for one large cup. He was soon handed his astonishingly strong cup of tea, which he proceeded to sip with relish. With each sip his hands seemed to tremble less and, by the time he'd finished, he was a different man. His eyes had become normal and his speech moderated. He asked where we were from, how long we were staying on the island and what our intentions were, then suddenly stood up and said, 'Thanks guys, you saved my life. I will not forget it.'

We were so pleased to see him leave that we gave him a bottle of vodka and a couple of meat cans before he disappeared silently into the darkness.

When we were sure he had gone, I asked our friend how he knew about such strong tea. He told me that, as a foolish young man, he had become involved in a gang fight, was arrested for his part and served a six-month jail sentence. There he had learned about prison life, the language they used and the structure of prison relationships. Some inmates used very strong tea as a drug. Our visitor, he presumed, must have been one of them, with a dependency on whatever it is in tea that gave him a lift.

The following day passed without incident, but that night two other strangers appeared from the darkness of the surrounding bushes and asked in rough voices if we had given a bottle of vodka to a man the previous night. Because our reply might mean trouble of some sort, we were at a loss as to how to respond.

Suddenly, one of our men said casually, 'Yes we did and so what?'

One of the strangers responded gruffly, 'One of you men come with us.'

I wondered why we had come to that remote place with such wild people about. We hadn't even seen their faces clearly, did not know what they wanted of us or what was about to happen to our friend. He was brave to follow them into the darkness.

Those of us left around the fire sat in eerie silence, wondering what would happen, when suddenly all three men dragged a huge flapping fish out of the darkness. It was a live sturgeon, the biggest live fish I'd ever seen. As it was laid on the grass, we all gathered around excitedly, shining our torches on its huge moving head and gills.

One of the strangers said, 'This is a present from the man you helped last night. This fish is full of caviar; do you know what to do with it?' he asked.

We replied eagerly, 'No, please show us.'

He asked for a bucket of boiling water, gauze, muslin and a lot of salt. Then followed what appeared to me to be a ritualistic performance, with the fire, the background darkness and the shadows of the two men handling special long knives with amazing skill, moving silently as we watched in spellbound fascination.

They cut the spine of the fish in two places, behind the head and close to the tail. Then, in one swift movement, they pulled out the spinal cord. They said this was necessary because of the heat. If not removed quickly, the spinal cord could rot and spoil the fish.

Then they deftly gutted it. The roe was removed in its membrane and placed on a muslin cloth; there was enough to fill half a 10-litre drum. Gauze was stretched over an empty bucket and the roe lifted onto it. Gentle massage through the gauze separated the roe from the membrane.

When the roe was free of membrane it was put into a muslin bag and dipped a few times, for just a few seconds, into salted boiling water. When that process was complete, it was taken from the cloth and placed in a basin.

Then they said, 'Eat!'

'What?' we exclaimed. 'But it's raw, it's only just been taken from the raw fish.'

At this, they broke down, howling with laughter at our ignorance.

'What kind of caviar do you people think you eat when you take it from a can?' they asked. 'This is exactly the same.'

With big wooden spoons, we gingerly took turns in tasting it. It was sensational and our spoons began to move in and out of the bowl with a little less concern.

We asked them what they intended doing with the fish, and they said it was for us. Being illegal professional fishermen, they were interested only in the valuable caviar. For us, the fish was just as much a treasure as the roe. We presented them with bottles of vodka, cans of meat and packets of cigarettes before our men folk gratefully escorted them back to their boat.

On the way to their boat, our men asked if they could get more sturgeon, or if it was possible to learn the art of fishing for them. They did not receive an answer.

When our men returned, we tucked into the caviar once more, but were frightened to overeat. Never having consumed the delicacy in such volumes before, we did not know what effect it might have on us. In retrospect, I think we were probably all a little concerned about the ease of its preparation and the fact that we thought it still raw.

Then our attention turned to the fish. Someone suggested we should have a barbecue, and we all thought that a great idea. The men started filleting the fish and we women found metal skewers that could be used to hold salted fillets of sturgeon over the fire.

It was delicious, but I found it a little rich and fatty. After eating just two pieces, I was sick all night with pains in my liver. Thereafter, I treated sturgeon with some circumspection and preferred to have it in soup form, with some of the fat boiled off.

That two-metre fish was to keep us busy and fed for the whole of the following day. We made soup, fish balls and fried fillets, and what was left we salted. Ordinary fish such as pike, perch and bream suddenly lost their appeal and didn't seem as tasty. We had been spoilt. After watching the fishermen, our men admitted that filleting sturgeon is an art they would need to practice – if they ever got the opportunity of doing so again.

It wasn't long before it happened. News had spread among the locals that there were visitors on an island happy to swap vodka and cans of meat for sturgeon. Fishermen began arriving during the day with caviar-bearing sturgeon. Soon we were sick of sturgeon, and returned to eating the usual river fish, while longing for a simple piece of barbecued beef.

Apart from lazing on our sandy beach, there wasn't much to do. We continued to prepare *vobla* from perch and bream, salted sturgeon fillets and caviar, all to take home. Our men asked repeatedly to be taken sturgeon fishing by the locals, but without success. They were told that, under Socialist rule, only State organisations, in season, were legally permitted to take fish for the supply of caviar and sturgeon meat to the Soviet government.

Local private fishing had been practised for centuries, and was the only occupation available to the people of the region. In view of the fact that food was in very short supply in the few local shops, the temptation to take sturgeon illegally, as their forebears had done legally over many generations, was overwhelming. And because they subsisted on fish, they were eager to exchange it for other food or money. The number of fish taken by the locals would probably have been far smaller than those poisoned by the government's Volgograd chemical factory. We saw evidence of the damage done to some fish by the chemical plant every few days. We questioned the fairness of the restrictions put on the local people. How could any government expect its citizens blindly to obey such unjust laws?

A couple of days before we were due to leave, two locals arrived to discuss sturgeon fishing with our men. As with those visiting us previously, their faces bore the stamp of tough lives. It turned out that most of these men had served time for illegal fishing. When released, they returned to the same occupation – their only means of making a living. They said they recognised us as genuine tourists and could clearly distinguish us as not being undercover police.

From our three men, they chose the one who had served a jail sentence 20 years earlier, although he had never revealed this fact to them. They were to fetch him in the middle of the night.

The following morning, we listened eagerly to the story of what had transpired. The local poachers fished only under cover of darkness. They were very territorial and any invasion of territory was likely to be met with severe resistance – so severe, in fact, that two-time offenders were likely to disappear in a watery grave, never to be heard of again.

Our friend was instructed to sit very quietly in the bottom of their boat and to stay out of sight of anyone else they might unintentionally encounter. By shining a light onto the water and gaffing sturgeons unfortunate enough to approach out of curiosity, they caught two fish. Because of the great size and power of the quarry, able to upturn the boat if handled incorrectly, it was obvious that experience and skill were required.

With two fish on board, they suddenly became aware of the silent approach of another boat in the darkness. It was a State fisheries officer who, when close by, shone his torch onto the faces of the two local fishermen, whom he recognised and greeted. His light had then fallen on the frightened face of our friend.

'Who is that,' he demanded?

One of the fisherman said, 'He's my cousin, here on holiday.'

The officer said, 'Look here old man, we've had enough of your "cousins". We have a file on you, so watch out.'

With that, he checked the boat and found the two sturgeons.

'One fish is enough for you today, so give me the other and get out of here now,' he demanded.

After handing over half their catch, the fishermen proceeded to row in silence to an island. They disembarked on the bank, made fast the boat and explained to our friend that they were going to give the other fish to somebody else. Our friend noticed a gathering around a fire of what appeared to be hoboes and fugitives of one sort or another. He concluded that outsiders probably seldom glimpsed this indigenous society.

Our friend learned that the local population was a very close-knit bunch of renegades, all familiar with one another. Poachers were well known to the law and the law to the poachers. It was a cosy setup. They had co-operated together for years, sometimes lived in the same houses, and were even intermarried.

Their code had been derived from practicalities. A poacher could take fish, but should respect the unwritten rules and not be greedy. Of course, as long as he abided by the rules and gave the requisite share to the law, everything was fine. The poachers made sure they fished only when they knew one of their mates in the police force was on duty. Among the 'Volga Sturgeon Mafia' it was a comfortable arrangement. If avarice overtook anyone, he either went to prison for a three-year stretch or, if he was the law, he was reported for taking bribes and a similar fate befell him. Such was our lesson about the secrets of the Mother Volga and those who lived on the banks of her lower reaches.

Our last day finally dawned and it was time to pack up. Each family had many bags of *vobla*, buckets of salted sturgeon fillets and glass jars full of caviar. At the promised time, the boat arrived to take us to the island on which our cars had been left.

Once there, we loaded everything into our cars and trailers, and left by ferry for the mainland. What was left of our vodka and cans of meat we divided among our new friends, the fishermen, the ferry captain and those people who had taken care of our vehicles.

There was one more obstacle that we had to negotiate. Police roadblocks were set up in Volgograd to search all vehicles for caviar and sturgeon. Circumventing the roadblocks was out of the question since there was only one road out of the area. If caught, we could face prison terms, but luck was on our side. They gave our vehicles only a cursory check and waved us through. Maybe having children in our cars made us look less like poachers.

Home was a most welcome sight. Our parents were happy to see us back, and even more so when they were given *vobla*, a few big jars of caviar and fillets of salted sturgeon. They had never been fortunate enough to have such quantities of caviar, fish and especially sturgeon. We packed what was left into our freezer and were happy to be able to offer it to guests.

Our 1987 island holiday was very interesting, and I wonder what that area is like today. From the news, I understand that there have been no changes beneficial to the environment in the area, and the numbers of fish have dwindled dramatically.

That means there will be progressively less caviar available. Perhaps the day is fast approaching when there will be no sturgeon left, and no more black caviar.

22

Perestroika

ARLY ONE MORNING IN MID-1982, I WAS HURRYING TO LEAVE
for work, but switched on the radio to catch the news. Instead
of the usual news broadcast I was surprised to hear the saddest part
of Tchaikovsky's *Swan Lake*.

At the office, heavy classical music continued to be broadcast all
day without explanation. Only on the evening news were we told
of the death of the General Secretary of the Communist Party of
the Soviet Union, Comrade Leonid Brezhnev.

The date of the great State funeral was announced and the
country plunged into official mourning. He had led us through an
18-year period of 'political stagnation' and we waited anxiously for
what was to happen next.

It was finally announced that his place would be taken by a
'relatively young', 68-year-old, ex-KGB Communist leader,
Comrade Yuri Andropov. His short period of leadership would be
memorable on account of his imposition of a virtual Police State.

Suddenly, people in cinemas, shops and even on streets, were
obliged to produce documents for police inquisitors to prove that
they had the right to be where they were. Anyone found shirking
their duties was arrested and charged for being in violation of the
constitution, which prescribed that every person should be
productive on the State's behalf.

Another memorable feature of Andropov's rule was that it
occurred at a time when video machines had just become available.
A few people in Kalinin had somehow acquired these very desirable
machines and delighted in inviting visitors to view movies.
Everyone, including the KGB, knew who had video players.

People could be reported for watching erotic movies by anyone with a grievance against them. The police could arrive at the homes of video machine owners, switch off the electricity at the mains boxes that were always located in stairwells in public areas, demand entry to the home, and check to see what kind of movie was being viewed, and if there were an audience.

If it was considered erotic or bordering on any kind of pornography (such as *Basic Instinct*), the owner would suffer confiscation of the video machine and be issued a fine. In more serious cases, where films were considered to be positively pornographic, owners would face prosecution in a court of law and suffer the indignity of having the matter publicised.

It was also announced that Andropov had initiated a campaign against corruption, but if it were true, it was so far from the lives of ordinary people that no beneficial effect was ever felt.

Fourteen months from the time of his inauguration, we were subjected once again to a broadcast of heavy classical music on all radio and television channels, and speculated as to the cause. It was announced in the evening that Andropov had died and that another period of official national mourning would take place before his magnificent State funeral. We could only guess at what our lives might have become had he continued to rule.

The 72-year-old Comrade Konstantin Chernenko succeeded him. He managed to distinguish himself by doing nothing worthy of public notice. Most Russian citizens remember the name and that's about all. In March 1985, after just one year, he, too, died quietly in office. We were subjected to heavy classical music once again, but by then we were sure we knew what must have happened.

As a result of having been subjected to so many Five-Year Plans, the people dubbed that period in their history '3P', from the phrase *'Pjatiletka Pishnigh Poghoron'*, which, roughly translated, means 'five years of extravagant funerals'. Brezhnev had surrounded himself with ageing colleagues, which resulted in the average age of Politburo members being 68. So it was not that unexpected that a few should die in a relatively short period.

Of course, none were prepared to retire, as was expected of

ordinary citizens. Rather, they were 'required' to be faithful and responsible to the Party – while living off the fat of the land and enjoying the privileges that came with office. Dying in office also meant immortalisation by having one's ashes interred in the Kremlin wall.

This sequence of aged leaders passing away at their desks showed that something was amiss. For years we had been 'led' by the aged, sick and infirm, who had done little of benefit for us or for their country. A vigorous, young and healthy leader was obviously needed. It was finally announced that our new leader would be the general secretary of the Communist Party of the Soviet Union, 54-year-old Mikhail Gorbachev.

He was a mere 'youth' compared to most Politburo members. Every Russian citizen responded in delight, hanging on his every word. It was the first time in our lives that we had had a leader younger than his equivalent in America; we were excited and proud of the fact.

He was dynamic, educated, erudite, intelligent, and had travelled. The man came across as kindly and approachable – quite a change from his predecessors. It filled us with hope of pulling out of our stagnation and building a new quality of life. The difference was written on Gorbachev's face. He actually smiled, which seemed to herald an era when we, too, would smile.

Another noticeable difference in his approach was that his wife often appeared with him. We had never seen most of his predecessors' spouses. We wondered whether the Gorbachevs were responding to the requirements of international politics or whether they simply loved each other. The mere thought of our Communist Party leader showing this simple and indulgent human emotion, especially towards his own wife, astounded us.

He announced that he intended to make positive changes to benefit the lives of ordinary people. His timing was perfect. Citizens were no longer prepared to continue their old way of life under orthodox Communism as prescribed by Marx, Engels and Lenin.

Gorbachev announced the adoption of the policies of *perestroika* (restructuring) and *glasnost* (openness) in February 1986. According to statutes in place at that time, he should have had those policies formally adopted at the twenty-seventh Party Congress, where the future Five-Year Plan would have been formulated and ratified, but he had jumped the gun.

One can only imagine the difficulty he would have encountered in persuading the Congress to alter direction so radically: political and cultural reforms, even within the framework of Communist policy, were not easily introduced. Under this new system, party leaders, right down to provincial level, were going to have to forego some of their taken-for-granted privileges.

The press were to be given the freedom to investigate and publish as they saw fit. Entrenched corruption and inefficiency were likely to be exposed and, once it happened, the genie would be out of the bottle. His stirring up of the cosy Communists' nest gave rise to wide public speculation about the extent of his growing unpopularity among his colleagues. We welcomed his policy changes, but thought they would be impossible to achieve within a Communist framework.

Around that time, our living standards began deteriorating further. Serious economic revitalisation was obviously called for. The Communist Party continued in the traditional way, spending huge amounts on congresses, military parades and self-indulgence.

People woke up to the fact that it was their money footing the bills for the glorification of those in power, and began to question more seriously the necessity for keeping such huge military arsenals. We didn't want to fight anyone; we understood the need for some kind of national defence force, but resented the fact that so much was apparently being wasted on unjustified mega-military power.

Gorbachev was busy building relationships with other countries, particularly those in the West, and we all greeted with enthusiasm his announcement of reductions in our military capacity. It was the first such edict in Soviet history.

Our material quality of life may have been deteriorating, but our spirits were rising daily. There was less tension, people were no longer scared to visit churches and, for the first time in my experience, Orthodox services were being advertised on television. By 1986, just six monasteries and 10 convents remained in Russia, compared to the combined total of 1 105 that had existed in 1917. But faith was on the rise again. Big Brother had fallen down a manhole, or so it seemed.

Glasnost was slowly taking root. Previously censored books were going into print and movies hitherto restricted were eventually screened. Artists and musicians previously banned from performing were busy drawing crowds to theatres. This engendered a spirit of excitement among people at work, at home and in the streets, but time would be required before the old system of censorship relaxed to what could perhaps be regarded as an 'acceptable' level.

Around 1988, investigative journalists were able to access some previously restricted State Archives, and ugly details of the horrors of the Revolution and civil war were beginning to come to light. Those responsible for the murder of Tsar Nicholas II and his family were named. For the first time, that evil deed was officially called a 'crime', creating feelings of great guilt among Russians and probably providing the stimulus for the later canonisation of the Romanovs.

Articles uncovered in archives about victims of Stalin's repression appeared in our newspapers, describing the horrors suffered by many who had disappeared. The seventeenth congress of the Communist Party that had taken place in 1934 was now, publicly if unofficially, to become known as the 'Congress of the Murdered'. Of the 1 961 delegates at that congress, 1 108 had been murdered in one way or another and, of the 139 members elected to the central committee, 98 suffered the same fate.

Those who were killed had been honest enough to voice their dissatisfaction with Stalin as their general secretary and had simultaneously proposed Sergei Kirov, the very popular First Secretary of Leningrad province, as his replacement. Kirov, understanding the inherent dangers, wisely declined the position. It didn't help him though; he was assassinated on 1 December 1934.

Stalin had put a spin on the killings to arouse anger in the populace against 'enemies' of the Soviet State. He claimed it was they who had committed the foul deeds. Now terrible stories were emerging from lucky survivors of gulags who had kept silent for so many years.

Georgy Zhenov, one of Russia's best-known actors, published the story of his nine years in a Siberian gulag, from the young age of 20. It appeared in a popular magazine called *Ogonyok* and described his suffering hunger, dystrophy and being worked almost to death in freezing conditions. The article shocked me. I was amazed that he had had the will to survive and go on to reach the heights he achieved as a performer, while maintaining complete silence about his terrible past experiences.

Freedom of expression was indescribably sweet, like being released from a dark, airless cellar in which the atmosphere had been regarded as 'normal'. Relatives of those repressed began applying to special commissions for the rehabilitation of their family members.

My mother's uncle, Nikoli, who had disappeared after being arrested in 1938, had an only daughter who, in 1988, applied for information about her father in the hope that he might be rehabilitated posthumously. After a number of years she received a document stating that her father had been charged with a crime under Article 58.10, 'Agitation and Propaganda against the Soviet State'. Millions of Soviet citizens had been charged under that most infamous of laws, because any innocent comment could be manipulated or misconstrued by someone bearing a grudge. He had been found guilty, and sentenced to hard labour on the mines in Syktyvkar, where he died in 1940. The commission declared her 'the daughter of a victim of repression' and, only in 1995, at the age of 65, was she granted some small social benefits consisting of a minor discount on her flat rental, medicines and public transport.

As a teenager, my mother had taken the disappearance of her favourite uncle and Communist idol very badly and, with the commission's finding, was relieved to tell everyone that she had always believed in his innocence and, all her life, had known that his arrest had been a simple error, which had finally been recognised. What the total cost in human suffering had been was incalculable.

TV became the main purveyor of *glasnost*, with broadcasters gradually obtaining more rights from the censors to express criticism and behave in a less constrained manner. We appreciated the more relaxed, open programmes being aired. It was the first time news items critical of government and State systems were broadcast, and presenters were actually able to draw comparisons of our situation with those in other countries. Progressive commentators, previously banned on air, were freely broadcasting alternative opinions.

Singers and artists were able to perform in clothes of their own choice and in a manner not necessarily dictated to them. Previously, in Brezhnev's time, male artists had been required to dress formally and stand at attention to perform patriotic acts.

Valery Leontjev, one of the most popular artists, had previously been banned from performing on television or in front of large audiences. He had earned the ire of the censors by dressing like a clown and jumping about on stage while singing a *Komsomol* song. To the great joy of his many fans, he was back.

In October 1987, a new television series called *VZGLJAD* (meaning 'LOOK') was launched, and met with immediate success. Without any Communist ideological bias, three young men regularly discussed subjects relating to politics, history or art, with unfettered freedom of expression. Interesting guests put forward refreshingly unusual views, which often provoked public debate in the week that followed. Although deliberately broadcast at midnight on Fridays, most people stayed awake to watch. We, the people, were beginning to learn to talk freely and accept different points of view. (However, about eight years later, the anchor of that very popular television series was assassinated on the stairs of his block of flats.)

Uncensored, live shows with real audiences were another innovation. Opinions were openly solicited from audience members who, without rehearsal, often made the entire country rock with laughter. One incident remains etched in my memory.

In a live show between audiences in St Petersburg, Russia and Seattle, Washington State, USA, talk revolved around our different lifestyles, letting some light through the previously opaque iron curtain.

From Seattle came an unexpected question: 'What about sex in your country?'

'Sex' was a word never before mentioned on television or in any public debate, and now it made the Russian audience cringe. It took some time before anyone brave enough to answer came forward. A woman of about 50, who looked like a university lecturer and no doubt understood every principle of Communist ideology, stood up and announced confidently, 'There is no sex in our country!'

We, together with American audiences, sat open-mouthed for a moment before bursting into peals of laughter. Her response pointed eloquently to the joylessness of life under Communist rule, and sparked a rash of popular jokes on the topic.

For the first time, our media began showing Western leaders in a positive light. The April 1987 visit of Margaret Thatcher to Moscow left an indelible impression on observers. We watched an interview with her on television by three Moscow journalists, specialists in international affairs. Their demeanour irritated us, because it was obvious they were acting on instructions from their Communist bosses, trying to belittle her and lay the blame for Russia's woes at her and other Western leaders' feet. Russia had no women in positions of political influence, and the journalists did their best to make it look as if she belonged in the kitchen and not the corridors of power.

But they were unable to confuse the erudite Iron Lady. She dominated the programme, having the last word on all questions, and earned the sympathy and respect of viewers. She was one of the first world leaders seen to be supporting *perestroika*. She also conveyed the impression of being willing to promote our cause among other nations.

The end of Margaret Thatcher's time in office coincided with the beginnings of *perestroika* and the end of the Cold War. She was the first foreign leader heard expressing confidence in Gorbachev, praising his announcement of *perestroika*, and offering to open a window on the rest of Europe for us. She certainly earned our affection and respect. Her sharp intelligence, charisma, natural grace, poise, charm and success were an inspiration to Russian women. Russian men recognised and respected her ability too, and her popularity snowballed to the extent that, in 1989, readers of a publication titled *Moscow News* named her 'Woman of the Year'.

We hoped desperately that Gorbachev would improve our lives. We saw *perestroika* as the controlled elimination of our sick, dictatorial administrative system, with the gradual adoption of a new democratic social base. He took the first step in that direction by announcing that multi-candidate presidential elections were scheduled for March 1989.

A storm of political activity broke, involving masses of ordinary citizens. For the first time, we were legally able to form parties capable of putting forward candidates for the Presidency and Public Deputies of the Supreme Soviet, who would be expected to formulate a new Constitution. Political parties were sprouting like spring onions and debates raged as to the suitability or otherwise of candidates. The media constantly broadcast political news items.

Former dissidents, hard line Communists, moderate democrats and even recently released convicts were suddenly putting themselves forward as public protectors, fighters for the rights of the people, and capable of improving our lives. It was a dizzying experience for people not previously exposed to such political solicitation.

A smiling Gorbachev announced on television, with his distinctive Ukrainian accent, 'The process has begun ...' – a phrase that, in itself, became a celebrated saying, quoted by all in their determination to ensure that change was irreversible.

It dawned on us later that reconstruction did not necessarily mean that the new would be an improvement on the old. The so-called 'new democracy' was to have a very painful birth. Gorbachev may have been brave enough to initiate *perestroika*, but not to rid the country of the heavy ballast that was the formidable old Communist bureaucracy.

Gorbachev was elected First President of the Soviet Union and Boris Yeltsin, who had earlier resigned his membership of the Communist Party, was elected President of the Russian Republic (the largest of the 15 states making up the Union of Soviet Socialist Republics).

Many progressive professional people, such as teachers or doctors, were elected to positions of public office. Among them were the nuclear scientist turned dissident, Andrei Sakharov, together with the lawyer Anatoly Sobchak and Mrs Galina Starovoytova, the latter two being popular figures from Leningrad (soon to revert to the name St Petersburg). The election of Mrs Starovoytova and other intelligent, energetic women, as public deputies of the Supreme Soviet, contrasted sharply with the old guard who had held sway for so long.

But, althought the Communists had undergone serious setbacks, there were still enough of them around to wreck moves towards democracy. Sakharov, in particular, suffered greatly in the Supreme Soviet (the equivalent of parliament) at the hands of the Communists, who launched verbal barrages against his every utterance. He died from a heart attack a couple of years later. Similarly, Sobchak, persecuted by Communist leaders in Leningrad, died of a heart attack before he turned 60. An unknown assailant shot Mrs Starovoytova in front of her home, and the crime, as with most killings of that type, was never solved.

The flame of hope that had briefly burned so brightly in our hearts and minds grew somewhat dimmer. The promises made by many candidates prior to their election to high office seemed to be secondary to the influence of a high life in Moscow, with State-provided cars, substantial salaries, power and publicity.

Groups of deputies banded together in the Supreme Soviet and fought each other in efforts to wrest power and influence for themselves. Now, in addition to the old Communist Party of the Soviet Union, we had the newly established Communist Party of the Russian Republic, together with the newly formed Supreme Soviet of the Russian Republic, called the Russian Parliament. Then there was the Supreme Soviet of the Soviet Union that we called the Parliament of the Soviet Union. The number of public servants was multiplying with amazing rapidity.

Inside these august institutions, as well as between them, there broke out nasty arguments, fist fights and mud slinging, all of which were exhibited for the first time on television and in other media. The shocked and disappointed public began to polarise, gravitating into either one of the spiders' nests that were the democratic or Communist camps. Each claimed that the other didn't care about the people and was not really interested in creating a better life for all.

The promised new Constitution and democratic laws took an interminable time to be promulgated. Meanwhile, arguments raged and bickering over the finer points appeared endless. Many old

Communist office bearers, because they were recognised as administrators, had been re-elected to new democratic positions as public deputies, but continued to govern from the same chairs in the same offices and, more often than not, with the same bureaucratic Socialist mindset.

In addition to the positions they already held, some managed to obtain other administrative responsibilities, such as chairmen of the executive committees of their regions. If successful, they were virtually their own bosses. They wielded immense power and often their main priority was to protect their personal, elitist interests. They then paid even less attention to the needs of ordinary people than they had before. Those office bearers, it appeared, often tried to 'white ant' democracy throughout the country. We stood by, confused at the way things seemed to be moving in the wrong direction.

A joke, popular at that time, concerned the friendship between a wolf and a dog. The wolf lived free in the forest while the dog, looked after by his master, was kept on a leash. The wolf heard that the dog's life had changed because his master had announced *perestroika* and *glasnost*, so he rushed over to enquire what difference it was making to his chum. The dog told him that, before the announcement, he had not been allowed to bark and, whenever he did, his master gave him a little food to keep him quiet. He could now bark freely, but his food bowl was being placed just beyond the stretch of his leash.

Our economy was sliding down a slippery slope; there was talk of an 'economic crisis', and ever-increasing prices were blamed on 'inflation', a word new to our vocabulary.

Feelings of dissatisfaction were escalating slowly among the people. Violent crime was on the increase, with little attention paid to it by anyone until a well known and much respected Moscow priest by the name of Alexander Men was viciously murdered. Once again, the police were unable to solve the crime. The media, for the first time, dubbed it a 'political assassination'.

The USSR had become far more difficult to govern and I recall feelings of sympathy for Gorbachev. He was doing his best, even attempting to reduce the incidence of drunkenness by restricting the sale of alcohol; but this particular curb didn't last long.

Although one might think that the people would be upset by such a restriction, it didn't bother most because they were accustomed to producing their own homemade vodka and wine from berries grown at *dachas*. The worst consequence of the ban was the destruction of grapevines in many areas of wine production, resulting in serious shortages. We had never been spoiled by the availability of good wine but, after the vines were destroyed, what was offered us was undrinkable.

On 26 April 1986, the Chernobyl catastrophe unfolded. Thousands of people still consider Gorbachev guilty with regard to this, because his government first announced it more than a week after it had happened. Meanwhile, on Labour Day (1 May), crowds were encouraged to take part in celebratory parades and public gatherings in the open, unwittingly exposing themselves to radiation. One wonders how many lives might have been saved had the catastrophe been publicised immediately and appropriate action taken.

In 1988, an earthquake in Armenia left 80 000 dead. The rescue effort stretched the resources of the fledgling democracy and tested the mettle of its leaders. On another front, splinters started to show in the fabric of the previously iron-clad Union: three Baltic republics demanded independence, which they were later granted. The same year, an astonishing two million Russians of German extraction emigrated to Germany to reunite with their families – a measure of the pent-up yearnings of ordinary Russians for a better life.

In 1989, Gorbachev ordered the total withdrawal of Russian troops from Afghanistan, which brought to an end a bitter war of attrition. (Although Russia withdrew in 1989, the war dragged on until 1992.) And, in an act of enormous symbolic importance that was screened on television world-wide, the Berlin Wall was torn down by frenzied crowds who had suffered its divisive rule for 28 years.

Then, in 1990, Gorbachev was awarded the Nobel Peace Prize. His popularity outside of the USSR soared. While he may have been seen as a hero by the outside world, we continually tightened our belts, holding onto the hope that his promise of a new life would one day be fulfilled.

23

Personal *perestroika*

IN 1988, AT THE AGE OF 33, I HAD RESIGNED MY POSITION AT THE Agricultural Project Building Institute. Nobody understood why. It appeared to outsiders as if I were approaching the pinnacle of my career: my group were happy with me, the institute satisfied with my work, and the Communist Party considered me a disciplined member.

My colleagues expressed regret that I was leaving and my bosses were at a loss, thinking it had to do with money. Truth was, it had nothing to do with money; I simply didn't want to work for the government any longer.

Eugene took it reasonably well, thinking me merely capricious, and said that, if I needed a rest, I could stay at home for a while. However, my mother took it badly and couldn't understand why, at my young age, and without children, I had decided to stay at home and do nothing. Mother, having had three children, had hardly ever missed a day working for the interests of the State. She was embarrassed by the thought that her daughter might be considered lazy by society, and her staunch Communist mind viewed me as being unworthy.

When I tried to explain my decision to friends, however, they appeared not entirely unsympathetic; many were equally unhappy working for the government. Most people of my age had begun grumbling about the government and their miserable lives, and theorising on how they might bring about change.

Giving vent to their emotions may have made individuals feel better, but, as a rule, they returned to their grinding lives the following day. But I was going out on a limb. Most considered it just a temporary aberration.

On the contrary; it turned out to be a watershed in my life.

I spent much time reflecting on what I'd done and analysing the reasons for my dissatisfaction. My past life came to mind like a movie. I could see scenes of myself as a child, asking my father about Communism and being unhappy about having to be the same as other girls. I remembered a boy at school being sent to Artek, and for the first time becoming aware of *blat*. I recalled the row of government-owned black cars outside Moscow University, and recognising bribery and unfair privilege. I remembered feeling like a second-class human being in a Prague underwear shop, together with the resultant loss of dignity. I realised, as was made evident on my visit to West Germany, that from a young age I had been fed false propaganda about the outside world. I pictured the injustices of my grandmother's life; old women having to work *dachas* to survive, *kolkhoz* duty, queuing for basic necessities, inadequate salaries and crowded living conditions.

I thought about the government turning a blind eye to vodka as an opiate; creating laws that, in some instances, had to be broken if one was to survive, as in the case of the sturgeon fishermen; all-powerful provincial Party leaders treating citizens as vassals; valid criticism of inept systems being dubbed treasonous; and high walls dividing those struggling to survive from the elite of the Party, who were living privileged lives. It was like an evil kaleidoscope, a horrendous montage.

Eugene and I had worked hard to get where we were. He was deputy director of an organisation employing more than 2 000 people. I had held a high position for a female engineer and, on aggregate, we were well paid. But what did we have after 12 years of hard work for the government? The same two-roomed flat, left to us by his parents, on the fifth floor of a building without an elevator; old furniture, also given to us; and insufficient money to replace or even renovate. A *dacha* that we were forced to work over weekends; our only 'luxuries' being a second-hand Zhiguli, used mostly to get there. We at least enjoyed the pleasure of a seaside holiday once a year – but we didn't have children, and those that did could not afford what we had.

What could the future hold if I continued working as before? The struggle for survival would be ongoing and I would be giving my health, strength and most productive years to a system in which I had lost faith. I was convinced that I could not carry on working in the rotten, artificial State economy, and I no longer wanted to continue my membership of the Communist Party and Trade Union. The all-pervasive bureaucratic atmosphere had become anathema to me.

What I didn't want was abundantly clear to me, but I had no idea of how I would go about creating a different life for myself. Whatever I was going to do had to allow me to live in peace with my conscience.

After not working for a while, my nervous system returned to normal and I was able to think more clearly. In principle, I concluded that I was going to do whatever made me happy and earn my own living without any reliance on the State. Fashion designing had been my dream from a young age, but it was too late now to go to university. I decided to take a two-year course in professional dressmaking. I so enjoyed that course, that I joined a one-year machine-knitting course that ran concurrently during the second year. The courses occupied three of my weekdays, so I looked for additional things of interest to fill the rest of my time.

With great enthusiasm I would jump out of bed in the mornings, knowing that the days were entirely my own. There were no Party controls, forward production plans or bosses looking over my shoulder, and, for the first time in my life, I felt really free. So free, in fact, that I did numerous other things that I hadn't considered previously.

I took driving lessons and got my licence, joined a gardening society enabling me to work at the *dacha* with a higher degree of proficiency, and took an interest as part of a group studying the rearing of chickens and rabbits. While still attending dressmaking lessons, I started breeding rabbits and raising day-old chicks at our *dacha*. I was busy and loving it, and Eugene was satisfied with the way things had turned out. What's more, my good animal husbandry and improved vegetable production provided food for our families when the government was rationing it.

In addition to those activities, I took an evening English language course. I didn't know why I was doing it, but I had a feeling that it could be useful later in life. I even suggested to Eugene that we should consider emigrating; I'd lost faith in the possibility of a good future in Russia. He thought we couldn't afford to leave. I accepted his response, but neither of us knew what the future held.

I was still registered as a member of the Communist Party with the Agricultural Building Project Institute, although I was deliberately missing what were supposedly compulsory monthly meetings. It appeared that they had lost interest in me anyhow, because there was nothing they could ask of me as far as their projects were concerned, and they were not interested in rabbits, chickens or dresses. I stopped payment of my monthly dues in 1990, so was automatically out of the Party. The Communist Party had more important things to worry about at that time and luckily forgot about me.

The end of my two-year course was fast approaching and I had to decide what I would do next. It was the end of spring 1990, and the first private companies were being allowed to trade. The new green shoots of capitalism were sprouting. Everyone appeared to accept the change that most considered essential for the establishment of a better economy.

I found a small, private clothing manufacturing company that needed to outsource additional production by using home dressmakers. They were prepared to allow me to make my own designs at home, so the idea appealed to me.

After working with them for a couple of months, I heard that the owner was having a problem regarding registration with the authorities. Those causing the bureaucratic problems turned out to be friends of my husband. As I also knew them well, I offered to help. Once the problem was resolved, I began to wonder why I hadn't thought of starting a company myself. I didn't want to sit in front of a sewing machine for the rest of my life, so the idea of having my own company was very appealing. It would tie in perfectly with what I'd been learning over the past two years.

That evening, I discussed the subject with Eugene. I needed to register, find capital, premises, machinery and workers. He was keen to help and his experience enabled him to give me good advice.

In January 1991, my new life as one of the pioneer capitalist businesswomen in Kalinin began. It was my personal *perestroika*.

24

Free enterprise

P RIVATE BUSINESSES WERE SOMETHING COMPLETELY NEW TO US
in Russia. Every business entity in our lifetimes had belonged
to, and been run by, the Communist government.

There was great excitement in the early 1990s, with people
believing that a good life under capitalism awaited them. Ordinary
citizens were starting to establish their own businesses, run them in
ways of their choosing and achieve an unprecedented degree of
independence.

The most important topic of conversation among young people
was what they intended doing to take advantage of their new-found
freedom to enrich themselves. The foreign word 'business' suddenly
became an everyday part of the Russian vocabulary and no effort
was made to use the Russian equivalent. Everybody dreamed of
elevating themselves to the lofty status of 'business person'.

Eugene was general director of a large wholesale business in
which I had always been interested – but now we discussed little
else. I was determined to absorb as much knowledge about business
as possible, and listened to male conversations on social occasions in
preference to idle women's chatter. The only way to learn was from
the experience of others, because we had no school, college or
university to teach us theory. I was gaining in confidence and really
believed I was in the right place at the right time to enjoy success.

While continuing to work at home for a small, privately run
clothing manufacturer, I began the difficult task of trying to register
my own company. It was fraught with bureaucratic pitfalls that had
me scampering for days on end from one office to another.

I had decided on what I thought was a good name for my

enterprise, 'Tverskaya Mozaika'. It means 'Tver Mosaic', flexible enough, I considered, to give me the leeway to produce a variety of products and reflecting my city's much-loved original name, to which it reverted that year (1991). I intended to start small with a few sewing machines, outsourcing excess orders to unemployed women. As profits permitted I would expand the business, but had no intention of it getting too big.

Demand was surprisingly buoyant, because government shops had had so little stock over the past years that the people were crying out for supplies.

A few days after I finally managed to get my company registered, a lucky break occurred. Eugene heard of one of the first private companies to go into liquidation. It was about to be broken up for disposal. A small factory with 25 workers, cutting tables, sewing machines, presses and a truck with a driver – it was ideal for my purposes. All I had to do was find the cash to buy it.

Eugene suggested that his company, which had capital available, could buy it, lease it to me and, once it was paid off, I would own it. It would be one of his company's satellite enterprises, and I could produce items required by his divisions and his staff. It was a great idea and, with pounding heart, I agreed we should go ahead.

I took over the factory in April 1991. Having bought the stock and equipment, the first thing to do was to get premises. I found a cellar in the centre of town, adequate for my purposes and at a reasonable rental. Eugene's company moved and installed the equipment and stock in the new premises. Staff, together with the manageress, Alla, from the defunct company, agreed to join me. It was a huge leap into the unknown and every day presented me with new challenges.

I opened a company bank account, signed documents such as contracts and agreements with which I had hitherto been quite unfamiliar. A part-time accountant and company lawyer had to be appointed. Deep down, I was concerned that my sewing courses would not prove adequate to enable me to manage the company successfully.

There were machines among those we'd purchased that were unknown to me, and I didn't have any idea of how to set up a production line. I knew that I could learn progressively, but it was going to take time. For that reason, I was very happy to have Alla. It was common sense to let her organise and oversee production, and I took it upon myself to be responsible for the administration, buying raw materials and selling finished products.

It wasn't long before I realised that we were going to need a full-time accountant. Terms like 'debit', 'credit' and 'balance' scared me witless, but I didn't want a bean counter who was going to be too smart. From the little knowledge I had of other small businesses, I understood that 'clever' accountants had sometimes landed their bosses in jail. On the other hand, taking an inexperienced person would leave us lacking in the necessary know-how.

I discussed the matter with Eugene, who explained how I might go about finding a full-time accountant and what I should or should not be prepared to sign. Through his organisation, I managed to find someone I considered right for the job. Her name was Alexandra. She had 20 years of experience and had last been employed as the chief accountant in a big State-owned company.

After *perestroika* was announced, accounting and tax laws changed almost daily, making staying on the right side of the law a nightmare. Not wanting to end up behind bars, she had decided it best to resign and find employment at a similar salary level in a smaller, less complicated, company.

When we first met I was drawn to her immediately. She appeared straightforward, warm and kind, and impressed me at once as being trustworthy. I wondered how I was going to match her high salary requirement and explained my future intentions for Tver Mozaika.

We were going to grow as profits permitted, and diversify into other products such as knits, furs and wedding dresses. We would then open our own shops and get the best fashion designers to work with us. The day would come when we would have our own fashion shows, employing our own models, and our company would become a household name in Leningrad and Moscow.

She agreed to start with us on a lower salary, with the prospect of earning more at some future date when the company was on solid ground and could better afford her. In all the time we worked together, Alexandra never belittled me for my lack of knowledge or experience. In fact, she always did her best to assist wherever she could. Consequently, we formed an excellent working relationship, with her making an invaluable contribution to our success.

With a full compliment of staff and the factory working eight hours daily, I was like a hamster on a treadmill. A number of small enterprises had opened, only to close after a few months for a variety of reasons, not least among them bad management and high company taxation. It meant that many people found themselves unemployed, leading to scepticism and distrust of small private companies in our community.

For that reason, it was imperative for me to imbue my employees with faith in our future and, from the beginning, I had to ensure that, no matter how difficult, they were paid in full on the last day of every month. In return, I was able to maintain discipline, achieve good quality standards and stick to promised delivery dates.

Because of their previous experience of working in private organisations, they understood the need for flexibility, and could switch with relative ease from producing one type of product to another. We went from ladies' dresses to a container of workers' gloves, to bed linen and then a contract for men's trousers. Of course, it was a far cry from working in the huge, State-owned 'sausage factories' that produced the same product year after year, regardless of market demand, which had made jobs so repetitive that workers could carry on with their eyes closed.

Our biggest customer was Eugene's company, which also supplied us with raw materials and, because of its size, was able to provide us with big enough production runs to make switching products viable. Their every wish was my command, because I needed everything they could provide by way of orders and raw materials to generate the profits necessary to pay off the lease as quickly as possible.

Rampant inflation provided problems on the one hand, but, on the other, enabled me to pay off the lease in 10 months instead of the originally budgeted two years.

I took my first salary after six months of operation. Eugene's salary was adequate for both our needs at that time, which had allowed for this interruption in my earnings. When I held that first salary in my hand, I felt joyous relief. Not because of the money, but knowing that we were on our way gave me a great deal of personal satisfaction. It was a most wonderful feeling of achievement.

The business had become my sole obsession and had my complete attention, often to the detriment of other aspects of life, such as what I wore. Every day I climbed into jeans and jerseys, without giving any thought to my appearance. I always returned home exhausted, and household chores had become pure drudgery. I needed a housemaid to take care of the boring side of my life, but nobody I had ever known had had a maid.

Schoolchildren in Russia had learned a popular slogan arising from the Revolution: 'We are not slaves, slaves are not we.' Despite serious unemployment, workers not being paid and pensioners not receiving their pensions, it was unthinkable for anyone to be a 'house slave'. Cleaning anybody else's toilet, even for good money, was beneath everyone's dignity.

As two business people, working long hours when necessary, even over weekends, it was becoming essential that we find outside assistance before our domestic position disintegrated totally. We approached certain of our relatives who seemd to be in need. Some were unemployed, others simply unpaid, but they refused to do domestic work, even if I promised to pay them well.

Even my mother saw fit to give me a lecture on being a childless woman living in the luxury of a two-roomed flat, and being too lazy to clean and cook. Trying to explain that I was happy working for my own benefit, and that by day's end I was physically and mentally exhausted, was futile.

'What was so bad about Communist times and who do you think you are, some big shot? I am ashamed that you are becoming so fond of making money, even losing control of your working hours,' Mother would say.

Her words really stung and the only explanation I could give her was, 'My business is my baby, nothing to do with money. But since you talk about money, what's wrong with earning it? I'm 36 years old and at the prime of my working life. It may be the only opportunity I will get in this country to create my own business. If I earn enough, I will be able to help you in your old age and look after myself too, but with nothing in my pocket, how will I be able to help either of us?' It was useless arguing with her.

After looking around for a few weeks, we came across an elderly woman, recently widowed, who couldn't stand being alone at home. She happened to like our dog and accepted us as her own family. We paid her four times her monthly pension, but she said it wasn't for money that she would work for us; it was because she wanted to help.

She was a wonderful person and I was able to breathe a sigh of relief. I'm almost certain that I was the first woman, after Soviet rule, to get a domestic maid in the city of Kalinin.

Six months after starting my business, I felt it was stabilising, the initial roller-coaster ride having levelled off somewhat. Working on administration and sales still filled my days, and there were times when all I could do was stick my head around the factory door to say 'hello'.

I relied on Alla to run the production, which she did satisfactorily. However, she was not an easy woman to understand, and sometimes I felt she was withholding things from me. Her eyes were too shiny on occasion, as if she were suffering a fever or had been drinking. As far as I could tell, she never smelled of alcohol, so I had to consider the possibility of her being on drugs. When her enthusiasm for her work began waning, it worried me to the extent that I decided to discuss it with Eugene.

In view of my being unable to spend more time in the factory, he thought it might be wise to consider making her a shareholder, which should increase her level of interest.

'Don't be greedy,' he said. 'Give her a third of your shares; the other two thirds is enough for you. It will be to the business' advantage.'

So I transferred a third of the shares into her name, giving her a year to pay, but no voting rights until the money was forthcoming. For a while it appeared to have done the trick, but none of the books I'd read mentioned what the negative side of such generosity could be.

The space we rented in the cellar was only part of what was available; with the rest standing empty, I always imagined that we would one day expand and fill it. Eugene somehow got possession of a brand new industrial knitting machine that he had been offered as part of a barter arrangement. Because of high inflation and the time it took for the bartered machine to reach Kalinin, it was cheap. He had no use for it and agreed to sell it to us, with payment over three months.

It was a very exciting development and I became involved in putting it to profitable use. I had to obtain raw materials, find a machine minder, an extra worker and markets for our new knitted products. Realising that the addition of knitted products to our range was creating more work than I could efficiently handle, an assistant was fast becoming a necessity. I racked my brain, trying to think who would be able to do the job and fit into the team.

An idea came unexpectedly to mind. Both of my brothers, who had married and been working in Siberia and the Urals since leaving university, had returned to live in Kalinin. At a family gathering, Tamara, one of my sisters-in-law, had been complaining about her job and mentioned that she was looking for another position. Although we weren't close, she was adequately qualified for our needs, having passed knitting courses and gained the necessary experience. I thought it advantageous, from the point of view of trust, to employ a family member rather than an outsider. I invited her to come and see me at my office the following day.

She started with us 10 days later and, with great enthusiasm, set about planning future knitting production. I gave her all my contacts with suppliers and customers, and she began her tasks, promising to be an asset.

But once she discovered that Alla owned a third of the company, she requested a third too. She felt it was unfair that an outsider should hold a third, while she, a trusted family member, owned none of it. In due course I capitulated and signed a third over to her on the same terms and conditions as Alla enjoyed. For a time, the arrangement seemed to work.

There is an old Russian expression, 'A wolf's legs feed him', which means that, if he doesn't run, he doesn't eat. I knew that nobody was going to take me by the hand and lead me to success, so I would have to make it myself. I phoned the directors of big clothing production plants in our town and province and made appointments to visit them. At these meetings, I offered to help them with production and, in the process, gleaned valuable information that they let slip in conversation.

In addition, I planned to visit at least one of the 40 companies similar to mine each week. Listening to their experiences was like dipping into an encyclopaedia of the 'do's and don'ts' in clothing manufacturing. It was lucky that nearly everyone in Russia, until that time, had retained their Communist thinking, otherwise they may not have allowed me through their front doors.

I had been fortunate that my husband's company had patronised us. We both discovered relatively early on that working together was going to be of mutual benefit. Eugene's company was one of 130 branches of an enormous wholesale industrial centralised supply system, covering all of the Soviet Union. His responsibilities included supplying Tver province and northern areas as far off as Archangel.

The system had been devised 40 years earlier and comprised conduits for channelling goods from manufacturers to industrial consumers. As with most nationwide systems, it was controlled by a head office in Moscow. They stocked all components needed by huge manufacturers of products, ranging from earth-moving equipment, to books, to kitchen cleaning items. It meant keeping a vast range of goods, controlled in 19 specialised divisions, employing some 2 000 people.

Storage was on open territory measuring 70 000 square metres, or in covered warehousing of 34 000 square metres, with gantries for moving heavy goods, such as iron ingots or timber, and forklifts for handling bulk chemicals, or sugar, or toilet paper.

When Eugene was appointed general director in early 1990, the company was still organised along Soviet bureaucratic lines. Dealing with them was a nightmare. There were no computers and the paperwork needed to take any item from stock required so many signatures, that long queues of customers waited for hours.

Eugene was determined to change all that, but came up against stiff resistance from the 'old guard', some of whom had been there for as long as 30 years. Being young, aggressive and stubborn, he was determined to implement improvements such as computerisation and the freeing up of delays caused by the multiplicity of paperwork. He could see that this would increase turnover dramatically.

He had welcomed Gorbachev's announcement of *perestroika*, but could not break free of the constraints of centralised control. The best he could do, for the promotion of capitalism, was by way of assisting the mushrooming new, small, privately owned businesses like mine, which he set about with vigour. He took about 30 under his wing, some of which collapsed, but others flourished.

Sadly, the entire economic system in the USSR was disintegrating. Imports had disappeared from store shelves years before, and many Russian manufacturers were cutting production or closing down. Inflation was growing and the previously unknown problem of unemployment was gaining pace. It was becoming evident that the huge unwieldy State structure was coming apart at the seams.

Eugene's company, as part of the malaise, began running into operational difficulties. On the one hand, they could not get certain vitally required supplies and, on the other, increasing numbers of customers were unable to pay. Valuable connections, established over decades, were breaking down.

By 1991, the government had decided on a policy of privatisation that included Eugene's organisation. It was very satisfying talking policy, but nobody appeared to know how it was going to be implemented or achieved.

We keenly awaited a plan, schedule, instructions or anything that might give some direction to the process, but nothing was forthcoming. Eugene drove to Moscow on numerous occasions, always returning frustrated and despondent at the lack of official action. It took some months, but a deal was finally put forward and Eugene took over his branch of the organisation, which he turned into a private company named 'Russnab'.

The association of my little company with Russnab was of great benefit, especially from the point of view of security. With the advent of small private companies, there was a growth in criminal rackets, many relying on extortion for 'protection' as practised decades before by American hoodlums. Being under the Russnab umbrella made life a lot easier and safer for my company.

Robberies were occurring more frequently, with small private businesses seen as soft targets. Racketeers and robbers were not necessarily associates; more often than not they were small groups of ex-soldiers or ex-convicts unable to get gainful employment. The real mafia, or organised crime, only got going later.

The police did nothing to bring the situation under control; in fact, I don't recall ever hearing of an instance where they apprehended the perpetrators. We were not immune, despite maintaining a low profile and letting it be widely known that we were associated with Russnab.

Through developing connections, I discovered a variety of small producers that needed marketing assistance. There was a deaf school, for example, where students made small items such as tea cloths that they wanted to sell, because the government had cut their subsidies and they needed the money. Disabled women were turning out cotton dressing gowns and nightdresses for sale.

Between large or contract orders, we were also making short-run items to dispose of an excess of short-end cloths. I needed to sell those too. I offered to sell the disabled women's products, but we couldn't do it from our basement factory site, nor could we afford to hire premises in town, so I compromised by buying a kiosk from the municipality, situated in the town centre.

Trade was brisk, but after a few months the municipality forced us to buy a new structure because they maintained that the one we were using was in bad shape and spoiled the atmosphere of the town. They hadn't mentioned this just three months earlier when they took our money.

I got wind of a new kiosk for sale, which had been left by the government in a small town in our province, and travelled the 150 kilometres to strike a deal with the town authorities. What I found was a brand new kiosk, of modern design, bigger than ours. It even had an electric heater for the winter months.

The price was a joke, so I bought it, but how was I going to transport it to Kalinin? I measured the base in order to make a foundation for it on our site and a few days later returned with a flatbed truck and crane, hired from Russnab. It took the entire day to take it back over the bad roads and offload it at our site in Kalinin. I was so pleased at the sight of it that I even let our factory workers leave their jobs to go and admire it. It was the last time we saw it, though – the following morning it had disappeared.

When I reported the theft to the police, I was told it was my problem and that they could not help. Their attitude was that the new businesses were to blame for rising crime in the town and they, the police, were not going to assist. I remonstrated with them, demanding that they do something; after all, it wasn't an item that could be easily lifted and carried away. The thieves would have needed a big flatbed truck and crane and, furthermore, it had been taken from the centre of town, where there were always people about. Someone must have seen something.

The police said investigating the crime was a waste of time. Anyone who had seen what had happened would not get involved for fear of reprisals from the criminals. They refused even to open a file, which made me furious. For what purpose did we have police?

Insurance was not an option, because everything had previously belonged to the State, and systems for private insurance were not yet up and running. There was a system of insurance run by the State, but it was a complete waste of money. Paying premiums was fine, but claiming was like trying to steal the jewels out of the Kremlin. So I ran out of enthusiasm and money for another new kiosk, in addition to which the municipality soon allocated the position to somebody else. We didn't give up though; when our truck wasn't busy we sent it loaded with merchandise and a sales lady to hawk products nearby.

Establishing our knitting business took about a month. Tamara and I had liaised closely on how we would set up and manage it, but as time went by, I found that she was communicating less frequently with me. She appeared, instead, to have built up an alliance with Alla, the factory manager. I watched her behaviour and tried to understand what was motivating her independence. Was she so confident in her own ability that she considered it unnecessary to discuss matters with me, or had she decided to demonstrate that I no longer meant much to her?

I shared my concerns about Tamara and Alla with our accountant, Alexandra. Her explanation amazed me.

'My darling, are you blind? Can't you see what's going on in our company? Alla is an alcoholic. She encourages our workers to drink in an effort to garner their support. Tamara has joined her and they are plotting against you, with the workers in support. I haven't said anything before because Tamara is your sister-in-law and I didn't want to be the cause of a family feud. You obviously haven't noticed because you are out trying to find work for us most of the time.'

Alexandra was right. A day or two later, after a meeting that had dragged on late, I went back to the factory, expecting to find the place locked and alarmed. To my surprise I found Alla, Tamara, our driver and a few workers drinking vodka on the factory floor. They maintained that it was the birthday of one of the workers. I said I didn't mind their having a party, but the factory was not the place to hold it. The reason for Alla's shining eyes was then abundantly clear, although I had never smelled liquor on her breath; but I wondered how or why Tamara had become involved. Nobody in the family had ever mentioned that she enjoyed a glass of vodka.

The following week I had to go to Moscow on business. As a rule, I would go directly home thereafter, arriving late in the evening, but, on that occasion, I decided to get back earlier and visit the factory. The same people were drinking in the same place, which prompted me to have it out with my co-directors. They promised that it would not recur.

Their attitude, to me, was strange. They apparently found it difficult to grasp that they were just as responsible for the business as I was, and behaved as if they were workers in a State factory talking with their State-appointed director.

For the next three months it looked as if the problem had, to all intents and purposes, been resolved, and then the story took a new turn. One day, a young man of about 25 arrived at the factory premises. His manner was tense and his eyes chameleon like, taking in everything in sight. He asked to see Alla or Tamara, but I explained that they were not at work because they'd had to go somewhere. He wanted to know who else could help him. I told him I would try and asked what he needed. He refused to talk in front of Alexandra, with whom I shared an office, asking if he could speak with me alone in the passage. Adopting a very confidential tone, he whispered that he needed fabric.

'What fabric?' I asked. 'Selling fabric is not our business.'

Because I was younger than my co-directors and Alexandra, he took me for an assistant and said, 'Come on girl, don't mess around, I'm desperate for that fabric.' And he proceeded to describe a particular cloth with which we were working at the time, making up an order of ladies' jackets and skirts.

'There's no way we're selling that fabric,' I said.

'I'll pay you a good price per metre in cash,' he confided. 'I need a few pieces.' (A piece was a 60 metre length.)

Suddenly, I realised he was offering to pay *me* the cash.

'Who do you think you're dealing with?' I asked. 'I'm the director of this company and, in any case, that fabric costs double what you want to pay me for it.'

'Okay,' he said. 'I'll increase the price, but remember I'll give you cash.'

By that time I was so angry I could hardly talk. 'How can you talk to me like that?' I managed to ask. 'I'm a director of this company.'

'Director, so what?' he insolently replied, 'Alla is also a director and she gave me the fabric at an even cheaper price. I'll wait until she gets back.'

He turned and walked out, leaving me utterly furious. It was obvious that he was accustomed to wheeling and dealing with directors of State-owned establishments, not private companies where the stock belonged to the shareholders – in our case, the directors. Alexandra and I went immediately to check the stock in our raw materials storeroom and, sure enough, there were pieces missing. What on earth were my partners doing? We were all in the business together, benefiting equally from profits generated, yet they considered it clever to sell the fabric we needed in the business, at a lower price than it cost us, and put the cash in their pockets.

More than 70 years of Soviet government had successfully eradicated all feelings of private ownership from the psyche of citizens. The only conclusion I could come to was that my partners were simply not able to grasp the fact that the company was theirs, and not a state within a state where everything still belonged to the government.

Under Soviet rule, people were told that everything belonged to the State and the State belonged to them, so in their minds, taking what belonged to them never appeared criminal – unless, of course, they were caught. Lying, cheating and being in opposition to the boss had become firmly entrenched as normal behaviour, and it looked as if they had chosen me as boss because they understood no other behaviour.

Perhaps people had been waiting for a better life to materialise when Gorbachev announced *perestroika*. But the announcement, in itself, meant nothing unless people grasped the nettle and tried to understand what was required of them as individuals.

That was the last straw. I could not continue with them as partners. My next move had to be a visit to an attorney to discuss a possible dissolution.

It was a unique period in Russian history, when laws were changing from the old Soviet to a new capitalist system. Everyone, including the lawyers, understood the old laws well enough, but the new were still in the process of being formulated, in many instances without precedents on which to base judgements and decisions.

From the time private enterprise had been permitted, thousands of enterprising individuals had rushed to establish ownership of their own companies, and Articles of Association had been hurriedly formulated with the object of getting into business as quickly as possible, enabling new entrepreneurs to make 'a quick buck' legitimately. I was one of those.

Many had failed before really getting started properly, which meant, in many cases, that there were no assets worth arguing over. Others, like mine, survived a little longer and had accumulated assets that became a problem to divide among shareholders if the company were dissolved for any reason. Finding an attorney able to advise me on such procedures was to prove difficult.

After some research, I managed to find an attorney reputed to know what she was doing. She explained that, according to our written agreements, if Alla and Tamara put in the money owing for their shares, I could be out-voted; together they would hold a majority stake in the company. On the other hand, should they neglect to put the money in before one year was up, they would have forfeited their voting rights, but I would still be entitled to only a third of the assets.

Whether she was absolutely correct in her assessment, I had no way of knowing, but taking the matter to the overburdened, bureaucratic courts was not an option because a judgement would likely take years and cost a great deal.

I alone had signed security for everything and the company still had creditors, so there was no point in trying to break it up until our debts had been expunged. The attorney's only suggestion, for my protection, was to give Alla and Tamara letters reminding them of their debts to the company and that, if they failed to pay by the end of the period allowed, I should return to her with details of the company assets for division among us.

The attorney displayed sincere sympathy for the position in which I found myself, and I will always remember her advice. 'Don't feel sorry about material things,' she said. 'They come and go, but the real asset is a person's mental capacity. Without it, no windfall will help in the long term.'

I left her office thinking how difficult it had been living in a Socialist society without money. Now it appeared that living with money in a capitalist society wasn't any easier. With or without money, there were always going to be headaches.

Even times of struggle invariably end and, despite signing letters of intent, Alla and Tamara didn't come up with the money in the time provided. I had paid off all of the company debts, cancelled our lease on the factory premises, ensured that we used all of our raw materials and then returned to the attorney with full details of our assets. Oddly enough, it was easy to divide them into three parts. Due to the liquidation of the factory that previously owned them, the original factory machinery and truck had been purchased at a very low price a year before and, because of hyperinflation since the date of purchase, the total value was now approximately the same as the value of our industrial knitting machine, which also equalled the value of our new truck.

Of the three parts, I chose the new truck, because I thought it would be the best thing to assist me in any other business I might buy or start. Had I chosen either of the other two, it would have been bound to create an argument. I simply wanted to be rid of the business and get on with something new. My colleagues' reactions were exactly what I'd expected: joy and bewilderment at the choice I'd made. Alla took the factory machines and the old truck, Tamara the knitting machine, and we said our goodbyes.

I took stock of my situation. Alexandra had stuck with me and I had retained the company name and a new truck, but, in truth, I had a lot more. Through all of the problems with my previous partners, Alexandra had proved her value as a true friend. I had made many useful connections in a variety of associated fields, such as banking and advertising, and I knew my company name, Tverskaya Mozaika, had goodwill as customers and suppliers alike held it in high regard.

Over our year of operation, I had worked and established a good rapport with Russnab, who would be very important to me in the continuation of business. More importantly, I had a year's experience in which, despite problems, I had gained knowledge and confidence. I would not have to begin again feeling ignorant or naive, nor would I make the same mistakes with people.

Weighing it all up, I determined that starting afresh and being confidently in command of my own business destiny was going to be a pleasure. I felt that Tverskaya Mozaika had a lot going for it.

25

Privatisation

BY THE BEGINNING OF SUMMER 1992, I WAS FREE OF ALL TIES TO my previous partners, and my dreams, hopes and enthusiasm for a new business life had been rekindled. But this time it would be different: there would be no partners, not because I was greedy, but rather because they might turn out to be so. Experience had been an excellent teacher. In addition, I was not prepared to start small with just a few sewing machines, rather preferring the idea of acquiring a complete, up-and-running factory.

A few months prior to this, in January 1992, the government had announced 'avalanche privatisation', although privatisation had in fact begun at least a year before, when they had initiated the change themselves by giving minority shares in big companies to employees.

Eugene's company had been involved in that process, enabling him to acquire a limited shareholding. However, overall progress had been too slow, which gave rise to dissatisfaction on the part of those involved in medium and small government industries.

Not only had the government stopped supporting those organisations, but the people involved in them had no idea of where to look for alternative assistance in their efforts to continue operations. It had led to serious breakdowns in the supply of goods and services, resulting in what can only be described as chaos. We felt ourselves falling into an economic abyss.

Simultaneously, it became clear to many of us that this was a historic moment in time, when what had previously been regarded as government property was about to be given to the people. That may have taken place centuries before in other countries, but

Russia was one of the few not to have followed suit. The kind of opportunity presenting itself would likely never be repeated. We had to get what we could, while we could.

Seizing the moment, I decided to visit the Committee for Privatisation and try my luck. That committee happened to be housed in one of the grandest buildings in central Tver, together with the provincial Communist Party committee and the *Komsomol* committee. The same people who previously served Communist ideology so zealously were busy now establishing an entirely different form of social structure, although nothing discernable had changed in their bureaucratic approach to the task.

Absolutely no initiative could be expected from them after the years of punishment visited upon those who had displayed any aptitude for original thought. Instructions still had to be awaited from Moscow, without which little or nothing could be done.

One thing had definitely changed, though, in our new democratic State. Instead of a policeman at the front door controlling visitors, there was just one old woman who chose to ignore me. Getting into the offices of the Committee for Privatisation proved easier than I had anticipated.

On entering, I was confronted by an elderly, thick-browed man of extremely grumpy disposition.

'Good morning,' I said, very politely. 'Please can you tell me where I can get a list of government industries about to be privatised?'

'There's no such thing,' he said, glancing briefly in my direction and continuing with whatever preoccupied him.

'But there must be, because my husband told me that at the last city administration meeting it was announced that the lists were complete,' I continued.

'Who are you, that you think you know everything, and who is your husband, anyway?

'The lists have not been signed yet by the administration chief and you are here already trying to spy. In any case, you ought to know that the list is not for everybody,' he thundered.

When I opened my mouth to try to reason with the man, he

just kept on ranting. I was shown the door. It was obvious that I wasn't going to get any further.

On exiting the building, I asked the old woman at the door if she could identify the grumpy man in the privatisation office.

'He's the chairman,' she told me in a deferential tone.

Confused, I left the building wondering where I'd gone wrong and why the lists were so secret.

Perhaps I should explain how I came by the information relating to the list. A year prior to this, Eugene had stood in the local elections, representing an area of our city. After he was successfully elected, he became involved in municipal meetings at which decisions were made regarding privatisation.

When he arrived home that evening I related my experience to him and asked why the list was so secret?

'Rubbish,' he said. 'How can you privatise if you keep it a secret? In fact, it is quite the opposite; by law, the list must be published in the press.'

A week later I decided to give it another shot, although I wasn't looking forward to another confrontation with 'old eyebrows'. I thought I had to get in early 'while stocks lasted' and, without braving the grumpy old man, I would likely never have a choice.

In my mind I went over and over our first meeting to recall how I had been dressed and what I'd said, finally concluding that it had been a good thing that I had not introduced myself or given him the name of my husband.

In order to make a different impression, I coloured my hair and changed the style, wore no make-up and borrowed glasses from a friend. Making friends with the old man was an imperative if I was to get what I wanted, and I realised that to achieve it, absolute concentration was going to be necessary.

Composing myself in front of the door, I knocked and entered casually with a broad, friendly smile. His reaction was completely different on this occasion. He offered me a chair and asked if I would like a cup of tea.

In response to his more reasonable questioning, I told him I was the owner of Tverskaya Mozaika and needed to expand my company's activities. To my great surprise, he said he'd heard of my company and the good quality of our production. Then, on request, he promptly produced the list I'd sought and began giving me fatherly advice on how to go about getting what I needed. I concluded that he must have had horrible indigestion on the first occasion I'd encountered him.

Listening to his opinions, I nodded in silence, while studying the list. Surprisingly, there was not one business located in the city centre earmarked for privatisation.

'What has happened?' I asked. 'Has a bomb dropped in the city centre that precludes businesses there from being privatised? I don't see one on this list.'

Without blinking he said, 'They are all privatised already.'

I had to bite my tongue to prevent asking when and how it had been done, because the list had been signed only a few days earlier and had not yet been published, which was required by law. Suspicion of corruption came to me instantly; someone had been smart enough to get in before anyone else was given the chance.

From the list of less desirable businesses, I chose a medium-sized factory producing men's suits and trousers, located in a three-storey building of 1 000 square metres, situated on the periphery of the 'bomb crater'. Some 130 people were employed there in two daily shifts, but, due to supply-side problems, the factory was about to close.

They had been one of 40 'spokes' in the production wheel of a big organisation that had in the past provided the necessary raw materials, enabling the 'spokes' to make products that were taken up immediately by the central 'hub' company for distribution to government retail outlets. The hub company had been obliged to close, leaving the spokes without supplies or the know-how to keep running by themselves.

The situation was typical of many other industries in the previously centralised Soviet production system, but no new system had successfully evolved to facilitate continuity. Privatisation was expected to supply the remedy. The weight of responsibility would be removed from the shoulders of the government and placed squarely upon those of the new private owners.

Before finally agreeing to take the factory, I thought it prudent first to check the place. The following morning I paid the director of the company a visit. She was a woman of about 30 who, on first impression, appeared sufficiently intelligent and energetic. I told her I had come from the Committee for Privatisation and was considering bidding for her factory.

While showing me around, she complained incessantly about the problems she'd encountered from the time the hub company had closed. Before, she said, this had been a good job, with all raw materials being supplied and instructions received on precisely what to do; the 'hub' had even fixed broken equipment or replaced it if necessary. They had collected finished products on a daily basis, but now, she complained, the place had become a nightmare: toilets were leaking; the building was in need of renovation; the raw material store was empty, while the finished product store was overflowing with reject goods; the workers had not been paid for three months; and money was owing for electricity and water.

When we arrived on the factory floor, it was obvious that a number of operators were missing from the production lines. They were temporarily on involuntary, unpaid leave, she explained, due to the lack of funds to pay their wages. The equipment looked as if it should have been installed in a museum at the end of the nineteenth century, and the technology they were employing in the manufacturing process looked primitive too.

The impression I had gained was not good, but I wasn't frightened of taking it on because I knew that most other factories in Russia were pretty much the same. At least the factory was situated in a good position relative to the city centre, and had enough space to diversify production and open a retail shop on the ground floor.

I asked the woman why she didn't want to take over the factory herself and, to my surprise, she launched into a tirade of criticism of *perestroika*, Gorbachev and Yeltsin, blaming democracy for ruining a life she had previously enjoyed. She had not had to worry before, and had been perfectly happy with her adequate salary.

What shook me was that I had thought that only old people were unhappy with the changes in government policy, and that all young people should embrace them. It appeared, though, that I was wrong. To some extent, it depended on what people had been doing before *perestroika* was announced, and I realised that, if I were to take the factory, it would be difficult for me to keep her on as a director.

In view of the fact that the employees were not interested in acquiring it themselves, the Committee for Privatisation had told me that the business would be auctioned off in August, just two months away. A special commission would evaluate the assets, which sum would be the reserve price, but bidders should be aware that, if successful, they would also have to pay the separately scheduled debts of the company. In addition, they would have to negotiate with the local council about specific demands, which would be explained prior to the auction.

A week later I was advised that the factory had been valued at 10 million roubles. Along with this startlingly high price, there was added pressure: according to them, there was another party from Moscow province interested in bidding.

Where was I going to raise 10 million roubles? Russnab was likely to be my best bet and, after discussing the matter with Eugene, he approached one of the banks, offering Russnab as guarantors.

With a letter confirming Russnab as Tverskaya Mosaika's backer, I met the deputy director of the bank. After our introduction, I asked for 10 million roubles to be repaid over five years; he asked if I knew what the current interest rate was.

'It's 120 per cent per annum,' he announced. I was shocked to hear this, but I couldn't step back now and had to cling to the hope that rampant inflation would work to my advantage.

I got the loan at an interest rate of just 90 per cent per annum, confirmation of which I took to the chairman of the Committee for Privatisation who, while having treated me better on my second visit, now appeared positively servile. But it was a little premature to celebrate; the other interested party had also produced a guarantee for 10 million.

Right on cue, the fawning chairman came out in his true colours.

'Our municipality,' he said, 'has made clear its requirements for the successful bidder. It needs 10 kilometres of tram rails, five kilometres of plumbing piping and 60 tyres for the city trolley buses. It has money to pay for the items, but if the price is too high, you will have to pay the difference.'

'Are there any more conditions, or is that the last?' I asked.

'That's all. And the one who supplies the items will get the factory,' he answered.

When Eugene heard my story that evening, he was incensed.

'Saltikov-Schedrin was quite right,' he shouted. 'Russia will always have fools and bad roads.'

The great author had made that statement in the eighteenth century and nothing had changed.

'Why didn't they pick up the phone and ask me? Our storerooms are full of those items. I'm going to give my staff a talking to; they ride on the trolley busses, but don't see that there are fewer and fewer operating because of the tyre shortage, and, instead, they look for business in other provinces. And can't they see that the trams are no longer able to travel the old routes because the rails have worn out? Now, instead of selling to the municipality at the normal prices, I'm expected to give them goods at a discount because my staff aren't doing their jobs properly.'

Three days later, I arrived back at the Committee for Privatisation offices with copies of receipts for the items requested, signed for by the municipality's goods receiving department. The man from Moscow province was out of the running. I had won the 'auction' and got the factory.

With the title deeds firmly in hand, I walked out of that office as the first person in my family, since the Revolution, to wholly own a business. The new era of capitalism had begun and I was one of very few businesswomen in the city of Kalinin, although I didn't realise it at the time.

26

My factory

AFTER TAKING OWNERSHIP OF THE NEW TVERSKAYA MOZAIKA, I was bound by a rule that dictated that I had to keep the staff employed as seamstresses for a period of at least 10 years, regardless of output, in addition to which I was not permitted to reduce staff through retrenchments. The only way of getting rid of workers was by natural attrition, or through the courts if they behaved in a criminal or negligent way, which was usually difficult to prove.

I started work by calling a meeting of staff. They were almost all women, unhappy about the lot they had in life and apparently prepared to blame anyone in a superior position for their lack of achievement. Their attitude may have been justified in some respects, but facing them in the conditions of the time did not make it easy for me to promise them a brighter future.

The best I could do was say that, as circumstances in the country changed and more free-market enterprises took root, there would be opportunities for advancement, but in the meantime we should work as a team in order to survive. Thieves and slovenly or undisciplined people were not going to be required, and from that day forward we were going to sew whatever would bring us money, meaning salaries for them and a profit for the company.

Right now, I told them, the market does not require big volumes of men's suits and it is going to be difficult to dispose of those we already have in our finished product storeroom. A few people would continue making them, but some others would start producing ladies' clothes. The rest would be busy producing linen bedclothes and tablecloths, because we had large orders for those items. I also explained that we needed to take care of our equipment because it was fundamental to our financial success.

When I had finished talking, I looked at their faces expecting some reaction and was disappointed to realise that their expressions hadn't changed at all. They continued to look at me with hostility, as if I were an enemy.

Goosepimples broke out all over me and I thought I'd made a bad mistake in buying the factory. How was I possibly going to lead and control such an unhappy and aggressive crowd?

The following day we received a large consignment of linen and cotton for use in the manufacture of the products I'd detailed. A day after that, worker dissatisfaction in the form of a near riot broke out. My office was suddenly invaded by a shift of furious women with distorted faces, shouting and shaking their fists at me in a violently threatening manner.

I was frozen with fright. For the first time in my life I was faced with a serious management problem. After taking a deep breath I stood up and shouted with all my strength: 'Shut up and get out of here! If you want to talk to me, select two people to speak for you and the rest leave my office; I can't talk to all of you at the same time.' I don't know how dangerous I appeared to them, but they all slowly backed out, grumbling among themselves.

As the door closed, I fell back into my chair and took a few deep breaths. I had somehow brazened out the challenge and it had worked.

A short while later, two of the most vocal workers came back into the office and explained that they, as was the case with most of their comrades, had worked in the factory for as long as 30 years, and many had achieved distinction as sewing workers, and had been recognised by the State with certificates and medals. Making sheets and pillowcases, they said, was offensive, and they were not prepared to suffer such indignity. They simply refused to comply and, furthermore, were not prepared to recognise me as their director. While they had remained loyally at their posts for 30 years, many directors had come and gone, so what made me think I would be any different, they wanted to know.

'Comrades, you'd better forget what you have done all your lives,' I said. 'I respect all of your certificates and medals, but a new era has dawned in the country and you should understand that your previous recognition is not, unfortunately, going to feed you. What I'm offering you is a way to survive in these changing times. We have big orders for bedclothes from our Russnab supporters, which means we will have salaries and capital to continue the business. Believe me, we will be okay.'

But my words had fallen on deaf ears, and one of them said, 'You look out, we will all resign.'

'Do as you please,' I told them.

When, half an hour later, a group of them came in one by one to tender their letters of resignation, I signed each one in silence and handed them to the accountant for paying off. But when that task was completed, an ugly crowd of women returned to my office.

'How could you just sign and let us go so easily?' they demanded. 'We are honoured workers and we have been here for up to 30 years. We are not going to simply accept it and will go to the authorities to bring you to their attention.'

What could I tell them? They had resigned of their own volition and it had all been done in accordance with the law. What's more, there was insufficient work to keep them all busy, and I was not about to re-hire their, or anyone else's, services.

Collective action by the proletariat in the past would have been likely to cause a serious problem for the boss. The Communist Party, Trade Union and a representative of the central authority, to which the satellite company responded, would immediately have become involved, attempting to reconcile the problem by, in most cases, taking the side of the workers. It was easier to get rid of the boss than to replace all the workers.

Highly qualified workers had adopted the habit of threatening bosses, secure in the knowledge that, in the end, they would likely get what they wanted. So, throwing letters of resignation in the faces of bosses was not that uncommon.

What they couldn't grasp was that the situation had changed. The Communist Party no longer had teeth, private companies did not accept the Trade Union, and there was no central organisation to which I responded. Only the law was above my decision and all procedures had taken place perfectly legally, which left no recourse for the frustrated workers.

I really felt sympathy for the women; they could not understand that we were at a point in time when it was essential to their survival as factory workers that they co-operate.

Together with Alexandra and newly employed Irena, our commercial deputy (my ex-colleague at the Agricultural Building Project Institute), I had a meeting to formulate a strategy for repaying our debt in the shortest possible period. Our main problem was the fact that our so-called 'democratic government' continued to be influenced by old Communist philosophies, thinking that the answer to all problems was to impose higher taxes.

Alexandra calculated that, if we paid all taxes, as laid down, 97 per cent of all profits would go to government and province, leaving just three per cent for the improvement of our working capital. No company could survive in those circumstances and we, like everyone else, had to try to hide profits, walking a tightrope between being lawful and managing to survive. Having grown up as honest citizens, it was hard for us to accept that staying that way would lead to the starvation of our workers and their families.

We believed that the economic crisis was temporary, that the government would soon come to its senses and reduce the crippling taxes. Sadly, it did not appreciate the urgency needed. It was no wonder so many companies were going belly-up, adding to the growing unemployment problem. In order to remain partially operative, some factories tried to continue on short time, with workers going unpaid for months.

Someone had come up with the idea of using a product made by the workers to pay them for their labour. A factory producing aluminium pots, for example, gave workers their equivalent salary value in pots. Another producing glass tumblers paid in tumblers, and a soap producer, in cakes of soap. They had no choice, so workers accepted what they were given and went out on the streets to convert their 'pay' to cash. In instances where there was only one factory in a town, it created problems. Everyone in the town had pots, glasses or soap that they could not convert.

On a national television news broadcast one evening, we were surprised to learn that miners in Yakutia had been paid, month after month, in gold. The miners were incensed because they were surrounded by thousands of square kilometres of uninhabited tundra, with absolutely no way of being able to convert their 'pay'. Nobody was jealous. For what was perhaps the only time in history, gold was decried as payment when, on so many other occasions, people had murdered to acquire it.

As sometimes happens, necessity became the mother of invention and the State forced us to give birth to new ideas: in this instance, barter – one of the oldest systems of payment known to mankind. It had the added advantage of finding a loophole in the tax system. (Later however, this was noticed by the government and also taxed.)

At a meeting, we concluded that, for the time being, barter was an option and not necessarily only with goods of our own production. We had already done a few small deals, but it was essential that we enlarge on them if we were going to be able to meet our commitments to the bank. Barter business required little by way of overhead costs. If successful, a few phone calls to the right people could bring about the exchange of containers of products, without our being involved in loading, storage or off-loading.

In a country where the centralised system had disintegrated, people were grateful to receive any assistance in obtaining what they desperately needed to keep going. How, you may ask, did we make money out of the exchange of goods? We simply charged for our services, which were not designated as profits and therefore attracted less tax.

Alexandra was a financial guru to us. She calculated all risks and determined the profits expected on each deal. Without her go-ahead, we did not enter into any deal. Irena worked with me from the beginning, but after a period took it upon herself to create her own goods exchanges. Happily, we had also found an honest, hard-working manageress, capable of fully overseeing the factory operation, who turned out to be a great asset.

Every day was a merry-go-round of product swapping, selling and buying, with some deals involving as many as four swaps before reaching finality. We traded over a large geographical area encompassing Murmansk, Saratov, Ivanov and towns in Moscow province. At times Russnab was part of the deal and at others not, but the volumes traded continually grew.

A huge variety of goods were being exchanged, but mention of a few should suffice as examples. We were approached by Russnab to produce a large order of special gloves and uniforms for the metallurgical industry. They said they would supply the materials and all we had to do was produce the items for delivery back to them. The finished products were important because they desperately needed them to trade for certain metal products in great demand. We didn't tell them that our sewing machines were not capable of doing the heavy-duty job required in making asbestos-type gloves, but we nevertheless agreed to take it on.

Our research uncovered a women's penal colony in Tver province capable of doing the job. I made an appointment to see the colonel-in-charge and, early the next morning, was on my way there with a couple of bags full of presents.

The prison authorities were very pleased to receive orders for any goods, particularly if the raw materials were supplied. The prices quoted me were unexpectedly low, they liked our 'presents', asked for more and the deal was concluded. This production facility was an auspicious find as far as I was concerned, because they were capable of producing many other products such as padded jackets and mattresses, which immediately raised new business possibilities.

Russnab, to their satisfaction, received delivery of the gloves and uniforms on time. Instead of payment in cash, we asked for heavy cotton fabric, which we sent to the prison to have jackets and mattresses made. We bartered the finished jackets in the north of Russia for domestic electrical goods and fresh fish. The fish was easily sold in Tver, but the electrical goods went directly to another town in exchange for glass tumblers. Mattresses went to Saratov where they were swapped for rustproof kitchen pots made in a converted military factory now producing domestic products (because of the sudden drop in demand for military goods). The quality of the pots was very high and they were in demand all over the country. They went straight from Saratov to Ivanov, where we exchanged them for cotton fabrics needed by our factory. From each transaction, we received cash deposited in our account, and Alexandra calculated that our barter business was, by this stage, more profitable than our factory of 70 workers.

While we understood that we could prosper without the headache of keeping our factory busy, there was no way out. We could have considered selling it, but that would have left us without protection from racketeers. From our point of view, there were two kinds of racketeers: criminals and the State. Either way, there was no escaping payment.

Criminals used 'protection' for extorting money. They provided what they called a 'roof', but we preferred not being involved with criminal elements and chose rather to pay taxes to the State. The State, however, was as bad as the criminals, in the sense that they took nearly every kopek of profit from businesses.

With the introduction of capitalism, the State created new taxes almost daily, constantly increasing the liabilities of private companies and causing financial strangulation. Companies, as a consequence, had to be inventive at finding ways to survive. While State taxation could hardly be termed criminal, the way new taxes were being introduced was so unfair that it bordered on extortion.

Let me provide an example. Rumours emanating from Moscow suggested that the government was about to introduce a new tax. Alexandra visited the tax office in Tver in January, begging for information to enable us to plan for our liabilities. At the tax office, they were aware of the rumours, but hadn't received official notification of the new tax.

Months passed without any official briefing. Then, all of a sudden official publication appeared in the mid-year press, making payment of a 12 per cent tax mandatory on all purchases of raw materials and goods from private individuals. Most of our supplies were obtained in that way. Our initial reaction in this case was one of acceptance – until we realised that Yeltsin's signature was dated December the year before. The tax dogs were then turned loose.

They virtually ransacked our office, examining every document to ascertain the tax applicable, and then penalised us for late payment. The total liability in respect of that tax alone was so great that it took three months to cover and, had it not been for the profits generated from bartering, we may well have had to close.

After this incident, Alexandra again approached her 'friends' in the tax office in an effort to establish why we had been so heavily penalised when, in fact, she had asked about the tax six months earlier. Their bureaucratic reply simply pointed out that the law had not been published at that time and, when it was, it was dated six months before the current date, so it had to be applied retrospectively. There was nothing they could do.

Barter, attracting less tax, was our mainstay and, had it not been for that, we would have been very hard pressed to keep our factory workers fully paid and our business afloat. Financial suffocation led to the demise of many businesses at this time, adding to the misery of the ever-increasing numbers of unemployed family breadwinners.

Whether unfair government actions, of which this is just one example, were deliberate or the result of simple incompetence, will probably never be known. If it were a merciless State racket, as opposed to a criminal one, at least we were not physically abused, nor were we threatened with having our factory torched.

Criminals knew perfectly well, from their informers in the banks, who was paying tax to the government and who was not. They also knew that it was pointless trying to take money from tax-paying companies because, after paying taxes, they were left with nothing for the criminals. So they concentrated their illegal efforts on the 'underground' businesses or those dealing in cash takings. Reports of factories burned, individuals shot and companies robbed were all too common. We considered ourselves immune because of our legal tax-paying status.

Even though we paid taxes, it did not give us protection from other vampires of authority, such as the fire department, the ecology authority and the consumer rights department. Instead of assisting us to establish a responsible business, they became unwanted parasites.

I will never forget the fire inspector who came to our factory door enquiring, at first, what we produced. Then she inspected our premises to assess our ability to fight fire. The fire-fighting equipment had been passed on to us a month earlier, when we had bought the complete factory from the government, but instead of helping us with expert advice on what we should install or service, she wrote a heavy fine that equalled our total monthly wage bill. Obviously we wanted to work in a safe environment, but she did not give us the opportunity to determine what exactly was required to create one.

When asked where we could buy the necessary items that she was penalising us for not having, she said it was of no consequence whether we could afford them as they were unobtainable. The manufacturers had either closed down or reduced production to the point where the equipment was in such demand as to be virtually unavailable. She then produced her report and asked me to sign acknowledgement. After some 'discussion', she reduced the fine to about two per cent of the original, in exchange for a set of bedclothes. Thereafter, she visited us regularly, every month, to exact tribute. She knew perfectly well that we could never be properly equipped and that suited her just fine.

The ecology authority was no different. It decided that our sewing business was polluting the town's atmosphere because of what it termed an 'ineffective ventilation system', also taken over from the government. We could not afford to replace the expensive system and the best we could do was encourage our workers to clean their surroundings more frequently with damp cloths.

Of course, we all understood that our small sewing factory could not possibly be responsible for even moderate pollution. The real culprits were chemical plants, plastic manufacturers, leather tanners and the like, whose chimneys constantly spewed visible pollutants. But what use were chemicals or raw plastics to the inspectors? After accepting the promise of a free tailor-made jacket, the inspector smilingly cancelled the fine and promised to visit us again.

For reasons unknown to us, the sanitary inspector was dissatisfied with our three toilets. He left our premises in possession of one of the electric samovars we were in the process of bartering. We had made another lecherous 'friend' who visited us regularly.

The biggest headache, though, came from the inspector for the city administration's consumer rights department. He didn't offer to fine us, but threatened to close us down for being in contravention of the privatisation conditions. According to him, we should be working two shifts and be open for business from 8 a.m. to 9 p.m. weekdays, and 8 a.m. to 5 p.m. Saturdays, as had been the case before we took over.

We had reduced the factory to one shift and the hours of business from 9 a.m. to 5 p.m. weekdays only, because there was insufficient work to run two shifts and nobody came to do business on Saturdays. Everyone was busy at weekends growing essential food on their *dachas*. However, he insisted that we were infringing on consumers' rights and claimed to have letters of complaint about our shortened working hours, which he said he would show us – but, of course, failed to do. He was of the opinion that our privatisation deal should be cancelled, which would have left us in huge trouble with our bankers.

Trying to reason with the man proved futile. He did not want to understand that we would have been perfectly happy to remain open 24 hours a day if we had had the work to justify it. With the population becoming more impoverished daily, they were unable to provide the demand we needed. Offers of bedclothes and samovars, which had satisfied others, were ineffective in his case. He was a higher-class parasite, but his threats evaporated when he was offered a tailor-made genuine leather coat.

Two months later, he called as if I were a close friend, saying how much his wife admired our work and also wanted a genuine leather coat. Two months after that, it was the turn of his daughter.

The only purpose those inspectors served was to further the already serious problems we had as manufacturers. They were taking advantage of the grave economic disorder and using their positions for personal gain. We were powerless against them; they could have closed us down at any time had we not 'given blood'.

So I was forced to learn new behaviour. Working in a State-owned organisation had not equipped me with the essential diplomacy necessary to run a private company. Humouring the people on whom our business depended was essential to our survival, not only as far as inspectors were concerned. There were suppliers and a host of others on whom we depended for one thing or another. The responsibility for the well-being of our 70 workers and office staff was weighing increasingly on me.

I redecorated my office to create a more comfortable ambience for visitors. We also installed a refrigerator, stocked it at all times with caviar, snacks, chocolate, champagne and vodka, bought good quality crystal glasses and fine China tea and coffee sets. Surrounding myself with these props provided me with confidence in negotiating with our more difficult customers. I had to calculate the importance of each visitor and treat them in accordance with the benefits they were able to bring us. There were times when I even drank vodka at 10 in the morning in an effort to placate someone or enhance the possibility of gaining one kind of advantage or another.

My colleagues, Irena and Alexandra, understood that I wasn't behaving in a manner that I necessarily enjoyed. Our workers, I realised, were less likely to grasp the point. They would occasionally barge in during such meetings, without first knocking, then stand with a look of amazement, staring at the laden table. I felt that trying to explain that generating a profit was not simply achieved by pressing on the pedal of a sewing machine, would likely not only be an exercise in futility, but also might further fuel the fires of their frequent discontent.

The fact was that they were well off in comparison to others, better paid than most doing the same jobs and unfailingly paid in cash on due date. In addition, we offered them goods at cost price that were in the process of being bartered when shops were empty, inflation rampant and the items not otherwise available. Our fabric store was open, permitting them to buy at cost and make up garments in their own time to sell for their own profit. Irena often exchanged our manufactured goods for food items such as frozen chickens, butter, sugar, cheese or meat that allowed our workers to buy at lower prices and get better quality than was generally, if at all, available.

Many of our women were single mothers or sole providers for

broken families; others had unemployed husbands. Knowing that they often had heavy responsibilities encouraged us to be charitable, but the government saw it differently. I could not understand where they got the idea that higher tax percentages would be of benefit to the populace. They were simply ruining businesses and creating unemployment at a frightening pace.

Despite the odds, we managed to diversify into leather and natural fur, plus employ a professional fashion designer and a few highly qualified specialist machine operators. We had decided to offer a greater variety of higher quality products, even though it increased our manufacturing costs. Our dream was to be in the fashion business and market our own exclusive fashion label.

To better manage our company, we bought a used computer from Russnab and ordered a program written for our specific needs. However simplistic that may sound now, in 1992 Tver there was no other company of our type and size employing such technology.

An increasing number of companies and individuals were recognising our name, and more clients were knocking on our door. The time when I could afford to dress in jeans and jerseys had long passed; it was now a case of modelling our products to show off in public. In our efforts to create interest and fuel the demand needed, Irena, Alexandra and I deliberately wore our best products when visiting potential clients and places like banks and city administration offices.

While my life and business were growing and developing, my mother continued to have strong Communist ideals. One day, when she saw me wearing a particularly beautiful leather coat, she questioned why I was wearing it and asked if my workers had the same?

'Not all, Mother,' I replied. 'It's a pity, but many can't afford to.'

For her pure Communist mind, it was just the answer she wanted.

'Olga, you exploit people,' she cried. 'You pay them less than yourself, you rob them, is that what *perestroika* means? And why did your forefathers create a Revolution? It was a waste of time; I am ashamed to have a daughter like you.'

I adored my mother and she me, but we should have known better than to argue on this topic. Our political viewpoints were widely divergent and obviously irreconcilable.

'Do you think my workers stay awake at night worrying how to feed me? I lie awake. I lie there thinking about the money I owe the bank, how to get orders to keep them employed, and how I'm going to pay their wages and taxes to the government. Do you think those things bother them? We shouldn't have the same incomes. While personally still owing the bank a lot of money, I went away for a night and the workers left an iron on that could have destroyed our entire factory. And do you think anyone would accept responsibility? Forget it! You know we can't get insurance; only God knows how we escaped being ruined. I believe that the political situation has righted itself now. We are being paid according to the work we do and the amount of effort we put into it. There will never be equality between mental and physical work. Responsibility and irresponsibility cannot be rewarded in the same way as it used to be in Soviet times.'

She turned quietly and, with a toss of the head, walked away.

In mid-May 1993 I received a call from our local television station. A pleasant voice informed me that they were putting together a show called 'Tver Businesswomen'; they would like me, as director of a recognised company, to take part.

I was struck by a mixture of emotions ranging from pride in our achievement to fear of exposing ourselves to racketeers. My initial response was negative and I explained that I felt too inexperienced to provide advice to others, but she persevered until I finally agreed that if she called back after six months, I would reconsider.

When she hung up, I was thrilled. I knew then that I had achieved something and, in doing so, found my way in life. Despite the difficulties I'd had, I felt confident that I possessed the energy, strength and know-how to grow the business successfully and continue enjoying it for many years to come.

I was happy that I had been privileged to have been born in peaceful times, had had the benefit of a good education and the opportunity of running my own business. How different this was from the lives of my mother, and especially my grandmother, who had had so little in their disadvantaged lives.

27

Russia 1991/1993

O N THE MORNING OF 19 AUGUST 1991, WE AWOKE TO HEAR
sad music on the radio from Tchaikovsky's *Swan Lake*. It had
occurred so often in the past few years that we had little doubt that
someone must have died.

The lunchtime TV news featured a small group of high-ranking
Communist hardliners who had appointed themselves the State
Commission for Emergencies (GKChP), headed by Vice-president
Yanaev, who announced to the world that President Gorbachev
had been taken seriously ill and was unable to fulfil his
responsibilities in leading our country. A State of Emergency had
been declared and, for the protection of the Soviet Union, they
were sending an armoured division to Moscow. The nation was
told that, should the situation warrant such action, a curfew would
be imposed in specific areas.

We were stunned. Just the night before we had been well on our
way to democracy, only to wake up that day and find we had
retrogressed to the old Communist Party dictatorship. Did it mean a
return to black 'voronoks', arrests, closed courts, gulags and being
scared of expressing an opinion? Was it a serious coup d'état?

All communications, TV, radio and telephone between Moscow
and Kalinin were then cut. Hour after hour, we tried to call
Eugene's parents in the capital to find out what was happening, but
could not reach the city.

Eugene met with his democratic colleagues to try to decide on
the best course of action. One of them reported that the local KGB
and police had orders to prepare lists of supporters of democracy
for later arrest, to ensure that enough handcuffs were available and

to make space in the prisons.

Anger welled. United by their determination not to lose their new-found democracy, people in Kalinin began gathering in groups, and had soon decided to go to Moscow to show their support for freedom.

The police were bound to have closed the roads, but, oddly enough, the railways still appeared to be running. It came to light later that thousands of angry people from all over Russia had made their way, by whatever means possible, to Moscow.

To our great relief, television and radio broadcasts resumed that evening. The Supreme Soviet confirmed an attempted rebel coup d'état by a minority group calling themselves the GKChP. Spokespersons for the majority Supreme Soviet distanced themselves from the rebels and denounced their actions. They told the nation that Gorbachev was in good health and on holiday in the Crimea.

It was revealed that the rebel GKChP junta, which had also intended arresting Yeltsin and taking into custody all supporters of democracy in the country, had placed Gorbachev and his family under arrest. Using the excuse of 'protecting' the Soviet Union, the junta had also put the army on alert and sent an armoured division into Moscow, where they were now approaching the Kremlin and Parliament (the White House).

Events well known to the world then unfolded in Moscow. Members of the public surrounded the tanks and reasoned with their crews, who decided not to go against the majority public opinion.

Yeltsin, as President of the Soviet Russian Federation, stepped in and took leadership of the mass democratic movement, freeing Gorbachev and his family from arrest in the Crimea and arresting the members of the GKChP. The coup had not lasted long, but had cost three young men their lives.

Gorbachev returned to Moscow; he looked pitiful. His indecision, trying to 'wear two hats' or 'sit on two chairs', as the Russian saying goes, may have been his downfall. Perhaps he had been unable to envisage life without a Communist Party. It had nearly cost the lives of many democratic supporters and had ruined his political career in Russia. Our hearts were heavy because he had had the backing of the majority, yet he had not been able to gauge the feelings of some of his closest colleagues.

Then Yeltsin made his famous speech from on top of a tank, calling on the people to unite in support of the young democracy in our country. He became an instant hero, enjoying the support of the majority of citizens. The mood among the general public was one of elation, prompting many changes. A new blue, red and white flag was approved, replacing the old red hammer and sickle Communist banner. New lyrics replaced the old in the national anthem and a new national coat of arms was approved.

Towns and cities, previously named after Communist bigwigs, reverted to their pre-Revolutionary names (as a strident protest at their having ever been changed in the first place). In September 1991, Leningrad reverted to its original name of St Petersburg, Sverdlovsk became Ekaterinburg again and my hometown of Kalinin, after 60 years, reverted to Tver, the name it had had since time immemorial.

Square and street names in every town and city, given in honour of people like Lenin, Marx, Engels and a host of others, or of Communist ideology, such as Soviet Square and Revolution Street, were also changed.

On 8 December 1991, the presidents of Russia, Belarus and Ukraine signed the Bialowieza Treaty in Belarus that proclaimed the end of the Soviet Union and the creation of a Commonwealth of Independent States (CIS).

Although the dissolution of the Soviet Union may have come as a shock to people in the outside world, in Russia we accepted it calmly, considering such changes mere acts of political convenience. We continued with our everyday lives. Giving individual states independence could assuage some of the resentment and prejudices built up over the years between different republics of the Soviet Union.

Yeltsin, then the most powerful man in the region, initiated the next major change. He banned the Communist Parties of the

Soviet Union and the Russian Soviet Federation. Then, step-by-step, he began abolishing the State structures of the Soviet Union, such as the KGB of the USSR, the Office of the Military Prosecutor of the USSR and the Foreign Ministry of the USSR.

What about Gorbachev, our first 'President', and previously general secretary of the Communist Party of the Soviet Union, the most powerful man in the USSR? By this stage, Gorbachev was busy writing a book titled *August Putsch: Reasons and Consequences*, which was launched on 12 November 1991. Gorbachev was now something of a king without a kingdom; president of the USSR, which hardly existed after most republics had bailed out.

At 7 p.m. on 25 December 1991, Gorbachev appeared on TV to announce, officially, his resignation as President of the USSR and to hand the nuclear trigger to the President of the Russian Soviet Federation, Boris Yeltsin. From that day, the word 'Soviet' was dropped from the country's name. Gorbachev later established the Gorbachev Fund for socio-economic and political studies; his *perestroika* was over and, from then on, he rarely appeared in the media.

My feelings towards the man were mixed. On the one hand, I was grateful and proud of his bravery in announcing *perestroika* and for what he did for us in the period of his leadership. Most importantly, he set us on the path to democracy. On the other hand, his humiliating departure from high office left me with a feeling of pity for a man I'd previously admired and considered strong. He was simply not quite the superman we had once considered him to be. His humanity may, sadly, have been his downfall.

All over the Christian world, people were celebrating Christmas, while we in Russia suffered ever-increasing shortages of basic necessities, blamed on the prevailing economic crisis. After the August *putsch*, we patiently awaited decisions from the government intended to alleviate the position.

The failed *putsch* had encouraged in us a belief that we and our government were at last moving in the right direction. The constantly deteriorating situation spurred Yeltsin into openly asking advice from economic scientists and politicians on how matters could be resolved. Everyone in Russia seemed to be spending their evenings glued to their television sets, watching debates between different groups of economists, scientists and sociologists, and speeches by well-known figures, demanding action. They all appeared to agree that a free-market economy was the answer, but how to arrive at one was a problem.

When asked why it was not possible to use the experience of other countries that had overcome similar problems, Russian economists invariably stated that our circumstances were unique to our country. While they debated the issue, we were obliged to run from one shop to another, desperately trying to find something to cook for dinner. It really didn't matter to us who won the debate or whether they adopted ideas from other countries; all we wanted was change for the better. The longer the debates lasted, the more dangerous the situation was likely to become.

Gauging the mood, Yeltsin hastily decided that a group of economists headed by a man called Yegor Gaidar would be given responsibility for overseeing reform. Gaidar was a young economist and sociologist, the grandson of a famous author of Soviet children's books. He appeared to be a committed democrat, without being a professional politician, and nobody doubted his ability to extricate us from our economic misery. In any event, we were accustomed to being used in socio-economic experiments of different kinds.

The foundation of his reform plan was privatisation and the establishment of a free-market system. The vast majority of the population embraced Gaidar's scheme of 'shock therapy' as being the least uncomfortable of a lot of bad alternatives, mainly because of its planned 500-day duration. We were prepared to suffer for that period, as long as we were assured of a decent life thereafter. Gaidar suggested that the quicker we passed through the difficult period, the better. In one night the government shut down all State supply structures and trading systems, effectively destroying the entire distribution network. It simultaneously announced 'avalanche privatisation', together with abolition of price controls.

New money was printed and everyone had to change their currency, which worsened the position of people; throughout history, changing currency had been to the detriment of the man in the street. After 70 years of dictatorial economic regulation and the last five years of instability, Gaidar's programme turned into a massive shock for everyone.

Inflation shot up 26 per cent and whatever had been available on store shelves vanished. The costs of water, electricity, gas, heating and public transport rose exponentially.

The government reduced subsidies to State-controlled organisations such as schools, hospitals, police and other administrative offices, resulting in employees going unpaid for months on end. Even frail and aged pensioners went without their small handouts for many months.

Then the government increased taxes, which, in addition to other increased operating costs, forced factories to cut staff and reduce production. In many cases, they eventually threw in the towel and closed down. We were riding a downward spiral.

At the beginning of 1992, one US dollar equalled 80 roubles, but it wasn't long before the Russian currency dropped to 241 and, by October, it was down to 309.

Industrial production declined by 18 per cent in 1992 and 16 per cent the following year. Every stratum of society was badly affected, from newborns to the sick and dying. Talk of the time always seemed to revolve around the same topics: unemployment, bankruptcies, inflation, and the shortage of food and money.

My family was no exception. My parents were already elderly and retired, going for months without pensions that, when eventually received, had devalued dramatically. Two cousins with children to support lost their jobs, with one finally having to accept work as a cleaner. The other tried to sew clothes, but couldn't find anyone with enough money to buy them. For their poor children, a piece of white bread became a luxury.

My elder brother, Victor, with a scientific doctorate, was retrenched, along with the other 2 000 employees of a State scientific research institute at which he had been employed for many years. After a few months of battling to find any kind of employment, he teamed up with one of his old colleagues from the institute, and resorted to baking bread at home to sell on the roadside. The profit generated wasn't enough to feed either of them, let alone their families.

My younger brother, Evgueni, was in charge of a State-owned power station that provided heating to children's schools and kindergartens. When the government reduced subsidies to the schools, they were unable to pay their heating bills, but Evgueni could not cut off the heating or the children would have frozen to death. He continued supplying them, wanting to believe their promises to pay as soon as they received the money they expected from the government.

This resulted in his frequently being taken to court by the government, who threatened to have him imprisoned for non-payment of monies owed to them, when they themselves were withholding payments from the schools and kindergartens owing money to the power station. It was a confusion of disorganised government departments, unable to get their acts together and blaming him, in his personal capacity, for their own ineptitude. After two years of being subjected to this bureacratic impasse, he resigned. He was mentally exhausted.

I bumped into Irena, a former colleague from the Agricultural Building Project Institute that I'd left four years earlier and scarcely recognised her. She looked gaunt and unhappy. The institute had closed, pitching her, her husband who had also been employed there and 400 others onto the streets. Her husband was over 50 and stood little chance of finding a job, while the only offer she had had was as a flower seller on the town square. Despair was etched on her face as she told me that they could not afford to feed their only son, aged 10.

She asked me how I had known what was going to happen as far back as 1988, and what had prompted me to resign to start my own business. I told her that I had honestly had no idea of what was to come, and would not have imagined such deteriorating conditions in my worst nightmare. Fortunately, I was later able to offer her a job as commercial deputy in my factory, where she still works, and is now one of the directors.

Inflation ran amok. In 1992, according to official statistics, it was 300 per cent per annum. It was pointless asking someone what something had cost without asking the date on which it had been purchased. Every day, prices escalated significantly.

Being married, childless and having fairly good incomes, we were luckier than most. Compared to our relatives, who were gradually becoming impoverished, we were very well off. We decided it was necessary to try to help those members of our families most in need.

When we understood what inflation was doing to the buying power of our money, we decided it prudent to spend what we had as fast as possible, which resulted in our flat becoming a warehouse for consumer goods. The overflow went to members of our families and remained there for their use.

Then Eugene came home with the idea that we should borrow as much money as possible because inflation, being what it was, would make loans easy to repay and leave us with appreciating assets. He had heard that the State Bank had begun providing 18-year bonds on new private houses to approved applicants.

A few days later, I nervously signed documents at the bank for a bond of 12 million roubles. The amount was enormous as far as I was concerned. I couldn't imagine what it would look like in bank notes. In a few days, we'd bought a plot near the Volga and building materials to the total value of the bond.

Fortunately, the gamble proved a winner; in just two-and-a-half years we had repaid the full amount. (The house is nearly finished now and Eugene will move into it.)

It was a frightening time in Russia. Masses of people were becoming catastrophically poorer by the day. The majority, especially the aged, could not grasp why it was happening.

An old friend visited us one day and cried like a child. His mother, he told us, had secretly hidden small amounts of money earned by getting extra part-time jobs and selling vegetables from her *dacha*. Over the years, she had accumulated 40 000 roubles, which, prior to *perestroika,* would have bought four Zhigulis (small cars similar to a Fiat). She determined that, before dying, she would give the money to her only son. The poor woman could not understand what inflation meant and, by the time she decided to tell him about it, the money couldn't buy a 50-kilogram bag of sugar, which by then cost 50 000 roubles. It's hard to imagine how many similar tragic stories could be told, or the rivers of tears cried as a consequence.

Increasing numbers of beggars appeared on the streets, asking for money and food. Many were obviously intelligent people who were so embarrassed by their predicament that they turned their faces away from those giving them cash or food. Teachers, doctors or state clerks, who had led decent, honest lives, did not want to be recognised as beggars, but had no alternative if they were to survive.

It was equally embarrassing for those giving, and I recall not quite knowing how to put something in their outstretched hands without making them feel shame. But ignoring them was not an option; those of us who could help simply had to do so.

The polarisation among us now into haves and have-nots caused unfortunate problems in our society, whereas before, such differences had been non-existent. Many individuals could simply not accept the bad hand that fate had dealt them. From being in a normal position, which certainly wasn't well off, people were now reduced to being unable to feed their families. It caused differing reactions.

Some continued to be friendly, others became jealous and aggressive. Some old friends came to borrow fairly substantial amounts, promising to repay us as soon as circumstances permitted, which we all knew was unlikely to happen. Whereas before, social discourse may have been concerned with cultural events like the ballet or literature, they now revolved around two subjects: how to make money and how to find food.

Crime increased alongside inflation. There had always been murders and robberies but, in addition, we now had political assassinations and well organised, large-scale heists. We were beginning to understand that we now had our own mafia organisation.

My husband's business was being targeted increasingly because it stocked everything from paper clips to large trucks and iron ingots. The guards he employed were a branch of the police left over from Soviet times. Unarmed, they were expected to summon the police in the event of break-ins, and when they went off-duty in the mornings, it was their responsibility to report the happenings of the previous night.

Eugene was sometimes surprised to find that stock of very heavy goods had disappeared overnight, without anything untoward being reported by the guards. Rolls of industrial plastic, weighing in excess of 20 tons each, vanished one night. The following month, 25- to 30-ton rolls of paper, destined for a print house, went missing. Then it was heavy engines and, thereafter, iron ingots.

To steal such items, cranes and heavy transport would have been essential; and the process would have been noisy, taken time and involved numbers of people. But security continued reporting that there was nothing amiss and swore that they had been awake the entire night.

In desperation, Eugene approached the police for help, demanding that they protect public interests. They said that, if the guard division could not help, there was nothing they could do. They were in any case busy and were not 'guards'.

Private security companies did not exist in Russia at that time. With no help forthcoming from the police, Eugene decided to open his own private security company, employing ex-army people, back from Afghanistan, as guards. Small losses stopped immediately, but well organised criminals were not put off so easily by unarmed ex-servicemen.

One night, the mafia arrived in strength, held guns to the guards' heads, tied them up, gagged them and proceeded to help themselves to everything they wanted, departing just before dawn.

Eugene went straight back to the police and demanded to be granted licences for his guards to carry arms.

'Out of the question' was their response.

'What do you want?' they asked. 'To start your own police force?'

Determined, Eugene went to Moscow to lobby support. By the end of 1992, he had official licences for the first armed security company in our province. From that time, the heists stopped, but Eugene had earned the ire of the local police.

While we struggled with life at the bottom of the heap, our politicians were having battles of their own. Yeltsin, his cabinet and parliament, appeared to be at odds over just about everything. There were power struggles going on among them that resulted in their real responsibilities being ignored. The Constitution was outdated and parliament seemed to be doing nothing, other than hindering progress.

By 10 November 1992, the rouble had dropped to 403 to the US$, many factories had closed and two-and-a-half million people were out of work. 'Shock therapy' had commenced for us, but the fat cats in parliament just kept on debating the need for reforms while combing their whiskers. They couldn't even decide if it was better to draw up a new Constitution or revise the old one.

On 18 February 1993, Yeltsin spoke on TV. He admitted a political crisis between himself and his supporters, on the one hand, and the predominantly pro-Communist parliament on the other. In order to overcome the problems, he called a National Referendum on 25 April. Fifty-three per cent of voters supported Yeltsin's policies, although dissolving parliament did not prove easy.

While the political upheavals were taking place, a horrible tragedy occurred in my husband's family on 8 July 1993, which was to alter our lives dramatically.

28

Tragedy

EVERY YEAR, IN EARLY SPRING, MY 62–YEAR–OLD FATHER–IN–LAW, Yuri, came from Moscow to spend the summer at our *dacha*. He had adopted the habit about five years earlier, because of his poor state of health. He felt that living in the fresh country air was beneficial; furthermore, he enjoyed the solitude and space – particularly since his wife, as a rule, preferred to remain at home, even in the hot summers.

There was a small wooden building, intended as our future sauna, in which the old man made himself at home, sharing the days in peace with our dog, Karrat. He had his red Zhiguli, enabling him to move around at his own convenience. If he wanted to shower, he usually visited our flat in town during the day, when Eugene and I were at work.

Normally I'd arrive at the flat first after work, with bags of food bought on the way. If we intended going to the *dacha* for the night, I would begin cooking dinner to take along, do the housework and wait for Eugene to arrive with his driver, who would then take us there. It wasn't unusual for Eugene to get to the flat after nine, change quickly into a tracksuit, then we'd pack our dinner and be on our way.

One beautiful evening in July, we planned a family dinner at the *dacha*. Yuri, my mother-in-law, Larissa, their nine-year-old niece, Anya, and I went to the *dacha* quite early, expecting Eugene to arrive much later, as was usual. All was peaceful there; the weather was idyllic, and our crops and garden were at their best. I was occupied in preparing a special dinner for everyone when Eugene and his driver arrived earlier than normal.

Before the driver left, Larissa asked who was going to take her and Anya back to the flat in town. She'd decided to spend the night there, in more comfortable circumstances. Her husband said he would take them in his car, as he knew how to operate the alarm system at the flat, and would see them safely inside before returning.

'Yuri, does that mean you will not be drinking with us at dinner?' I asked.

The driver, a very kind young man, cut in and offered to return later to take the old couple and Anya back to town. It was agreed and an arrangement made for him to be back before 10 p.m.

The atmosphere at dinner was unusually warm and festive. Everyone tried to make Anya feel welcome; she had not visited Tver before, so was a first-time guest at our *dacha*. The old man said how happy he was to be with us, and remarked that we spoiled him with good food and fine drinks.

At the agreed time, the driver arrived to pick up the party of three.

I tidied up after dinner and went with Eugene to walk the dog in a nearby forest. June and July nights are known as 'white nights' because sundown begins at only 10 p.m. and there is a long twilight time thereafter. We chatted about the lovely evening and how everyone had seemed so happy. On arriving back, we were surprised to see that the old man had not yet returned.

A short while later, the driver rushed in alone, asking us to accompany him back to town because the old man had taken a bad turn.

'What happened?' I asked as we hurriedly drove into Tver. 'Is there something wrong with his heart?' No reply was forthcoming.

At our block, we were met with the unexpected sight of many police and other cars surrounding the building. The stairs to our fifth-floor flat were crowded with men, some in uniform.

'What happened?' I asked.

Nobody answered. When we reached the fourth-floor landing, we saw our neighbours with Larissa and the old man, who was lying on the floor in a pool of blood.

'What happened?' I asked again.

A quiet voice from the crowd said, 'He was shot in the head.'

The driver had pulled the black Volga up in front of our block at about 10 p.m., a time at which Eugene may well have been returning home from his office. The old man had exited the car and proceeded slowly to climb the stairs to our fifth-floor flat, intending to disable the flat alarm and return to the car, while my mother-in-law fussed over the bags to be taken upstairs. After a couple of minutes, she entered the building with Anya. The driver was left sitting at the wheel.

Anya, who raced ahead, had just caught up with her uncle on the fourth-floor landing. They started up the last flight of stairs together, with the old man gripping the stair rail for support. Suddenly, a tall young man started down from the fifth floor. As he drew level with the old man, he quickly withdrew a silenced pistol from his bunny jacket pocket, placed the barrel against Yuri's left temple and pulled the trigger. Without uttering a sound, the old pilot dropped to the ground.

Anya, aware of what had occurred, began screaming, 'Uncle Yuri is dead! Uncle Yuri is dead!' while running in terror down to the protection of her aunt.

The old lady could not comprehend what had taken place and stood with her back to the wall, with little Anya's face buried in her skirt. Within seconds the tall young man, still with the murder weapon in his hand, sauntered down towards her, put the gun to her sternum and stared straight into her face. Larissa, usually fearless, was momentarily hypnotised with fright. Seeing that, the killer continued on downstairs, as if he were a resident out for his regular evening stroll.

The driver had heard Anya's screams, leapt from the car and hurried towards the stairs, coming across a young man with his hands in his pockets walking casually out of the building, as if completely unaware of the sounds of distress that had emanated from higher up just a few seconds earlier.

On the fourth-floor landing, the driver found the dead body of the old man, with his wife desperately trying to revive his lifeless form and the child shivering from shock.

Later, when the old lady, child and driver described the appearance of the killer, neighbours said that they had been aware of the tall young man hanging around the block for the past three or four days. He had been seen between six and 11 each evening, looking out of the fifth-floor stairwell window, as if waiting for someone to come home. Occupants of fourth- and fifth-floor flats could even give a fairly detailed description of the man.

Neighbours had called for the police and an ambulance. The police, stationed just a slow, 10-minute walk away, took 40 minutes to arrive. A number of unknown men in civilian clothing arrived simultaneously, filling the stairs, trying to find the bullet that had exited the right side of the dead man's head. It mysteriously 'disappeared', never to be found.

Around four in the morning, two detectives arrived and proceeded to question each of us individually in the kitchen. When it was my turn to be interviewed, the detectives showed little sympathy for the fact that I had been traumatised by the earlier events and, from the slant of their questioning, I felt that I was under suspicion.

Later, when I had the opportunity of comparing my questioning with the old lady and Eugene, it transpired that they had been treated in the same offensive manner.

While discussing what had taken place, we tried to recall where we had been for the past four evenings and why we hadn't noticed the presence of the stranger. On reflection, we realised that we had not been back to the flat on any of these particular evenings, but had gone from work to some other activity, and then straight on to the *dacha*.

It was obvious to us that the killer's intended target was someone arriving in a black Volga and living on the fifth floor. Eugene was the only occupant of a flat on the fifth floor with a car fitting that description. The assassin was probably given only the address, the usual time of arrival of his target, and a description of the car. If the killer did not know the face of his victim, we had to assume that he must have been hired to do the job. Whom had we offended and why would somebody want Eugene dead? We had no idea.

A police colonel phoned the following day. He was head of all investigations in our province, had been a friend of Yuri's, and was well known to us socially. He warned us against holding out any hope of the murderer being apprehended. 'His blonde hair was a wig,' he said. 'He has obviously already changed his clothes and washed off the tattoos. No doubt there was a car waiting for him close by, and he could be anywhere by now, even Moscow or St Petersburg. In any case, it seems he didn't achieve his aim; he killed the wrong person. He obviously came to shoot Eugene, and it's clear that he will have to fix his mistake before being paid or he may himself be killed. The police cannot defend you, so I suggest you leave town and hide as best you can.'

The attitude of the police was astonishing. It appeared that, though the body was hardly cold, they were already admitting incompetence and failure in finding the murderer. Moreover, they were refusing to provide us with protection from the man they thought would return to finish the job he'd botched.

Sensational headline reports were in every morning paper: 'KILLER MAKES MISTAKE — WRONG PERSON SHOT'. It felt as if they were advising the killer of his blunder, just in case he was unaware, and suggesting he return to put his error right.

The following day an identikit picture of the alleged killer was published and we offered a substantial reward for information leading to his arrest. The police would be monitoring our phone from that point on, in case the killer tried to make contact. Our neighbours, who had previously promised their assistance in identifying the murderer, suddenly developed amnesia, forgetting all details of the suspect and adopting an attitude of reluctance to become involved. Decent people though they were, after questioning by the police, they mysteriously declined to have anything further to do with the case.

That night, Eugene noticed a suspicious-looking man lurking near the flat. At this point, the police agreed to watch the entrance to our block that night, just in case someone attempted entry. Early the morning thereafter, the occupant of a first-floor flat on the opposite side of our block arrived at our door in tears, begging us to leave. She had found a dead tree pushed against her balcony. She had heard noises in the night and deduced that someone had tried to gain access to our flat through hers, out of sight of the guard. She said that all of our neighbours were anxious for us to leave as they considered our presence a threat to their own security.

Many things that were previously important now paled into insignificance. As this was the growing season, we would usually have concerned ourselves with the crops at our *dacha*. Our beloved dog, Karrat, had been taken to my parents' flat and we had no time to be concerned with his well-being. It felt as though my business was of no consequence, and Eugene went to his office only to catch up on progress towards finding the killer.

Our flat was strewn with his hunting rifles, cartridges, knives and flak jackets. The security guards from Russnab had become our personal bodyguards, working 24 hours a day on a roster basis, which meant there was always a man somewhere in our flat.

All roof entrances to our block had been securely nailed shut and were constantly checked by the guards for signs of tampering. A special steel door had replaced the usual entrance door to our flat, with a video camera installed in the passageway outside to monitor anyone approaching. The curtains were kept closed to ensure that snipers on surrounding rooftops could not see us.

Our telephone had been replaced with one that displayed the numbers of incoming calls and recorded conversations. When Eugene left the flat, he did so only in the company of a number of bodyguards. He now drove away in any one of three cars, the others transporting guards, and they would randomly swop vehicles.

Some of our friends called to convey their sympathies, others offered help, but many never made contact with us again. We'd had the same treatment in the 1983 hunting accident and understood that they were reluctant to get involved in an affair that may prove dangerous to them.

Even though a substantial monetary reward was on offer, nobody came forward with any meaningful information. Our lives had become akin to those of prisoners, guarded 24 hours a day and unable to move freely.

We began planning, in secret, to leave Tver on the day of the funeral. Staying there was not an option if the killer was still at large. Living through the highly publicised funeral would prove a test of our nerves.

Eugene, together with his close friends and bodyguards, planned his protection through every step of the ceremony. The body was in one of the city morgues on the outskirts of town, surrounded by pine forests. In accordance with Russian tradition, we had to go there to collect the coffin and drive to the cemetery some 40 minutes away. However, Eugene was advised not to go to the morgue, as providing protection there would be impossible.

Crowds of people had gathered at the morgue; many were strangers to Larissa and me as we greeted them through a tranquillised haze. One by one, they approached the open coffin to take leave of the deceased, who was lying as if asleep, with just a small star-shaped mark on the left temple providing evidence of the nature of his demise.

When everyone had finished paying their respects, the coffin was loaded into the hearse and we drove slowly to the cemetery, followed by a long line of vehicles. We were surprised to see a big crowd there. A priest began giving religious rites, because the old man had been baptised in childhood. It meant he was entitled to a Christian burial, despite having been a Communist throughout his life. The priest, Father Valery, told us after the event that he had been very nervous, thinking that a killer might well have lurked in the assembled crowd. We were most grateful to him for taking the service; others may well have declined. Whenever I visit Russia, I make a point of seeing Father Valery, who remains a friend to this day.

Just before the coffin was closed, a car with dark windows appeared and drove slowly into the crowd. Eugene exited from a rear door, walked quickly to the open coffin, kissed the old man on the forehead and, as the coffin was lowered, climbed back into the vehicle and was driven away.

We had asked two of the mourners to take videos of the funeral, and especially of the people in attendance. I had noticed their diligence during the ceremony, but one told us later that his video had not come out and would be of no use. Studying the other proved fruitless in finding anyone fitting the description of the murderer, and showing it to the police didn't help either. The video inexplicably disappeared from our flat and was never found. It was the only thing in the entire flat that ever went missing.

In accordance with Russian tradition, we hired a restaurant for the wake and served special foods appropriate to the occasion. Only vodka is drunk at Russian wakes. Three speeches are made about the deceased, with a small glass of vodka drunk after each one. Pies with rice are eaten, together with a glass of *kissel*, (a kind of starchy cranberry jelly). It is customary to finish the offerings.

While seated at a table in the restaurant, my mother-in-law opened her bag and produced some documents that had been given to her at the mortuary. One was a record of the results of the post-mortem carried out by the city pathologists and, to our great surprise, it was recorded that a bullet had entered the back of the head and exited through the left temple – the exact opposite of what had really happened.

We were shocked. Why would they deliberately get it wrong? All they had done was further complicate an already difficult investigation. In order to clarify the matter, the body, so recently laid to rest, would need to be exhumed. Who was behind all of this and why were we being targeted?

Only a few people were aware that Eugene and I planned to leave Tver during the wake, and two suitcases secretly awaited us in a bank-owned bullet-proof car parked nearby.

After half an hour, I made the excuse that I needed to visit the powder room. I met up with Eugene, who had also slipped out, and two bodyguards. We hurried out of the building, through a rear entrance, to the waiting car.

Planning our escape had proved difficult because all of our close friends and relatives lived in either Tver or Moscow. Only my father's relatives in Orenburg province were sufficiently distant to afford us some security. But travelling internally in Russia, using public transport such as trains and planes, or staying in hotels, required an internal passport (or ID book) that, when produced, would leave a trail wherever we travelled. Hotels were out of the question for that reason and, the more remote our location, the safer we would consider ourselves.

Father had promised to telegraph my cousin, Nura, in Orenburg, asking that she help us with accommodation for a month of 'annual leave', with no mention of our tragedy.

En route to Moscow we changed cars three times. It was like being in a James Bond movie. Reliable friends in Moscow had prepared secret accommodation for the night and two cars to transport us to the airport the following day.

Taking off for Orenburg was the first of our flights to 'safety'.

29

Orenburg revisited

WE LANDED AT ORENBURG AIRPORT IN THE EVENING AND rushed to the bus station, where we discovered that we had missed the bus that left twice weekly to our village of destination. The next was in three days' time. The bus station itself was filthy and full of beggars and poor refugees, probably from places like Nagorny Karabakh (land being fought over by Armenia and Azerbaijan).

Eugene decided we would take a taxi for the 200-kilometre journey, regardless of cost, and set about negotiating with the drivers. We learned later that drivers were reluctant to transport passengers such long distances at night, for fear of being robbed or killed by them. The largest and most vocal man finally decided he would undertake the journey for an exorbitant fee.

We sat dejectedly on the rear seat while our driver did his best to draw us into conversation. He could not understand how a young couple on their annual holiday could be so unhappy.

Night had fallen, but we saw no lights as we travelled. Villages are few and far between out on the vast Russian steppe, providing no clue as to one's whereabouts. This added to our apprehension.

We then discovered, to our dismay, that spring floods had washed away the bridge over the Ural River. It was now mid-July, and it hadn't yet been repaired. However, a sign directed us to a temporary pontoon bridge close by. When the taxi's headlights revealed the temporary bridge, it was evident that the river was flowing strongly and distorting it. At that point the river must have been about half a kilometre wide, but the bridge could be seen for only about 100 metres before it disappeared below the surface.

I tried to stop the driver from attempting to cross, but, overruling me, both he and Eugene decided to carry on.

Pictures from the closing scenes of a well-known old movie about the Civil War in 1918–1920 came to mind. During a pitched battle against the White Army, a Red Army commander, Vasily Chapaev, a favourite hero of Communist Russia, was wounded on the bank of the Ural River. Desperately trying to avoid capture by swimming across the river, his strength had finally given out and he had drowned in the swirling waters.

From our taxi window, I was horrified to see that the water was already covering our wheels. I prayed that our lives would not end like the legendary Vasily Chapaev's. We finally emerged on the other side, much to my relief.

By the time we eventually arrived at my cousin Nura's house, it was one in the morning. The driver wanted to return to Orenburg immediately, but we persuaded him to wait until we'd seen Nura and he'd had a cup of tea.

Nura finally responded to our knocking and opened the door in her dressing gown. During the 20 years since I had last visited her with my mother, I had not seen her on more than two occasions. When she realised who we were, she allowed us in. Her husband and son also came into the dining room to meet us. Father had told me that Nura had been appointed director of a large rural school and that her husband had advanced his career to a chief in the administration of the area. Their eldest son had married and left home, and the younger, at 18, was about to start university.

The sight of their large, double-storey house was initially comforting. I thought Father had been perfectly correct in saying that we would find the peace we sought without disturbing anyone. But the faces of our anticipated hosts confused me. Nura said that they had not expected guests and, in response to my question, said they had received a telegram from my father and had replied, declining to have us to stay.

My eyes met Eugene's; anyone in the telegraph office would by now be aware of our whereabouts, and the information could easily have been passed on to 'interested parties'.

I took out a bottle of expensive vodka and a box of biscuits, bought at Moscow Airport, put them on the table, and offered them a drink. After a glass or two, everyone felt better.

'I know your village is quite big,' I said. 'How many people live here?'

'Yes,' replied Nura proudly. 'Our village is one of the biggest in this area. There are 1 800 houses with 4 500 people here. We have a big modern school, a new shopping centre with a modern cinema, and our *kolkhoz* produces a huge wheat crop annually. Our salaries are good and each family has a house with domestic animals, orchards and vegetable gardens.'

'Nura, if you don't have room for us', I said, 'do you know anyone who would rent us a room for a month? We can get all the food we need at the shopping centre.'

'I'm not going to ask anybody,' she replied. 'They will think that we are such bad people, not finding a place in our own house for relatives.'

The taxi driver, who had said nothing until then, at this point leapt from his chair and shouted, 'It's quite clear, guys. Can't you see that they are too high and mighty? Let's jump in the car and I will take you back to Orenburg.'

With that, Nura relented and offered us an upstairs room until sunrise, but the driver had no choice other than to sleep in his taxi. Once upstairs, Eugene and I debated our next move and realised that we had little option other than to return to Orenburg. Nura woke us at sunrise. To our surprise, the breakfast she offered us was wonderful. There was a basin full of locally made ricotta-type cheese, another full of fruits and wild berries, home-made ham, bread and fresh milk straight from her cow. Other delicacies, such as locally produced sausages and smoked fish, also graced her table.

We ate our fill, then set off on the return journey to Orenburg, which was a lot less scary in daylight. The driver could not refrain from commenting on our reception at Nura's. As a local man, he was embarrassed and deeply offended by the behaviour of his compatriots.

'Bloody Communist pigs', he called them. 'They just take advantage of their position close to the feeding trough. Their powerful positions in society have done them no good. They now have rotten minds.'

When we arrived in the city, the taxi driver dropped us off at the offices of Orenburg Russnab, a local branch of the same organisation that Eugene ran in Tver. Eugene asked the secretary to tell her boss, Boris Ilyich, that we would like to see him. Within minutes the door was flung open and we were warmly greeted by the director.

Since the Moscow head office directors were familiar with everything surrounding the murder, it was pointless trying to hide it from our host. Eugene started relating the events of the past six days. As he did so, his colleague's face became ever more serious.

Having listened intently to Eugene's story, he said there had been many similar killings in Orenburg and he himself felt very insecure.

Finally he said, 'In my opinion, they are shooting us one by one.'

'Who are *they*, Boris Ilyich?' I asked.

'Who knows?' he replied. 'Unfortunately, in this country, the State archives are made public only after 30 years. I hope I live that long,' he added.

We explained that we needed accommodation without the obligation of showing our passports. He kindly offered us his own flat – he and his wife were about to set off for a two-week holiday in Austria. It was a great relief for us. We could maintain contact with Eugene's mother in Moscow, with the detective assigned to the murder in Tver, Eugene's office, and, if it became necessary, it would be easier to escape from the city than from a village in the country.

It was a large apartment by Russian standards, in one of the Stalin-type buildings in the city centre, well equipped and furnished. Eugene and Boris discussed arrangements for us to vacate the flat in the event of our having to do so before their return.

After their departure, Eugene called Moscow to speak with his mother and ensure she was okay. He asked her to contact my family and pass on the news that we were safe in Orenburg.

His second call was to the detective in Tver who was responsible for our case. However, the detective offered no response to Eugene's questions about progress in resolving the case and repeatedly asked for details of where we were.

After hanging up, Eugene was tense and unhappy. 'The man's manner was strange,' he said. 'He demanded our present address, wanted to know precisely when I would call him again, and insisted that I tell him whom I suspected of being the murderer. And when I asked if they had made any progress, all he would say was that they were busy checking some evidence. I asked the man why the autopsy certificate was incorrect and he told me not to worry because the detail wasn't important. What the hell are they playing at?'

Meanwhile, Orenburg was unbearably hot. We tried to keep the flat cool by closing the curtains during the day. The only times we ventured out were to buy food. Our days were spent discussing who could have committed the murder and why, and watching television, particularly the news.

Almost daily, there was news about murders, a number of which resembled closely that of my father-in-law's. It appeared almost commonplace for people to be killed, either on the way to or from their flats. The form was always the same, with the killers waiting on the stairs and shooting their unsuspecting victims in the head. Their targets were almost always well-known politicians, young businessmen, bank managers or owners of kiosks, probably all supporters of *perestroika*.

It was evident then that it wasn't just happening in Tver, Moscow and St Petersburg; it was happening in Orenburg and other cities too. What was going on in our country?

We had spent a week in the flat when, on two consecutive days, we saw a couple of men loitering in a position that gave them a good view of our windows. We felt it wise to move on.

Leaving money in gratitude to Boris, we set off for a nearby military airfield in a car provided by the company. The plane looked old and unreliable to me, but after the stressful situations suffered over the previous two weeks, I was not prepared to object. I closed my mind to the potential danger and climbed aboard.

30

St Petersburg

DESPITE MY MISGIVINGS ABOUT THE SAFETY OF THE PLANE, WE landed without incident at a military airfield on the outskirts of Moscow. A friend of Eugene took us directly to the railway station, where we took the Moscow–St Petersburg express.

A flat in St Petersburg had been organised for us, along with a lady, also named Olga, who met us at the station and took us to the flat. It was situated in the old part of town, built in the time of Peter the Great, behind the famous Nevsky Prospect. The building had a hollow core with arched entrances at the front and rear, originally intended to allow entry for coaches. There were no other entrances apart from the arches, and the hollow core did little to improve ventilation in the flat, which was situated on the first floor, directly above one of the arches.

Internally, it was impressive with spacious rooms, high ceilings and unusual arch-shaped windows. It appeared to have been recently renovated with new parquet flooring, a newly tiled bathroom, a toilet and a kitchen of European design, highly sought after in Russia. Everything was freshly painted and the front door was made of bullet-proof steel, a feature that had become popular in cities where people could afford such protection.

While the flat itself was perfect, it was totally unfurnished. There were no curtains, a refrigerator, not even a teaspoon. All we had were two suitcases with summer clothes. We took the necessary risk of going to the nearest kiosk to buy some food and drink. We also collected old newspapers, which we used as curtains, and a base that would be covered by our clothes to form a makeshift bed.

Having eaten, we lay down to get some desperately needed rest.

I was lying there, eyes wide open in the dead of night, when a noise erupted that nearly scared me to death. It sounded as if someone had tried to blast the steel entrance door open. Only after some time did we realise what had happened.

A police car had driven at high speed through the stone-paved hollow core of the building, creating a blast of noise exaggerated by the mineshaft effect of the structure. Architects in the eighteenth century had clearly not considered the possibility of motorised vehicles speeding through their buildings, designed for the slower, more stately passage of horse-drawn coaches. Many nights thereafter I was frightened by similar sounds, but at least knew by then that it was more than likely cars speeding through the building.

The following day, Olga arrived with mattresses, bedclothes and kitchen utensils, as she had promised, and even a small television set. These basic comforts helped to make our stay more bearable. We felt relatively safe in this large city. But our days in exile seemed to drag on interminably, with the topic of conversation always returning to the murder and speculation about the reason behind it. Every time Eugene called the detective responsible for our case, he ended up throwing the receiver back in the cradle and giving vent to his frustration.

'They have nothing new,' he would shout. 'They haven't even found the bullet, so there is no chance of identifying the gun. But they demand to know where we are, as if no further investigation can take place without this information. Whose side are they on?'

Our life was becoming increasingly grim, with the feeling that we were being stalked for the kill. All our instincts were sharpened to detect danger, while around us, life for others continued as usual in beautiful St Petersburg.

The city was full of summer holidaymakers, visitors and foreign tourists, but we could not venture out to public places like art galleries, museums or theatres. When we had to leave the flat to buy food, we covered our heads with hats or scarves and, even in the rain, wore dark glasses.

The only place we visited regularly was a nearby church, thinking that only neighbourhood residents would likely be there.

We prayed with all our strength and gave charity to those in need, thinking that our position may indeed not be the worst.

The pressure of constant stress was getting to me. My brain would not switch off. We were starting to run short of cash, so Eugene arranged for a trusted friend to bring us a substantial amount, providing not only relief as far as daily living was concerned, but also allowing us the independence to move about.

One Saturday, in late July, we switched on the television to see the usual morning news. To our dismay, a government spokesperson announced that new banknotes would be issued from Monday and that all existing notes would be worthless with effect from that date. People would be permitted to change only 35 roubles each, and the rest of their money would afterwards be worthless. Amounts in excess of that figure would result in scrutiny of the bearer, who would be obliged to present a passport and provide documentary explanation for the source of the money, which had to be exchanged by Monday at the latest.

What on earth was the the government doing? Thirty-five roubles was nothing and it was Saturday morning in mid-summer, when everyone was on holiday. Without prior notice, the perfidious authorities had once again impoverished the people. They had done that before. One could wake up any day to find that, in the name of 'financial reform', our government had decreed our hard-earned money to be of no value. Notwithstanding the other hardships foisted on them, the people now had to suffer another shattering of their hopes for improvement in their lives.

We set off immediately in search of a State savings bank, only to find that not all branches were open. We did find one on Nevsky Prospect, but what we saw there shocked us. Two huge security guards, armed with Kalashnikovs, stood on either side of the entrance at the top of a series of steps.

A crowd of mostly elderly pensioners was gathered, trying to get through the doors, while the guards pushed them roughly away with their weapons, shouting, 'Go away, the bank has closed now.' It was unbelievable that such a fascist act could be taking place before our eyes. I had to pinch myself and ask if this was really the beloved country of my birth.

We realised that it might not be possible to get even the 70 new roubles we needed for Monday's food. If there was a crowd of elderly people today, when most people were out of town enjoying themselves, on Monday there would be a multitude of seething individuals.

Rushing from shop to shop on Nevsky Prospect, we tried to find a place to spend the substantial sum we were carrying. Most shops were closing, many as we approached their doors, because they were reluctant to have too many old rouble notes on Monday.

As 'refugees' from our home town, there was little of value that we wanted – not furniture, nor a piano, nor a motorcycle. At the same time, we obviously didn't want to throw away our hard-earned money for the benefit of the State.

On the opposite side of the Prospect was a crowd outside a jewellery shop. We thought this would probably be the best way of using our money. We joined the queue and, after a long wait, were thoroughly checked by security guards before being allowed entry.

Chaos reigned inside the shop. People were running from one display cabinet to the next in a frenzied panic to dispose of their cash. Finding something worth buying was a challenge, but with every minute there was less available. Deciding quickly, we bought a diamond ring at a price equivalent to the amount we wanted to dispose of.

With a sense of relief, we left and made for the nearest food shop to try to get as much long-lasting canned or dried food as possible; at least we would be able to survive for a few days on that.

Once back in our flat, we examined the ring, wondering what our lives were really all about? I now had a diamond ring that I didn't need. It would not lend me protection from anything or anyone. I still have that ring and have never put it on my finger. I keep it as a symbol of the sadness experienced at the time and will never wear it.

For the rest of the weekend we watched television constantly, taking in the full impact of the government decree. They had created an atmosphere of revolt among the population. Programmes featured individuals displaying ever-increasing anger.

Reporters interviewed visitors who had come to the capital from all parts of Russia to enjoy their holiday. They were beside themselves with worry, claiming that, with the 35 roubles, which was the full sum anyone could change, they could not get home. A sobbing schoolteacher, caught changing trains in Moscow, was explaining how she had brought 25 children from the far north on a Black Sea holiday. Parents had entrusted her with cash to cover costs for their children (travellers' cheques or credit cards were unknown in Russia at this stage) and all she held now was worthless paper.

The most tragic interviews were those with old people. One after the other they described how, at every opportunity during their difficult lifetimes, they had battled to accumulate money for possible dark days in their old age. Suddenly, never having had sufficient faith to invest in State banks, and because they had kept their cash under mattresses with no documentary records of the source of the funds, their life's savings had been rendered worthless, leaving them destitute. The sad commentaries were endless.

Having listened for a day-and-a-half, we came to the conclusion that ours was not the worst problem; there were others in far less favourable circumstances. Yeltsin, who had been the nation's favourite just two years before, was likely to suffer enough criticism to unseat him from power.

On Monday, the entire country listened when Yeltsin addressed the nation. He claimed that, at the time the announcement had been formulated, he had been on holiday at the Black Sea, and was unaware that the Minister of Finance intended introducing such financial reform. He said the country needed reform, but not the way it had been announced, and that the minister would be taken to task for doing so. As president, he extended to the year-end the date by which money had to be changed, and recommended that the maximum amount that could be changed without explanation of the source be increased. That speech was obviously intended to pour oil on troubled waters and lift his image as national leader, but the people weren't that stupid. In the few years of political upheaval since *perestroika*, we had begun to be able to distinguish truth from fiction.

Having experienced an attempted *putsch* and a few changes of government, we understood that we could expect no guarantees, on waking up in the morning, as to what kind of people would be ruling us, or whether we would be free or in shackles. What kind of country was it if our elected president knew nothing about what was happenning in terms of national financial reform? Was real security in life just a dream?

At 42 and 38 respectively, Eugene and I understood that we were at an age of decision. Our futures were at stake. Doubts about life in Russia were forcing us to give serious consideration to leaving family, friends and everything we had worked so hard to build. We decided that we had to get out before it was too late.

I wanted to retain some self-respect as a human being. I did not want to wake up in the morning, frightened of what I would face during the day or worried about tomorrow. I wanted to be able to smile, be happy and sleep peacefully. From then on we concentrated on our return to Tver, with the clear intention of preparing to leave Russia. We had no idea of where we would go or how we would get there.

31

Leaving

THE COMMAND 'FASTEN YOUR SEATBELTS' RANG OUT. I COULD still not believe we were leaving Russia. Our beloved motherland had brought us such tragedy, bitterness and disappointment over the past three months. Now we were fleeing.

Recollections of our return to Tver from St Petersburg filled my mind. We had tried to return home as quietly as possible, but the newspapers had somehow got wind of it and the headlines brazenly proclaimed, 'Well known businessman Eugene Morozov returns home. Killer still on the loose.'

Back in Tver, we felt we were living on death row. While occasionally visiting his office, Eugene constantly worked at ensuring our safety, trying to come up with better ways to protect us.

Our bodyguards were young soldiers who had recently finished their training or had been demobilised after service in Afghanistan. They worked three at a time in two daily, 12-hour shifts. All knew how to handle weapons, but were learning how to be bodyguards.

Cars were checked for hidden explosives. Visitors were also checked. Bodyguards were not permitted to leave our block, or to leave Eugene's side, so they ate in our flat. My life revolved around washing dishes, cleaning the flat and helping prepare considerable quantities of food. A trusted driver was detailed to shop for us.

While our politicians, democratic Yeltsin supporters and pro-Communist parliamentarians, were fighting for power, they appeared to have completely overlooked the increasingly violent crime statistics.

Assassinations continued. Victims were shot outside their flats. Cars would explode. Gunmen would jump out and shoot individuals as they walked among the crowd in broad daylight, dropping their automatic weapons and leaping into getaway cars. Often other people, in close proximity to the victim, were killed or wounded. It was happening in shops and restaurants too. Snipers were even shooting people in their own kitchens. Nowhere was safe.

Anyone of prominence had his own personal bodyguards. There was a growing demand for bullet-proof vehicles, clothing, doors and television monitors. All apartment buildings had previously been open to the street, but now residents, even the poor, collected money for securing buildings with metal doors and access PIN codes.

Criminal groups had been virtually eradicated under the totalitarian regime, but with the move to democracy, bad elements had been able to take advantage by joining with certain political or administrative outfits. They then exploited the lack of governmental control for their own economic benefit. By the 1990s, industry, building, transport, trading and many other spheres of economic activity were largely under criminal control. Never before in Russian history had there been such criminality.

Some provinces, cities and towns were divided into criminal groups' control zones, with industries forced to pay tribute to their overlords. Many companies fell into the hands of criminals. Through corruption and threats, criminals engineered partnerships with official functionaries, and the banking credit system, manipulating borrowing rates for their own benefit.

The increased cost of borrowing and the ludicrous tax rates had to be allowed for in the costing of products, raising the price of goods and services disproportionately for the man in the street. This had the effect of increasing the cost of locally made products, making imports cheaper by comparison, and so contributing to the decline of local industry and the economy. Huge amounts of money were accumulated in the unofficial or shadow economy, outside of taxation, and therefore beyond State control.

The more criminals strengthened their grip on the economy, the more they were able to influence the political and social life of our society. It became widespread practice for associates of criminals to be insinuated into positions of power within politics or business, using any method necessary to eliminate those obstructing their plans, including blackmail, kidnapping or murder.

Criminal subjects became predominant in art, popular music, literature and especially in movies. And a compulsion arose among normal people to emigrate.

Eugene and I felt we had little choice other than to leave. Many decisions had to be made during the month before our departure, including what we should liquidate in order to get sufficient US dollars for travelling. We had never lived outside Russia, so had little idea of what our costs would be, where to go or how to get the necessary visas. Everything had to be done as secretly as possible, because we didn't know who our enemies were.

Initially, we tried to get visas for America. However, they refused us entry on the grounds that we were childless and were therefore likely to stay in their country. Our passports were stamped accordingly.

Once our passports bore American stamps of refusal, Canada also refused us visas and we realised that our chances of getting into another country had been adversely affected. We considered the possibility of applying for new passports, but that procedure would take time and alert people as to our intentions and whereabouts.

Help arrived out of the blue. Eugene's cousin, Katya, had called to inform us that she was on her annual visit to Tver, with her Lebanese husband. When we told them about our difficulties regarding visas, they offered to organise visas for us for the Lebanon, as they had friends in the embassy. Within a few days we had our visas, although we were woefully ignorant of anything to do with that country. In our position, we didn't really have much choice and were anxious simply to get out of Russia.

Now we were on a plane to Beirut; it was 30 September 1993.

I reflected sadly on the fact that I had left Russia without seeing my beloved grandmother again. We had lived at opposite ends of the same town for the last 10 years, since she had gone to live with my aunt Lydia and her family. It had been more than three months since I had last seen her, before the shooting tragedy that had struck our family. And now I would probably never see her again.

Epilogue – Paradise found

THE REPUBLIC OF BOPHUTHATSWANA: WHERE IS IT AND WHY are we going there? I repeatedly asked myself. Can it be better than Russia or Lebanon?

We had spent a fraught three-and-a-half months in Lebanon and, although we had met and been befriended by some wonderful people, we had seen no prospect of settling in that country.

Back in Russia, the police investigation into the assassination of Eugene's father had been closed, without anyone having been brought to book. This meant the killer was still at large, and precluded any possibility of our returning there.

While in Lebanon, we recalled that some years earlier, in Tver, we had met a Russian businessman who had emigrated to South Africa. He had cast a magic spell over the evening we spent with him, telling of the golden life he now lived under that southern sky, and we had never forgotten the images of paradise he had conjured up. After some intensive research, we managed to find his telephone number and contacted him. He kindly arranged visas for us for the southern African 'Republic of Bophuthatswana' – a country we had never even heard of.

Now on our way to South Africa, we wondered if what we had been told in Moscow was true. Would we land in some wild, tropical place with lions on the streets, banana palms and monkeys everywhere?

The plane landed with a thud, but taxied to a smooth halt. It was 22 January 1994. The doors opened and stairs were wheeled into place. As I arrived at the exit door and looked out at this new and unknown land, an unexpected feeling of euphoria came over me. It was as I remembered it having been described back in Moscow. The sky was high, wide and very blue. The sun was shining brightly; the air was sweet, clear, fresh and full of aroma. There were pleasant smiles on white and black faces around the stairs, greeting us as if we were long-lost relatives.

At the immigration window I showed an officer our passports and faxed visas, trying to explain that the originals should be on their computer. They checked and gave us a couple of forms to complete. There was another spoke in our wheels: we couldn't understand the questions on the forms. Eugene suggested we ask permission to find our benefactor and request his assistance. To my surprise, the officers agreed, providing Eugene remained behind with our luggage. We would never have been allowed to do that in KGB-controlled Russian airports or post-war Beirut.

Even though two years had elapsed since our last meeting, I had no trouble recognising our Russo-South African benefactor, who readily agreed to help with the forms. The immigration officer, when stamping our passports, told us, in a very serious manner, that we could remain in South Africa for only three days before having to move on to Bophuthatswana.

'Yes, yes,' we responded anxiously, 'We will do everything according to the law.'

To our amazement, our friend appeared amused and actually chuckled.

As we drove away from the airport, my chameleonic eyes, assisted by a swivel neck, took in everything around us. Surprisingly, the roads were in perfect condition compared to Russian highways. They had white lines painted on them, which was unheard of, even on the main Moscow-St Petersburg highway. Drivers appeared to drive responsibly and gave way politely when necessary, without the constant hooting experienced in Beirut. Buildings were modern, well designed and tidy, with spaces between them planted with grass and pretty flowers in beds. There was only one building in Tver that could possibly compare – that of the Communist Party committee.

Our friend took us to his house in a suburb called Illovo and kindly led us to a room, which he explained we could use while we found suitable accommodation elsewhere. His house was surrounded by a large garden with huge trees covered with beautiful lilac flowers.

In all my life, I had never seen a tree of such size with so many flowers falling from its branches. All we had in Russia were flowering apple and cherry trees in early spring. Lebanon may have a cedar tree on its flag, but there weren't many trees of any kind in Beirut. I thought I'd arrived in the Garden of Eden; walking barefooted on warm earth, covered in lush green grass, overlaid by a carpet of lilac flowers, was what I imagined heaven to be. Later, I was told that these trees are called 'jacarandas'.

On our first morning in South Africa, I awoke to the singing of birds, the cooing of doves and the raucous call of what I later discovered to be ibises. In Russia there were just sparrows and pigeons in town; only in forests were singing birds to be found and Beirut didn't appear to have even a sparrow. And yet here, in the middle of a city suburb, were so many happy birds. I felt a healthy aura all about me. Surely God must have created this land for peace, I mused. I immediately resolved to do everything possible to remain in this wonderful country.

But the immigration officer's words haunted me. Would we really have to leave this paradise after just three days? Every time I raised the subject, our friend laughed and told us that Bophuthatswana existed on the map, but had no official borders. To prove he was telling the truth, our host decided to take us there. When we arrived at the Carousel Casino, he said we were on Bophuthatswana territory and asked if we were satisfied. Thereafter, with our fears assuaged, we stopped worrying about our visas.

In fact, the State of Bophuthatswana existed for only about another two months before the citizens of that country demanded, and received, re-unification with South Africa. By a miracle, our being in South Africa had been made perfectly legal. At last, some positive signs for our future were appearing.

Each day we learned more of life in South Africa and, as we did so, I fell increasingly in love with the country. In Beirut we had encountered our first supermarket, which was a small shop. In Tver we had only tiny shops, each with specific types of food such as bread and sweets, fruit and vegetables, or meat and fish. What's more, for the past few years of my life in Tver, the shops had almost always been practically empty. But here in South Africa, a food store could be almost half a kilometre in length and full of an incredible variety of different foods and other goods.

I had never seen so much food in one place. I walked down the isles bemused, looking at boxes, packets and tins with absolutely no idea of what they contained, unless of course there was a picture of the contents on the label. How could people choose from so many different kinds of sugar, milk, butter and bread?

In Russia, we had considered ourselves members of a modern, educated society, but in South Africa we felt about as developed as cave people. Everything back home had been purchased using cash. Now, in our forties, we began learning about things such as cheque books, credit cards, autobank machines, shares and stock exchanges, as well as medical aid, and life and short-term insurance.

Watching the behaviour of local people, I was delighted to see that women and children appeared loved and respected. Our upbringings had been different; we were spartans, prepared for a tough life, never spoilt or asked what we would like – food was simply put in front of us and we were glad to have it.

I don't regret my childhood, but it was wonderful now to see children treated with tenderness and asked their opinions, as if it were understood that they, for the rest of their lives, would be offered choices and should therefore get used to making decisions.

What impressed us most was the kindness displayed towards foreigners. So many times in banks, clinics or offices, I tried to communicate something to someone who honestly could not understand what I was saying. I would become terribly frustrated, but people were always prepared to make the effort to understand me.

When we rented an apartment from an Afrikaans-speaking landlady, we were surprised to find similarities between some Russian and Afrikaans words. Such words would have come into use in Russia in the time of Peter the Great, who visited Holland in the early eighteenth century to study shipbuilding and other

Western technology. In this way, far-flung people of the world are drawn together into one huge tapestry of history.

New Year celebrations here came as a revelation to me. I marvelled at shop displays congratulating peoples of different religions and nationalities – Chinese, Muslim, Christian and Jewish New Years freely celebrated by communities without fear of contempt from any quarter.

When we arrived in 1994, we were told there was a wave of emigration under way. We could not understand why. Local people explained that there were some who did not want to live under a black government. It struck us as odd, since millions of people in Russia were very unhappy with their white government. From the experiences of three generations of my family in Russia, I can confidently say that I don't care what colour government I live under. All that matters to me is that I should be able to live a secure, peaceful and happy life, unthreatened by authorities. After all we had been through, I am thankful to have found a place in the sun, in a peaceful democracy.

We have discovered, too, that democracy comes at a price. We paid dearly for it in Russia through the increase in criminal activity, which continues to this day. On a very personal level, crime took a dear family member and forced us to leave the land of our birth. South Africa, too, has undergone a similar upsurge in crime, which has taken its toll on the lives of ordinary people.

Something that disturbs me, though, is seeing people waving the red hammer and sickle Communist flag, wearing Lenin-type caps or shouting Communist slogans.

Three generations of my family lived a delusion while building Communism. 'Please, read my book,' I want to tell the flag wavers. 'If you really think it's for the good of all, you are deluding yourselves.'

Although in the grand scheme of history, Russian Communism came and went like summer lightning, it blighted the lives of generations of innocent people. May people never again be tempted to follow leaders who, out of ignorance or by design, peddle the fairy story that is Communism.

Bibliography

The following publications were used as sources of information:

Babusenko, S. & Arnevikh, G. 1990. *Politics can be Unjust*. New Time Magazine No. 49, Moscow.
Encyclopaedia Britannica 2002 Deluxe Edition. *britannica.co.uk*
Iljin, M. A. 1994. *Tver Province. Encyclopedia Reference Book*. Tver Province Book-Magazine Publisher, Tver.
Iljin, V. 1989. *Volga. Pain and Misfortune of Russia*. Planet, Moscow.
Kelly, Rosanna. 1996. *Russia*. Flint River Press Ltd., London.
Kudrov, V. M. 2002. *World Economy*. Beck Business Series. Moscow.
Moscow. Encyclopedia. 1980. Soviet Encyclopedia, Moscow.
Onikov, L. A. 1980. *A Brief Political Glossary*. Political Literature, Moscow.
Polak, G. B. & Markova, A. N. 2000. *History of World Economics*. Unity, Moscow.
Polynina, I. & Rodimtseva, I. 2000. *The Moscow Kremlin*. Red Square Publishers, Moscow.
Popov, V. 1990. *Political portrait of Margaret Thatcher*. Man and Politics. Magazine World Economy and International Affairs, No. 12, Moscow.
Putin, Vladimir. 2000. *First Person*. Hutchinson, London.
Radugin, A. A. 2002. *History of Russia*. Lecture course. Centre Publishers, Moscow.
Rutskoy, A. 1995. *About Us and About Me*. Science Books, Moscow.
Vorobjev, V. M. 1996. *History of Tver Region*. Constellation, Tver.

Glossary of Russian terms

Babushka	Old Russian woman (grandmother)
Bednjak	Small landowners (poor people)
Blat	Bribery
Bolshevik	Supporters of Lenin; later called themselves Communists
Bulochka	Small Yorkshire-type pudding
Cossack	Historically, frontier guards
Dacha	Piece of land used for private agricultural purposes
GKChP	State Commission for Emergencies; attempted a coup d'état in 1991
Glasnost	Openness
Junarmeetz	Junior soldiers, participants in Pioneer game called Zarnitsa
KGB	State security, previously known as the Cheka, OGPU and NKVD
Kolkhoz	Large collectivised farm
Kolkhoznik	Male collective farm worker
Kolkhoznitsa	Female collective farm worker
Komsomol	Young Communist League of the Soviet Union
Komsorg	A Komsomol organiser
Kopek	Unit of currency (rough equivalent of a cent)
Kulak	Wealthy farmers owning large tracts of land, usually hiring labour
Kyzyak	Pressed dried cow dung
Menshevik	Members of the minority Russian Social Democratic Party, who split from the Bolsheviks in 1903
Nagruzka	The word means 'load', but was used to describe the unavoidable purchase of unwanted items
Octyabryonok	Children of seven to ten years of age, preparing for entry into the Pioneers
Pelmeni	Siberian meat dumplings
Perestroika	Reconstruction/reorientation
Pioneer	Children from 10 to 14 years of age, members of Soviet Union Pioneer Organisation (similar to Boy Scouts and Girl Guides)
Pirozhki	Russian pies
Politburo	Russian Cabinet of Communist Party
Rouble	Unit of currency (rough equivalent of a dollar)
Russian Soviet Federation	The biggest republic in the Soviet Union
Russian Federation	Independent State after the dissolution of the Soviet Union
Samogon	Homemade vodka
Serednjak	Farmer of moderate means, able to employ labour sometimes
Shapka	Russian fur hat
Stanitsa	Large village in steppe area of southern Russia
Subbotnik	Day of voluntary unpaid labour
Tsar	Russian king
USSR	Union of Soviet Socialist Republics
Vobla	Dried and salted fish
Voronok	Black crow; popular name for KGB car sent to arrest people in the Stalin era
Zarnitsa	Soviet Union Pioneer game
Zemstvo	Elective district councils, before the Revolution
ZIL	Top-of-the-range car for the exclusive use of Politburo members